Praise for

SIMPLE RULES

"One of twelve leadership books to watch for in 2015." — *Washington Post*

"One of Wall Street's must-read books of the summer."

— *Bloomberg Businessweek*

"Whatever you want in life can be achieved if you break it down into a few basic rules. Well, that's the theory of these two business experts, and many influential figures think likewise." — *Times* (UK)

"Can't convey enough how important this is . . . *Simple Rules* is the nerd book of the summer." —Tom Keene, Bloomberg TV

"At last, a book offering an ingenious way to fight back against the relentless assault of complexity and its insidious spawning of untold confusions, costs, crashes, and calamities. *Simple Rules* offers an exciting framework for both understanding complexity and rendering it harmless. Whether you run an organization or are simply trying to survive modern life, this book is gold." — **Chris Anderson, TED curator**

First Mariner Books edition 2016

Copyright © 2015 by Donald Sull and Kathleen M. Eisenhardt

Library of Congress Cataloging-in-Publication Data
Sull, Donald N. (Donald Norman)
Simple rules: how to thrive in a complex world / Donald Sull,
Kathleen M. Eisenhardt.
pages cm
ISBN 978-0-544-40990-3 (hardback)   ISBN 978-0-544-70520-3 (pbk.)
1. Simplicity. 2. Conduct of life. 3. Decision making. I. Eisenhardt,
Kathleen M. II. Title.
BJ1496.S85 2015
650.1 — dc23
2014044513

Book design by Chrissy Kurpeski
Typeset in Minion Pro

Printed in the United States of America
21 22 23 24 25 LSB 11 10 9 8 7

To our parents, Kathleen and Norman Sull and Marie and Bill Kennedy, with much love and appreciation

Contents

Introduction

THE SIXTY-SEVENTH COMBAT SUPPORT Hospital, located 250 miles northwest of Baghdad, was not like most hospitals. For starters, the doctors carried guns. As officers in the U.S. Army, the physicians were required to wear sidearms, which were deposited in a lockbox before every shift. The hospital often treated Iraqi insurgents, who were known to spit in attending physicians' faces as they received treatment. If they (or a disoriented U.S. soldier) got their hands on a weapon, a firefight could break out in the operating room.

Built on the bombed-out remains of a farmer's field near the Mosul International Airport, the hospital, a cluster of buildings, trailers, and large green tents, was surrounded by concrete bunkers and blast walls to protect the staff and patients from mortar fire. The medical staff spent days at a time treating routine conditions like indigestion and dehydration (in summer, temperatures in the region could reach 120° Fahrenheit, hot enough to stick the contact lenses to the eyes of soldiers as they walked from one building to another). Lulls could be interrupted at any moment by an onslaught of wounded soldiers and civilians.

At noon on December 21, 2004, at nearby Forward Operating Base Marez, U.S. troops, Iraqi soldiers, and military contractors crowded into the mess tent for lunch. Sergeant Edward Montoya Jr., an Army medic who normally avoided sweets, was feeling homesick at the prospect of Christmas in Iraq and decided to console himself with a piece of cheesecake. As he headed for the dessert table, his buddies ribbed him about putting on weight.

At the same moment, a man wearing an Iraqi security services uniform entered the mess tent, approached a cluster of U.S. soldiers waiting in line for lunch, and detonated an explosive vest concealed under his uniform. Montoya was returning to his seat when he saw a flash out of the corner of his eye, followed by what he remembers as "the largest boom in the history of booms." Montoya dove under a table and, as the mess tent filled with smoke, pulled several disoriented soldiers to cover.

After assessing the injuries of a soldier lying next to him, Montoya got to his feet and moved quickly through the tent to evaluate and treat the wounded. One soldier had blood spurting from a femoral artery, and Montoya used his belt to fashion a makeshift tourniquet, securing it around the soldier's leg and applying table napkins to stanch the bleeding. As Montoya moved from soldier to soldier, he checked vital signs — pulse, responsiveness, blood pressure — to gauge the severity of the injuries, using a handful of simple rules to prioritize the injured for care.

The most urgent cases were sent to the Sixty-Seventh Combat Support Hospital. In the span of a few hours, the hospital admitted ninety-one casualties, an influx that overwhelmed its limited resources. Patients pressed up against the hallways to make room for passing medical staff. The less seriously injured had to wait in the parking lot until space freed up indoors. The doctors conducted some of the simpler surgical procedures outside the operating room, and judiciously allocated their dwindling stock of medical supplies. Like Montoya, the hospital staff used a set of rules to sort patients who required immediate care from those who could afford to wait.

Treating traumatic injuries is difficult under the best of circumstances, and combat is about as far from ideal as you can get. The injuries are often severe, the physical conditions bleak; medical staff work under the constant threat of assault, and critical supplies are limited. In 2004 the Army had about fifty surgeons in Iraq to serve 140,000 troops as well as injured civilians and military contractors. Despite the challenges of medical care in wartime, by the beginning of the twenty-first century combat mortality rates had fallen to surprisingly low levels. Only one out of every ten American soldiers injured in Afghanistan and Iraq died of their wounds, well under half the mortality rate of soldiers wounded in Vietnam, and a world away from the 42 percent mortality rate of soldiers wounded in the Revolutionary War. This impressive survival rate is the culmination of continuous improvements in frontline medical care over the past two hundred years. In the grim arms race between medical improvements and ever deadlier weaponry, the doctors are pulling ahead.

Advances in drugs, surgical techniques, and diagnostic equipment are the obvious sources of progress in survival rates. Also important, but less familiar to most people, are improvements in how armies allocate scarce resources in the face of mass casualties. Medical professionals are trained to do whatever they can to help the patient lying in front of them, but frontline medics, medevac pilots, and military doctors must make hard choices about whom to treat first. In the wake of an attack or battle, medics and admitting physicians are forced to make life-and-death decisions about complex injuries, with limited information, under tremendous time pressure, and often under fire.

Throughout most of history, the allocation of medical resources was haphazard. The poet Walt Whitman, who served as a nurse during the U.S. Civil War, observed that the injured were cared for on a first come, first served basis, regardless of the severity of their injuries. The wounded sat in line, waiting patiently for their turn to be seen by a doctor or nurse. After the First Battle of Bull Run, the injured who were able had to walk the thirty-mile distance from the battlefield to hospitals in Washington for treatment, a system that failed those most in need of care, the soldiers lying on the battlefield.

In the Second World War, the U.S. surgeon general introduced a formal process for prioritizing care in order to reduce deaths. The system is known as *triage*, after the French word for sorting commodities, such as wheat or coffee beans, into categories based on their quality. Given the complexity of the injuries they encounter, you might think medics use complicated algorithms to classify the wounded. They don't. Instead they rely on a handful of simple rules, like those employed by Montoya and the Sixty-Seventh medical staff, to quickly sort injured patients into three or four categories, prioritizing them for treatment. When performing frontline triage, medics will typically spend less than a minute with each patient. Simple guidelines, such as whether the patient can follow instructions, has a pulse rate below 120, or a respiratory rate between ten and thirty breaths per minute, allow medics to quickly evaluate the wounded. The injured are then assigned a color-coded tag that categorizes them according to the severity of their injuries.

Those with stable vital signs are tagged with the color green — treatment can safely be delayed for these "walking wounded." At the other extreme, patients who are unlikely to survive even with heroic intervention are tagged with black and provided palliative care. The remaining patients are first in line for care, with the more badly injured given a red priority tag and the others a yellow tag denoting "urgent." Sorting the patients using these simple rules ensures that scarce medical resources are brought to bear where they can do the most good — on those patients who have a shot at survival, but only if they receive immediate attention. The rules of triage are widely used to allocate medical resources — such as intensive-care-unit beds or vaccines during a flu pandemic — in the face of mass casualties. After the Boston Marathon bombings, for example, a first-aid center set up at the finish line was transformed from treating sprained ankles and dehydration to performing rapid-fire triage, prioritizing the wounded for care and directing the most severely injured to nearby hospitals. The rules of triage are an excellent example of what we call *simple rules*, the rules of thumb that people and organizations use to make decisions and take action quickly and efficiently.

THE POWER OF SIMPLE RULES

Simple rules are shortcut strategies that save time and effort by focusing our attention and simplifying the way we process information. The rules aren't universal — they're tailored to the particular situation and the person using them. We all use simple rules every day, whether we're aware of them or not. You may have consciously decided never to check your email before you have a cup of coffee in the morning, for example, or never to go on a second date with someone who only talks about themselves. But chances are you also rely on simple rules to decide what to wear, where to invest, or how to stay fit, without even realizing you're following them. Simple rules allow people to act without having to stop and rethink every decision. That is why frontline medics use them to make fast and reasonably accurate decisions about who gets medical care.

Simple rules have proven highly effective in a wide range of activities beyond frontline triage. They help guide critical policy decisions, including how the Federal Reserve Board fixes interest rates, how the state of California protects its marine wildlife, and how the president of the United States approves targets for drone strikes. Tina Fey used simple rules to produce the hit comedy *30 Rock*, Elmore Leonard used them to write a series of bestsellers over sixty years, and the White Stripes used them to record one of the most acclaimed rock albums of the past twenty years in only ten days. Simple rules help judges decide whether to grant bail, and police officers to determine if a suicide note is authentic. In nature, starlings employ simple rules to fly in unison, and crickets use them to decide when to stop searching and settle on a mate. Sometimes simple rules can mean the difference between life and death. Ignoring them contributed to one of the most deadly days for climbers in Mount Everest's history, and one of the most lethal forest fires in U.S. history.

Simple rules work, it turns out, because they do three things very well. First, they confer the flexibility to pursue new opportunities while maintaining some consistency. Second, they can produce better decisions. When information is limited and time is short, simple rules make it fast and easy for people, organizations, and governments to make sound choices. They can even outperform complicated decision-making approaches in some situations. Finally, simple rules allow the members of a community to synchronize their activities with one another on the fly. As a result, communities can do things that would be impossible for their individual members to achieve on their own. Bee colonies, for example, use simple rules to find a new nest, and members of Zipcar relied on simple rules to share cars across thousands of users. In the next chapter, we'll expand on why simple rules are so powerful.

At first glance, the rules of triage have nothing in common with, for example, the rules geese follow to flock in tight formations. But a deep unity lies beneath the variety. Whether they are used by rock stars or crickets, effective simple rules share four common traits. First, they are limited to a handful. Capping the number of rules makes them easy to remember and maintains a focus on what matters most. Second, simple rules are tailored to the person or organization using them. College athletes and middle-aged dieters may both rely on simple rules to decide what to eat, but their rules will be very different. Third, simple rules apply to a well-defined activity or decision, such as prioritizing injured soldiers for medical care. Rules that cover multiple activities or choices end up as vague platitudes, such as "Do your best" and "Focus on customers." Finally, simple rules provide clear guidance while conferring the latitude to exercise discretion. Central bankers, for example, use simple rules not as a mechanistic tool to dictate interest rates, but as guidelines within which they exercise judgment. Rules come in all shapes and sizes, ranging from implicit heuristics we use to make snap decisions to voluminous regulations affecting small businesses. Simple rules, as we use the term, refers to a handful of guidelines tailored to the user and task at hand, which balance concrete guidance with the freedom to exercise judgment. The dozens of diverse examples of simple rules provided throughout this book all share these four traits.

THE DISCOVERY OF COMPLEXITY

Simple rules provide a powerful weapon against the complexity that threatens to overwhelm individuals, organizations, and society as a whole. Complexity arises whenever a system — technical, social, or natural — has multiple interdependent parts. The human body, bees in a hive, a soccer team, and international banking are all examples of complex systems — they consist of many components and interdependencies that can change unpredictably and frequently.

To visualize complexity on a small scale, you need look no farther than your living room. A home entertainment system consists of multiple components — screen, DVD player, game console, cable box, and speakers — that need to work together. Integrating more parts into the system opens up new possibilities, such as binge-watching *House of Cards* on Netflix, but also increases the number of things that can go wrong and the number of remotes (three per household on average) required to manage the system. The defining issues of our time — climate change, the global financial crisis, international terrorism, the shift toward emerging markets — all arise out of the churning interactions of complex systems.

Complexity itself is not new — the Roman Empire was one of the most complex political systems in history — but our recognition of complexity has vastly increased in the past six decades. A search for the word *complexity* in five million books published since 1800 shows that the term was initially rare, rose gradually for 150 years, and then exploded just after the Second World War. The upsurge in interest coincided with the publication, in October 1948, of an eight-page article entitled "Science and Complexity," written by an unassuming mathematician named Warren Weaver.

Warren Weaver is not a household name, but he may be the most influential scientist you've never heard of, actively shaping three of the most important scientific revolutions of the last century — life sciences, information technology, and agriculture. In

1932 Weaver joined the Rockefeller Foundation to lead the division charged with supporting scientific research. Funding was scarce during the Great Depression, and the Rockefeller Foundation, with an endowment nearly twice the size of Harvard's at the time, was one of the most important patrons of scientific research in the world. Over his three decades at the Rockefeller Foundation, Weaver acted as a banker, talent scout, and kingmaker to support the nascent field of molecular biology, a term he himself coined. Weaver had an uncanny knack for picking future all-stars. Eighteen scientists won Nobel Prizes for research related to molecular biology in the middle of the century, and Weaver had funded all but three of them.

Weaver recognized the potential of computers long before most people even knew they existed. He wrote a seminal paper that laid out how computers could translate text from one language to another, sixty years before the creation of Google Translate and Babylon. While at the Rockefeller Foundation, Weaver also handpicked and financed a team that spent two decades developing high-yield varieties of wheat that were impervious to disease. Their work helped Mexico feed itself within a generation. When India and Pakistan faced widespread famine in the early 1960s, they adopted the practices pioneered by the Rockefeller team, and doubled their wheat production in five years, saving hundreds of millions of people from starvation.

As if spurring on three scientific revolutions were not enough, Weaver also pioneered the study of complexity. In his 1948 article, Weaver described science as progressing through successive eras, defined by the three types of problems — simple, uncertain, and complex — that they solved. Simple problems address a few variables that can be reduced to a deterministic formula. Isaac Newton's laws of motion (force = mass x acceleration, for example) were powerful tools to solve simple problems, such as how a satellite orbits the Earth or what happens when two billiard balls collide. Simple problems occupied scientists for most of the seventeenth to nineteenth centuries, and their solutions yielded life-changing inventions ranging from the telephone to the diesel engine. By the late nineteenth century, scientists shifted their attention to problems of uncertainty, such as the motion of gas particles in a jar, which consisted of large numbers of objects. While scientists could not track the movement of every molecule, they could use probability theory and statistical analysis to predict how large numbers of particles behave in aggregate, paving the way for advances in thermodynamics, genetics, and information theory.

Scientists can predict the path of two billiard balls with precision, and the average behavior of two million gas particles. But what about the messy middle ground, where twenty or thirty components interact with one another in unexpected ways? Many of the most critical scientific and social challenges of today — the aging of cells, or hunger in emerging markets — result from multiple variables that interact in numerous and often unpredictable ways. Complexity covers the untidy yet vibrant realm where so much of life unfolds. What makes a primrose open when it does? How do market forces influence the price of gold? How will an expectant mother's diet affect her child? When will a concussion permanently damage the brain?

The world was complex in 1948 when Weaver wrote his influential article, and since then it has become significantly more so. Since the fall of the Berlin Wall, the fates of the world's economies have become more interwoven, with the number of international trade agreements increasing sixfold since 1990. Over the same time, global air traffic has increased nearly threefold, facilitating the mix of people and commerce around the world. Capital has followed trade, and in the past few decades the correlation between countries' stock markets has more than doubled, while banks' exposure to debt beyond their home markets has nearly tripled. And of course the Internet has revolutionized interconnectedness in a way comparable only to the invention of the printing press or perhaps even the development of writing itself. It is easy to forget that Google is still a teenager, and Facebook is in elementary school.

Weaver argued that simple and uncertain problems have largely been solved, and that the greatest challenges of the future would be problems of complexity. He was right. At the personal level, many of us struggle to manage complexity every day. We have to call a teenager to navigate the three remote controls required to turn on ESPN, an accountant to fill out our tax forms, and the IT help desk for guidance every time Microsoft introduces a new version of its software.

On a macro level, the great issues of our day, almost without exception, arise from the unpredictable interactions of many moving parts. High default rates on subprime mortgages (which totaled less than 3 percent of U.S. financial assets) spread like a contagion through the global financial system in the late 2000s, infecting previously healthy banks around the world and triggering the most severe downturn since the Great Depression. Affordable and high-quality health care for an aging population demands cooperation among patients, doctors, hospitals, insurance providers, and governments, all of whom have different agendas. Across the Atlantic, Europeans struggle to retain their traditional lifestyles and national sovereignty even as their destinies are inextricably linked with others in Europe, the Middle East, and the rest of the world. And of course there is climate change, the mother of all challenges, arising from the interactions among technology, population growth, and the global ecosystem, and affecting everyone.

SIMPLE RULES FOR A COMPLEX WORLD

People often attempt to address complex problems with complex solutions. For example, governments tend to manage complexity by trying to anticipate every possible scenario that might arise, and then promulgate regulations to cover every case.

Consider how central bankers responded to increased complexity in the global banking system. In 1988 bankers from around the world met in Basel, Switzerland, to agree on international banking regulations, and published a 30-page agreement (known as Basel I). Sixteen years later, the Basel II accord was an order of magnitude larger, at 347 pages, and Basel III was twice as long as its predecessor. When it comes to the sheer volume of regulations generated, the U.S. Congress makes the central bankers look like amateurs. The Glass-Steagall Act, a law passed during the Great Depression, which guided U.S. banking regulation for seven decades, totaled 37 pages. Its successor, Dodd-Frank, is expected to weigh in at over 30,000 pages when all supporting legislation is complete.

Meeting complexity with complexity can create more confusion than it resolves. The policies governing U.S. income taxes totaled 3.8 million words as of 2010. Imagine a book that is seven times as long as *War and Peace,* but without any characters, plot points, or insight into the human condition. That book is the U.S. tax code. Such an exhaustive tome should leave nothing to chance. And yet, when forty-five tax professionals were given identical data to calculate one fictional family's tax bill, they came up with forty-five different estimates of the couple's tax liability, ranging from $36,322 to $94,438. The tax code is so confusing, even IRS experts give the wrong advice one time out of three. To navigate this labyrinth, U.S. citizens employ 1.2 million tax preparers, more than all the police and firefighters in the country combined.

Applying complicated solutions to complex problems is an understandable approach, but flawed. The parts of a complex system can interact with one another in many different ways, which quickly overwhelms our ability to envision all possible outcomes. To illustrate how quickly complexity escalates out of control, consider an apparently simple question: How many ways can you combine six Lego blocks? For one block, the answer is trivial: 1. With some work, most people can calculate that two blocks combine in 24 ways, but by three blocks the calculation becomes tricky (the correct answer is 1,560). When you get to six blocks, the number of possible combinations is daunting. For decades, the commonly accepted answer for six blocks was 103 million combinations, until two mathematicians revisited the problem with massive computer power and discovered 915 million combinations. If professional mathematicians, among the smartest people on the planet, struggle to work out the possible combinations of six Lego blocks, what are the odds that members of the U.S. Congress can envision every contingency when drafting legislation to cover banking or taxation?

Complicated solutions can overwhelm people, thereby increasing the odds that they will stop following the rules. A study of personal income tax compliance in forty-five countries found that the complexity of the tax code was the single best predictor of whether citizens would dodge or pay their taxes. The complexity of the regulations mattered more than the highest marginal tax rate, average levels of education or income, how fair the tax system was perceived to be, and the level of government scrutiny of tax returns. Or take retirement savings. According to the mutual-fund giant Fidelity Investments, fewer than half of all Americans are on track to cover their expenses when they retire. When employers offered two options for investment in their 401(k) retirement plans at work, three-quarters of workers signed up. As the number of options on offer proliferated, however, participation dropped (to 61 percent for plans with many choices) — even when employers matched their employees' contributions. Overwhelmed by complexity, people walked away from free money.

Books on complexity tend to fall into two camps. Thousands of science books explain theories of chaos, complexity, and adaptive systems, and complexity is currently a hot topic in scientific research. At present, there are at least a dozen scientific journals devoted to the study of complex systems, and more than thirty research centers, including the well-known Santa Fe Institute, and the Observatory of Economic Complexity housed at MIT's Media Lab. Science books on complexity are often fascinating, but rarely provide much practical guidance on how to manage it. A second camp of books veers to the opposite extreme, offering homespun advice on how to simplify your life by decluttering your closets, for example, or limiting the number of blogs you read. Self-help advice, while well-intentioned, lacks grounding in research and offers little insight on how to manage complexity in larger systems.

Simple Rules offers a fresh perspective on a fundamental question: How can people manage the complexity inherent in the modern world? Our answer, grounded in research and real-world results, is that simple rules tame complexity better than complicated solutions. *Simple Rules* presents a general framework defining what simple rules are, why they work, and the six types of rules that have proven effective across domains ranging from medicine to standup comedy. Much of the existing research on rules assumes they are fixed, either hardwired into our brains as decision-making biases or deeply embedded as social norms that defy change. One of our most surprising and important findings is that simple rules are not immutable — they can evolve in light of new evidence, shifting objectives, and changed conditions. The second half of this book provides concrete advice on how to actively develop better rules and continue to refine and improve them over time.

We started our research on complexity in the late 1990s, when Don was a professor at the London Business School, where Kathy spent a sabbatical. Kathy had just published *Competing on the Edge*, with Shona Brown. (Shona would go on, as senior vice president of business operations at Google, to successfully implement their ideas as the company rapidly grew from under $2 billion in 2003 to $46 billion nine years later.) *Competing on the Edge* argued that companies should avoid the extremes of too much or too little structure — an insight that we build upon in *Simple Rules.* Don was studying how complexity kept successful companies from adapting to changes in the marketplace, even when they saw the shifts coming. We came at complexity from different backgrounds — Kathy had studied science and engineering before switching to strategy, while Don had worked in private equity prior to entering academia — and our complementary viewpoints allowed us to tackle the problem from different angles.

We began an exploration of the winning (and losing) strategies of companies struggling with the complexity unleashed by the Internet boom. What we found surprised us. The most successful companies did not try to match technological, competitive, or market complexity with complicated solutions. Instead, they identified a critical process — developing new products, for example, or prioritizing potential customers — and used simple rules to manage that process. We wrote up our findings in a *Harvard Business Review* article called "Strategy as Simple Rules," which argued that a company's strategy does not live in thick binders on the CEO's shelf, but in the simple rules that shape critical processes on a daily basis.

In the subsequent decade, we have expanded our inquiry beyond business to study simple rules in a range of diverse settings, detailed in this book. In the chapters that follow, we will describe how DARPA, the secretive military organization that was behind the creation of the Internet, chooses which groundbreaking projects to pursue next, and how burglars use simple rules to decide where to strike. We will explain how the most distinguished chefs in Paris protect their signature dishes; how Stanford's brainy football team became the brutes of collegiate football; and how Don used simple rules to survive as an undersized bouncer in a biker bar. Simple rules allow locusts to congregate in thick swarms that can extend for miles, but also enable over one hundred thousand volunteer Wikipedia editors to collaborate on millions of articles, which are as reliable, on average, as those found in the *Encyclopaedia Britannica*. Simple rules are not new. As we'll show, ancient Roman jurists used them to make judicial decisions, and the Jesuits applied them to guide the explosive growth of their young organization in the 1500s.

We draw on our own research and work with colleagues including Chris Bingham and Jason Davis, using field studies, laboratory experiments, and simulations that show why some kinds of rules are harder to learn than others but can have bigger payoffs. These studies also describe how people can improve their simple rules and avoid sticking with dysfunctional ones. We also draw on research in other fields: studies of simple rules in psychology, economics, strategy, social biology, and medicine have yielded surprising and important insights. Simple rules help us understand why Parisians can eat a rich diet without gaining weight, while their counterparts in Chicago struggle with obesity. Research by financial economists has shown that a simple investment rule provides higher returns than complex financial models over 80 percent of the time and never loses money.

Don has road-tested simple rules with members of the Young Presidents' Organization (YPO), a global network of twenty thousand executives who have founded or run a sizable organization before the age of forty-five. Over the past four years, highly trained teams of MBA and PhD students have worked with dozens of YPO companies to develop rules, document their implementation, and measure their impact. The result has been the formulation of a three-step process to clarify corporate objectives, identify where simple rules can have the greatest impact, and then develop and refine the rules. This process has produced dramatic results (in many cases increasing profits by 20 to 50 percent) across a range of diverse companies, sometimes within the span of a few months. To our surprise, participants followed the same process to develop simple rules for their personal lives. In later chapters, we will describe the nuts and bolts of developing simple rules for both business and personal use. We've also tested and refined our ideas about simple rules in the classroom — Kathy at Stanford's School of Engineering and Don at MIT's Sloan School of Management.

COMPLEXITY IS NOT DESTINY

Many people accept complexity as unavoidable. Consider the example of early MP3 players, which featured hideous design flaws. Popular MP3 players were designed with up to two dozen buttons, some labeled with head-scratching titles like "exp" and "lib," or unmarked altogether. One bestselling device had a one-touch "delete" button placed right next to the "play" button. Reading reviews of these early products, the most depressing part is not the product flaws themselves, but customers' willingness to accept complicated interfaces as inevitable. Users believed that MP3 players had to be complicated because they integrated so many moving parts — hardware, software, various file formats, music sources, and a dizzying array of accessories.

Then came the iPod. When consumers first used the iPod's iconic click wheel, they realized, perhaps for the first time, that even a system as gnarly as personal music could be managed with an interface that was clean, intuitive, and effective. The iPod didn't just improve the music experience; it (together with iTunes) revolutionized how people listen to music on the go. At their best, simple rules do the same. Like the iPod's click wheel, simple rules allow people to control complex systems without succumbing to complicated solutions. Simple rules address a deeply rooted human desire for simplicity when dealing with a range of complex challenges ranging from the prosaic to the global.

For most of us, complexity is a problem we struggle to manage in our own lives every day. Simple rules offer a hands-on tool to achieve some of our most pressing personal and professional objectives, from losing weight or overcoming insomnia to becoming a better manager or a smarter investor. By limiting the number of guidelines, simple rules help maintain a strict focus on what matters most while remaining easy to remember and use. In a wide range of decisions, simple rules can guide choice while leaving ample room to exercise judgment and creativity. As you read through this book, we hope (and suspect) that you will identify at least one, and probably more, personal and professional challenges that simple rules could help you manage better.

For individuals, simple rules are a powerful tool, but for social systems their benefits border on the miraculous. If you've ever observed a colony of ants searching for food, you've surely marveled at how they adapt to unexpected obstacles and coordinate their activities with one another without ever losing sight of their overarching objective. The ants are not directed by any central authority. Instead, their behavior emerges naturally as each ant follows a handful of rules when foraging. Many of us spend our workdays in organizations — including corporations, family businesses, schools, or not-for-profit organizations — that require coordinated action in the face of constantly shifting circumstances. In the chapters that follow, we will provide examples of managers and employees who used simple rules to do their work more effectively and efficiently without relying on thick manuals of bureaucratic rules. Simple rules can also help solve some of the most daunting challenges we face as a society. This book documents thorny social problems where simple rules are currently used to great effect, and identifies challenges that could be addressed by simple rules in the future.

Fighting complexity is an ongoing battle that can wear us down. Disheartened, people tolerate complicated solutions that don't work, or cling to overly simplistic narratives ("Climate change is a myth," for example, or "Globalization is bad") that deny the interdependencies characterizing modern life. Simple rules can be a powerful weapon in this fight.

1

Why Simple Rules Work

AFTER PUBLISHING A STRING of best-selling books, including *The Botany of Desire* and *The Omnivore's Dilemma,* University of California professor and author Michael Pollan distilled his nutritional insights into three simple rules: "Eat food. Not too much. Mostly plants." By "food" Pollan means *real* food — vegetables, fruits, nuts, whole grains, and meat and fish — rather than what he calls "edible food-like substances" found in the processed-food aisles of the grocery store. This rules out anything your great-grandmother wouldn't recognize as food, any product with ingredients a third-grader cannot pronounce, or any meal that arrives through the window of your car. Pollan's rules for healthy eating, posted on family refrigerators around the world, illustrate the four common traits that define simple rules.

First off, the number of rules matters. Simple rules consist of a handful of guidelines applied to a specific activity or decision, such as deciding what to eat. They're intended to offer a limited amount of guidance, so there's no need for a lot of them. Keeping the number of rules to a handful forces you to focus on what matters most. You might think that capping the number of rules would result in guidelines that are too simplistic to solve complex problems. Not so. In many situations, a handful of factors matter a great deal, while a long tail of peripheral variables can be safely ignored. A comprehensive review of the scientific research on diet confirmed that Pollan's rules can reduce the risk of diabetes, obesity, and heart attacks. To be used, rules have to be remembered, and limiting the number to a handful makes this possible. Pollan's rules for healthy eating fit that bill.

Second, simple rules are tailored to the situations of the particular people who will use them, versus one-size-fits-all rules that apply to everyone. For example, Shannon Turley, whom we will discuss later in the book, has rules for healthy eating that differ from Pollan's. As director of sports performance for Stanford's football team, Turley's rules for his players are "Eat breakfast," "Stay hydrated," and "Eat as much as you want of anything that you can pick, pluck, or kill." These rules make a lot of sense for very large and very active college-football players, who have a tendency to stay up late and get up late, exercise voraciously, and easily work off the calories. But rules that encourage eating as much as you want, are certainly not for everybody.

Third, simple rules are applied to a single well-defined activity or decision, such as choosing what to eat or prioritizing injured soldiers for medical care. Simple rules are most effective when they apply to critical activities or decisions that represent bottlenecks to accomplishing an important goal. When people attempt to cover multiple activities or decisions with the same principles, the result is platitudes, not simple rules. The National Academy of Sciences, for example, commissioned a blue-ribbon panel of physicians, academics, and executives to identify ways to redesign health care in America. The panel developed ten principles, intended to cover tens of thousands of distinct diagnostic decisions, medical procedures, and administrative processes that compose the U.S. health care system. This list of all-purpose principles included safety as a system property, the need for transparency, and continuous decrease in waste. The committee's principles were certainly laudable, but they were far too vague to provide concrete guidance to an emergency room doctor prioritizing patients for care or a nurse administrator organizing hospice options. Overly broad principles are often dismissed as clichés, fodder for a *Dilbert* cartoon.

Finally, simple rules give concrete guidance without being overly prescriptive. Pollan's rules for healthy eating do not specify whether you should have blueberries or cantaloupe or kale for lunch. Just make it real food, include plants, and not too much. Simple rules leave room to exercise creativity and pursue unanticipated opportunities. A private equity firm based in Moscow, for example, developed simple rules to screen the cascade of investment opportunities that appeared during Russia's transition to capitalism in the 1990s. A potential investment should, according to the company's rules, have revenues of $100 million to $500 million and compete in an industry in which the firm had previously invested. Another guideline identified target companies as those offering products the typical Russian family might purchase if they had an extra $100 to spend each month. This rule was tailored to the firm's contrarian investment strategy, which favored opportunities in consumer-goods companies at a time when most investors were putting their rubles into energy and mining. A final rule was to work only with executives who knew criminals but weren't criminals themselves, which acknowledged the ubiquity of illegal activity in Russia while providing clear directions to avoid involvement with the Russian mafia. These simple rules contrasted sharply with the guidelines developed by another Russian bank, which included "Invest in undervalued companies" and "Look for companies that can grow," hopelessly vague platitudes that junior bankers dismissed as useless.

In this chapter, we look at why simple rules work, including how they lead to better decisions and allow people to coordinate their activities to achieve shared goals. But we start with another advantage of simple rules — they provide the flexibility to seize fleeting opportunities. Crafting rules to seize opportunities may seem like a modern innovation, but simple rules have been used throughout history for this purpose, as the story of the early Jesuits illustrates.

SIMPLE RULES TO SEIZE OPPORTUNITIES

As the sixteenth century began, Europe was experiencing a spike in complexity after a thousand years of relative simplicity. For a millennium after the sack of Rome, the Catholic Church had enjoyed a near-monopoly on religious doctrine throughout Europe. Monasteries preserved the classical tradition, religious universities educated Europe's elites, and the Church's extensive hierarchy of cardinals, bishops, and priests exercised political power across the continent. In the early 1500s, this monolithic structure broke apart, leading to a series of religious conflicts that culminated in the Thirty Years' War. One of the longest wars in modern history, it would ultimately leave eight million dead, including at least a quarter of all Germans.

As the Church fragmented, the known world expanded. Beginning in the late 1400s, Europeans began to explore and colonize the Americas, the Pacific Islands, and Asia. Within a few decades, the economies, societies, and politics of European states were densely interwoven with those of exotic lands unknown just a few decades earlier. The invention of the printing press — the Internet of the Middle Ages — increased the speed and volume of information linking formerly isolated corners of the world. Fewer than 5 million manuscripts were produced in the 1400s — all of them written by hand. Over 217 million were printed in the following century, during which time the price of a book fell by two-thirds.

The Catholic Church responded to this newfound complexity by increasing the number and variety of religious orders. In the 1500s the Church authorized several new religious orders, including the Capuchins, the Barnabites, the Ursulines, the Angelic Sisters of St. Paul, and the Society of Jesus (commonly known as the Jesuits). For the most part, these newly formed orders pursued traditional ministries, stayed local, and rarely grew beyond a few dozen members.

The Jesuits, in contrast, grew exponentially. Within two decades of its foundation in 1540, the fledgling order expanded from ten initial members to over one thousand priests, who ran forty schools and operated throughout Europe, India, Brazil, Japan, and the outskirts of Imperial China. The order survived the death of its founder — membership increased to more than eight thousand priests by 1600 — and the Jesuits remain influential to this day. The current pope, Francis, is a Jesuit from Argentina, and the Society of Jesus constitutes the largest order of priests in the Roman Catholic Church. The Jesuits run nearly eight hundred schools in seventy countries, including such well-known U.S. institutions as Boston College and Georgetown. The order remains global, with half its schools in Asia, including more than forty in India alone. Over the centuries, the Jesuits have exerted great influence through their schools, educating prominent intellectuals (Voltaire, René Descartes, David Hume), artists (Peter Paul Rubens, James Joyce, Alfred Hitchcock), and politicians (Bill Clinton, Charles de Gaulle, Fidel Castro).

The Jesuits' founder, Ignatius of Loyola, led a life so full of adventure that it could qualify as a plot line on *Game of Thrones.* Born the youngest of thirteen children into a family of ancient Basque nobility, Ignatius was first a page and then a soldier serving the Spanish Crown. While defending a fortress against an attack by French forces, Ignatius was struck by a cannonball that shattered one shinbone and badly injured the other. At some point during his convalescence, Ignatius experienced a religious conversion. Shortly thereafter he exchanged his sword for a pilgrim's staff and spent the next two years living in a cave, fasting and praying. Over the following decades, he made a pilgrimage to the Holy Land, preached in public squares, and twice landed in prison after arousing the suspicion of Spanish Inquisitors. He studied for the priesthood at the University of Paris, where he gathered around him a group of fellow students who would form the nucleus of the Jesuit order. After receiving his bachelor's degree (at the age of forty-three), Ignatius attempted to settle in Jerusalem with his companions. When their expedition to the Holy Land failed, the fellowship traveled to Rome and offered its services to Pope Paul III, who issued a papal bull officially recognizing the order as the Society of Jesus.

The early Jesuits were distinguished from other religious orders by the small number of rules governing their actions. Most religious orders promulgated detailed regulations to guide every aspect of their members' lives. The Benedictines, a monastic order founded in 529, were bound by a written constitution organized into seventy-three chapters and entailing hundreds of highly detailed rules that dictated everything from the arrangement of beds in the dormitories to the number of cooked dishes served at dinner. Rules prescribed the precise timing of prayers, work, meals, sleep, and all other activities, leaving little to chance. The Benedictines' rules became a model for later religious orders, such as the Dominicans, whose constitution specified hundreds of regulations, including prohibitions against wearing slippers outside the monastery, sleeping during lectures, breaking or losing utensils, and letting blood (a common medical procedure at the time) more than four times per year.

The Jesuits' foundational document, known as the "Formula," consisted of five paragraphs that laid out the order's mission to help souls, an all-encompassing mandate that could (and did) include nearly any ministry. The most striking element of the "Formula" was how few rules it entailed. That handful of rules left the early Jesuits with a great deal of flexibility in pursuing novel opportunities to help souls. Existing religious orders, in contrast, were bound to clearly defined missions specified in great detail in their constitutions. The "Formula," with its few rules, provided some guidance on which ministries the early Jesuits should pursue. The most important rule obliged individual Jesuits to carry out whatever task they were assigned, whether "to send us among the Turks, or to the New World, or to the Lutherans, or to any others whether faithful or infidel." While the voluminous rules of existing orders ensured stability, the Jesuits' rules explicitly encouraged mobility. A second rule dictated that the Jesuits favor education, a guideline that would steer them toward building schools, which became their signature activity. A third rule released the Jesuits from the obligation to recite their daily prayers in unison, at a time when most religious orders required all members to assemble six to eight times per day to pray together. Excusing the Jesuits from the requirement for communal prayer allowed them to work odd hours and pursue ministries demanding extended stays away from their residences.

The expanding world of the sixteenth century created new possibilities to help souls, and the simple rules of the "Formula" provided the Jesuits with the flexibility to seize these opportunities, something incumbent religious orders lacked. As a religious startup with few rules, the Jesuits were well positioned to experiment with novel ministries. The first generation of Jesuits experimented widely: they converted natives in newly formed European colonies; negotiated peace between Catholic and Protestant rulers; freed debtors from prison; ministered to repentant prostitutes; preached on the streets; brought apostates back to Catholicism; cared for disabled soldiers; nursed lepers; and brokered truces among feuding Sicilian families. Even sympathetic commentators have characterized the Jesuits' diverse ministries as a "grocery list" that "might be separated by only a hair's breath, or less, from opportunism." But opportunism is not necessarily a bad thing.

The Jesuits' simple rules also provided them the flexibility to adapt to local circumstances of time and place. In their first year, eight of the ten founders left Rome on missions. Francis Xavier, for example, traveled to India, Indonesia, and Japan before his death on an island off the coast of China eleven years after leaving Rome. Throughout his travels, Xavier adapted his preaching to local conditions without losing sight of the overarching mission to help souls. In India, he preached to the lower castes, walking through the streets, clanging a bell to attract children, and teaching them by setting prayers to music. When he arrived in Japan, then embroiled in a civil war, Xavier shifted tactics. He exchanged his ragged cloak for rich garments to impress the aristocratic shoguns whose permission he needed to preach to and win converts.

The Jesuit leadership recognized the importance of flexibility, and sought out candidates who exemplified this trait. A decade after the order's founding, Juan de Polanco, secretary to Ignatius, listed flexibility third among the qualities of an ideal Jesuit, defining it as the ability to adapt to different situations, accommodate the specific idiosyncrasies of people, and learn from one's mistakes. Early Jesuits were not monks praying within a monastery, but rather missionaries who often worked alone or in pairs in distant territories. Like members of other religious orders, the Jesuits took a vow of obedience, but their work required constant adaptation to local circumstances and precluded frequent guidance from Rome. Face-to-face meetings with superiors were seldom possible. Communication by post was slow, erratic, and expensive. A letter and response from Rome to Japan or India could take up to three years, assuming the ship carrying the correspondence was not sunk or captured by pirates (a common occurrence at the time). The Jesuits' simple rules attracted spiritual entrepreneurs who relished the opportunity to seize the initiative and exercise creativity in pursuit of missionary opportunities. And the early Jesuits were a remarkable group. Within its first century, the order produced thirty-nine priests who would go on to be canonized for their contributions to the Church.

The story of the early Jesuits illustrates a key benefit of simple rules: they allow individuals and organizations to pursue a wide range of possible opportunities. Yet their rules also gave the activities of the early Jesuits consistency and coherence. The Jesuits' ministries were wide-ranging but not random; the order favored education, missions beyond Europe, and activities that brought them in contact with the world outside the rectory walls. Compared to the comprehensive regulations of the Benedictines or Dominicans, the Jesuits' simple rules, few in number, erred on the side of flexibility by conferring on individuals the latitude to exercise judgment. As a result, the Jesuits were better able to adapt, innovate, and seize unexpected opportunities than traditional orders.

A hammer is just the thing for nails, but useless when it comes to sawing a plank. The same is true of simple rules: to be effective, they must fit the task at hand. Simple rules work best when flexibility matters more than consistency. For the early Jesuits, the flexibility of their simple rules allowed the order to flourish. Throughout this book, we will discuss dozens of other situations, including creative endeavors and entrepreneurship, where the benefits of flexibility trump those of consistency. Both flexibility and consistency have their advantages, but increasing one reduces the other. There are some situations where the balance tips in favor of consistency. Then a large number of highly directive rules, like the Dominicans' regulations, are the best tool to use.

Detailed rules are particularly useful for avoiding catastrophic errors, such as plane crashes, mishaps in nuclear power plants, and surgical deaths that result from known causes. Pilots are fond of saying that "checklists are written in blood," a reference to how these lists were developed in the first place. When an airplane accident occurs, aviation investigators retrieve the black box and pinpoint the accident's cause. If the cause is novel, the investigators add a new item to the preflight checklist to prevent a similar accident in the future. Similarly, every surgeon knows that three of the top killers in surgery are bleeding, infection, and inappropriate anesthesia. Although these errors are common knowledge, taking measures to prevent them is not always common practice. Even in well-respected teaching hospitals, surgical teams sometimes forget to take small but crucial steps — such as confirming the patient's identity and procedure or ensuring the pulse oximeter is on the patient and functioning — that mitigate these well-understood risks. A surgical checklist of a few dozen specific rules ensures that basic steps are carried out with complete consistency. And if you are going under the knife or boarding a flight, consistent execution of the basics is exactly what you want.

Detailed rules enhance efficiency in executing routine activities. Consider McDonald's, one of the largest fast-food chains in the world. The chain's selling point has never been the quality or innovativeness of its food. Rather, McDonald's offers low prices, predictable food, and a consistent experience across its network of over thirty-four thousand restaurants operating in 116 countries. Nine out of ten McDonald's stores are owned by franchisees (rather than the company) and staffed by a workforce where most employees have worked at McDonald's for less than a year. Across its sprawling network, McDonald's requires that each franchisee follow the 386-page operating manual. This document lays out in fine-grained detail the guidelines for operations, maintenance, marketing, working-capital requirements, and the training of new employees. This detailed rule book reduces discretion to a bare minimum, and tips the balance to consistency to ensure predictability, efficiency, and few mistakes. The choice between simple rules and a more detailed rule book is driven by the task at hand, and the same individual or organization can use both in different circumstances. A doctor, for example, might rely on a checklist to prep for surgery but simple rules to diagnose a disease.

Simple rules impose a threshold level of structure while avoiding the rigidity that results from too many restrictions. The resulting flexibility makes it easier to adapt to changing circumstances and seize fleeting opportunities. Simple rules can also produce better decisions than more complicated models can, particularly when time and information are limited.

SIMPLE RULES PRODUCE BETTER DECISIONS

Simple rules enable people to make quick, reasonably accurate decisions that require less effort than more complicated approaches. When there is not much time or when information is at a minimum — in frontline triage, for example — these rules of thumb can save the day. Simple rules work because they focus on key aspects of a decision while ignoring peripheral considerations. By using simple rules, people can function without constantly stopping to rethink every aspect of a decision every time they make it.

Rules of thumb are often viewed as second-rate measures for use when people lack the time or information to come to a more considered judgment. Indeed, the term *rule of thumb* refers to a rough and practical approach that is not particularly accurate or reliable in every situation. While the term's exact origins are unclear, it is thought to refer to the practice of carpenters using their thumbs to make rough approximations of length rather than measuring accurately with a ruler. Rules of thumb are ubiquitous. Some golfers, for example, use the rule "Tee up the ball on the side of trouble" to guide them in driving the ball away from hazards (like a creek) and onto the fairway, while parents use rules like "Never give in once my two-year-old starts a tantrum."

There are some situations where simple rules are not just quick and easy mental shortcuts, they also produce surprisingly accurate decisions. Counterintuitive as it may sound, simple rules can outperform more analytically complicated and information-intensive approaches even when there is ample time and information to make a decision. This is especially true in situations when the links between cause and effect are poorly understood, when important variables are highly correlated, when a few factors matter most, and when a gap exists between knowing what to do and actually doing it. Simple rules do not trump complicated models every time, but they do so more often than you might think.

Gerd Gigerenzer is at the forefront of understanding why simple rules often allow for better decision making. Gigerenzer, a psychology professor at the Max Planck Institute, has conducted (and inspired) dozens of studies pitting sophisticated decision models against simple rules (which he refers to as *heuristics*). One study looked at how police can identify where serial criminals live. A simple rule — take the midpoint of the two most distant crime scenes — got police closer to the criminal than more sophisticated decision-making approaches. Another study compared a state-of-the-art statistical model and a simple rule to determine which did a better job of predicting whether past customers would purchase again. According to the simple rule, a customer was inactive if they had not purchased in x months (the number of months varies by industry). The simple rule did as well as the statistical model in predicting repeat purchases of online music, and beat it in the apparel and airline industries. Other research finds that simple rules match or beat more complicated models in assessing the likelihood that a house will be burgled and in forecasting which patients with chest pain are actually suffering from a heart attack.

Why can simpler models outperform more complex ones? When underlying cause-and-effect relationships are poorly understood, decision makers often look for patterns in historical data under the assumption that past events are a good indicator of future trends. The obvious problem with this approach is that the future may be genuinely different from the past. But a second problem is subtler. Historical data includes not only useful signal, but also noise—happenstance correlations between variables that do not reveal an enduring cause-and-effect relationship. Fitting a model too closely to historical data hardwires error into the model, which is known as *overfitting*. The result is a precise prediction of the past that may tell us little about what the future holds. Throwing more data and computing horsepower into the mix doesn't necessarily resolve this problem, because big data mixed with little theory is a recipe for overfitting. IBM recently released a study, based on a hundred years of data, showing that the increases in the height of women's heels were a leading indicator of economic downturns. The flat shoes favored by 1920s flappers gave way to high heels during the Depression, 1960s sandals to platform shoes during the 1970s oil crisis, and the low heels of the grunge look were replaced by stilettos as the dot-com bubble burst. The correlation worked, until it didn't. In the aftermath of the 2008 financial crisis, heel height trended downward. If you crunch a lot of numbers without a good theory, you will find correlations—the problem is, they may be spurious.

In contrast to complicated models, simple rules focus on only the most critical variables. By ignoring peripheral factors and tenuous correlations, rules of thumb eliminate a great deal of noise. The absence of noise results in decisions that work reasonably well across a wide range of scenarios, rather than being optimized for a single situation. Recall the triage rules that medics use to quickly assess the severity of soldiers' injuries. Despite their simplicity, these diagnostic principles are remarkably effective at predicting medical outcomes across a bewildering diversity of injuries. In very complex systems, like the stock market or the economy as a whole, where causal relations are poorly understood and shift over time, the risks of overfitting past data are particularly acute. Statisticians have found that complicated models consistently fail to outperform simple ones in forecasting economic trends, and the accuracy of their predictions has not improved over time. When it comes to modeling complex systems, sophisticated does not always equal effective.

Besides avoiding the overfitting of data, simple rules also capture correlated information about context. For example, Kathy, along with Chris Bingham of the University of North Carolina, studied the internationalization decisions of entrepreneurs. One successful U.S. entrepreneur used the simple rule "Enter English-speaking markets" when he made decisions about expansion. While simple, this rule was actually a proxy for several other variables that were related to successful growth. The entrepreneur grew up in England, which gave him familiarity with the cultural background of former British Commonwealth countries, which as it turns out constitute most of the world's English-speaking states. Also, most English-speaking countries have high Internet usage, per capita exports, and per capita GDP, making them relevant marketplaces for this entrepreneur's technology-based products. So this simple rule was, in fact, about a lot more than language—it was a surrogate for deep cultural knowledge, and a proxy for economic attractiveness.

We often assume that the best way to make a decision is by considering all the factors that might influence our choice and weighing their relative importance. Psychologists have found, however, that people tend to overweigh peripheral variables at the expense of critical ones when they try to take all factors into account. One study, for example, asked college students to consider several factors (such as the required reading, syllabus, prerequisites, and past students' ratings) and weigh their relative importance before deciding which courses to take. A control group was given the same information and simply asked to choose their courses. The students who gave less thought to the variables tended to focus on a single variable—past students' ratings — in making their decisions. In contrast, their classmates who considered more variables actually made worse decisions (as measured by their ultimate satisfaction with the courses they took). By ruminating on unimportant details, the students failed to give the most important variables the weight they deserved. Simple rules minimize the risk of overweighing peripheral considerations by focusing on the criteria most crucial for making good decisions.

Simple rules also make it more likely that people will act on their decisions, because they are easy to remember and less cumbersome to follow than complex guidelines for action. A terrific illustration of how simple rules trigger action comes from the experiences of twelve hundred micro-entrepreneurs in the Dominican Republic. They participated in a study to learn basic accounting to run their businesses better. Each entrepreneur was randomly assigned to one of three experimental groups. The first group studied accounting the way it is taught in most universities, as a complicated body of knowledge to be mastered. A second group studied accounting as simple rules like "Keep personal and business money in different drawers" and "Only transfer money from one drawer to the other with a written IOU." The third group received no accounting instruction. The entrepreneurs who learned the simple rules of accounting were more likely to translate their knowledge into action. They improved their bookkeeping and cash management and also increased sales by 25 percent. In contrast, the entrepreneurs who were exposed to accounting as a complicated body of knowledge were no better off than those who were not taught any accounting at all.

Simple rules not only trigger people to act, they also keep them from abandoning a decision once they have made it. Dieting is a prototypical situation where quitting is all too easy. One study of dieting, for example, compared perseverance and weight loss on a simple diet plan versus a complicated one. While the dieters who stuck with the program lost weight on both plans, people were more likely to adhere to the simple diet and abandon the complicated one. When asked why they quit, the lapsed dieters cited complexity as the single most important reason for giving up. Simplicity is even more important when people are tired, stressed, or otherwise cognitively impaired.

Willpower, it turns out, is more like a reservoir than a river. If we deploy willpower on one decision, we have less self-control available for our next decision. Many of our worst dietary choices, for example, are made in periods of low self-control — at the end of a long day when a big glass of cabernet or a pint of Ben and Jerry's calls out our name. Self-control then demands reserves of willpower when the tank is dry. But research finds that people in periods of low willpower can pass up tempting calories, provided they follow a simple rule. Without any rules, dieters tend to lapse back into their same old unhealthy habits. One of our favorite studies demonstrates this point further — dieters who followed just one simple rule ("Use ten-inch plates for dinner") lost about two pounds per month. In contrast, people with no rules had no weight loss at all.

Of course there are situations in which complicated decision models work better than simple rules. Decisions that can be made by computers, such as automated trading programs, are better candidates for complicated models than those that rely on human willpower to implement. Complicated models also work particularly well when data is ample and the underlying causal relationships among variables are well understood. For generations, sailors relied on rules of thumb like "Red sky at night, sailor's delight; red sky at morning, sailors take warning." A hundred years ago, these rules might have been the best sailors could do, but today's mariners would be better off checking the Weather

Channel. Meteorologists make amazingly accurate forecasts, particularly in the short term, and have nearly doubled the accuracy of their forecasts over the past forty years using increasingly sophisticated models. Meteorologists succeed because they understand the laws of fluid dynamics governing weather patterns and can incorporate these physical laws into their models. Their predictions are still limited by the imperfect measurement of current conditions (like temperature or air pressure), and the enormous computing power required to run all the simulations they need to forecast the weather. But meteorologists understand fairly well how the pieces of the weather system interact, so they can model these intricate relationships with precision.

Heuristics are a powerful decision-making tool, often matching or even outperforming more sophisticated approaches. They are easy to remember and use, attributes that increase the odds that people will not only make the right choice, but translate their decision into action and stick with it over time. Simple rules not only help produce better decisions, they also allow individuals to synchronize their activities with one another to collectively achieve feats that none could accomplish on their own, as the example of honeybee nest-selection illustrates.

SIMPLE RULES PROMOTE COLLECTIVE BEHAVIOR

Of the twenty thousand species of bees in the world, the vast majority eke out a solitary existence, tunneling into the ground to build crude cells where they live and die alone. A few species of bees, such as *Apis mellifera* (better known as the western, or European, honeybee), have evolved to live in complex societies with tens of thousands of members. As individuals, these colony members are not much more sophisticated than their solitary counterparts. Collectively, however, they can build complex honeycombs to store food and house their young, maintain a steady temperature in the hive year-round, and direct one another to the most promising sources of food. Japanese honeybees defend their nests from giant hornets by swarming around the attacker, vibrating their wings quickly to create heat, and cooking the hornet alive, a defensive tactic sometimes referred to as *thermoballing*.

When we observe a sophisticated structure like a beehive, we tend to assume it is the product of a plan. We see a design and infer a designer. The queen bee, however, is no forward-looking monarch planning and directing large-scale construction projects. She is little more than an egg-laying machine. Instead, the bee colony's behavior emerges in all its sophistication out of the activities of individual bees, who follow simple rules to synchronize their behavior with one another. As an example of simple rules driving collective behavior, consider how western honeybees decide where to live, a matter of life and death for the colony. In late spring or early summer, a swarm of several thousand bees flies in tight formation around the old queen as they leave their nest to perch on a nearby tree. The swarm hangs in a beardlike cluster for a few days while the bees collectively evaluate potential spots to build a nest and decide where to relocate. If the bees make a poor choice, they will fail to accumulate enough honey to survive the winter and the entire colony will die.

Professor Thomas Seeley, in his delightful book *Honeybee Democracy,* describes how bees select their new home. First, a few hundred scout bees fly from the cluster in all directions to seek out promising nesting sites. They typically look for a cavity in a tree, sufficiently large to store honey for the winter and far enough from the ground to avoid land-based predators. Collectively, these scouts identify up to a few dozen potential nest sites. When a scout discovers a promising site, she returns to the cluster and reports her find by dancing in a figure-eight pattern (known as a waggle dance) on the backs of her sister bees in the cluster. The dance encodes critical information about the potential nest site she has discovered. The bee's orientation during the waggle dance indicates the direction of the site, while the vigor and number of dance circuits signal its quality.

Other scouts milling about the dance floor follow the first dancer that they see, fly out to assess the site independently, and perform their own waggle dance upon their return. Bees that have discovered more attractive sites dance for longer, thereby attracting more scouts and amplifying the advertisement for their preferred location. Independent assessments by multiple scouts minimize the odds that the colony will choose an inappropriate nest based on a single scout's enthusiastic but flawed recommendation. Returning scouts also head-butt scouts advertising other sites to persuade them to stop dancing. Eventually one nest site attracts a quorum of followers, typically about one hundred bees, and the entire swarm mobilizes to depart for the new home. Attracting more recruits to the most promising site and closing down alternatives through head-butting ensures that the bees do not find themselves deadlocked between two competing options. While hanging as a beard, they are exposed to predators and the elements, and they need to coordinate not only well, but quickly.

The bees' nest-selection process is impressive, identifying multiple opportunities, securing independent quality assessments, conducting an open debate on alternatives, converging on the best choice, and avoiding deadlock. Bees achieve this impressive feat of coordination by following simple rules, such as "Dance longer for better sites," "Follow the first dancer you bump into," and "Head-butt scouts promoting other sites." The rules provide individual scouts with guidance on what to do, while leaving them the freedom to explore unexpected opportunities. Coordinated action emerges from the individual activities of hundreds of lone bees. No single bee visits all the sites to make direct comparisons, nor does the queen weigh the options and make the final call. Instead, all of the bees collectively follow the rules that allow them to gather disparate pieces of information, process them as a group, evaluate options, and decide. By following simple rules, they collectively make better decisions than any single bee could make on her own.

In many situations, our fates are closely intertwined, and success, failure, or even survival can depend on what others do. Simple rules allow humans, as well as insects, to synchronize their activities with one another. Improvisational comedy troupes, as we will discuss in chapter 3, use simple rules to weave unexpected material into a smooth narrative, in real time, and do so without a script to follow or a director to guide the action. By following simple rules, the members of open communities like Indiegogo can mobilize thousands of people who have never met one another to fund innovative ideas. In each of these cases, the members do not follow a preexisting plan or look to a central planner for guidance on what to do. Instead, their collective behavior emerges from individuals following simple rules.

It's easy to imagine why simple rules would work for bees, since they are hardwired to do what is best for the hive. But what about with human beings, who tend to follow their own self-interests? Simple rules impose a minimal level of coordination, while leaving ample room for individuals to pursue their own objectives. To see how simple rules balance coordination with individual interests, consider the case of Zipcar, which was founded in 2000 by Antje Danielson and Robin Chase. Zipcar emerged as the world's leading car-sharing network, with approximately

810,000 members and over ten thousand vehicles in cities and on college campuses spread across the United States, Canada, the U.K., and Europe. Unlike car rental firms like Hertz or Enterprise, Zipcar has no drop-off centers or staff to clean, check, and refuel the cars. Instead, Zipcar relies on its members to ensure that the vehicles they used are fit for the next driver's use. The quality of each member's car-sharing experience depends critically on the behavior of the complete stranger who drove the car just before them.

To ensure smooth coordination, Zipcar could have employed a thick contract that few would read and even fewer would remember. It could have asked members to contact each other to negotiate the transfer. But who has time? Instead, for its first dozen years, the company used six simple rules for members sharing a car: (1) report damage, (2) keep it clean, (3) no smoking, (4) fill 'er up, (5) return on time, and (6) pets in carriers. (The company did have a more detailed member agreement, but that only came into play for the very rare situations that the simple rules did not cover). These simple rules, easy to remember and follow, set the basic expectations for users. The actions covered by these rules accounted for the vast majority of disputes among members, so by following the rules members could avoid most problems. As long as they obeyed these simple rules, moreover, Zipcar members were free to use the cars however they liked: students might use them to load up on groceries, film crews could use them to lug their equipment around town, and couples could rent them for weekend getaways.

When the rules that guide collective behavior are simple and clear, members of a community can monitor one another and sanction anyone who violates the social norms. Consider master chefs. A study of dozens of accomplished French chefs, most of whom had been awarded Michelin stars, revealed that their community relies on simple rules to protect their intellectual property while swapping tips on techniques and ingredients. Chefs cannot resort to legal remedies to protect their recipes — whoever heard of patenting lamb stew? Copyright law also offers limited protection. Recipe books as a whole can be copyrighted, but not individual recipes. To accomplish what formal laws cannot, French chefs enforce powerful norms in the form of a few simple rules, including "Do not copy recipes by other chefs," "Do not pass proprietary information from a chef on to others without permission," and "Always acknowledge the author of a recipe."

Although these rules are not written down anywhere, they are well understood throughout the global community of master chefs. And if they are violated, the consequences are severe. Protecting intellectual property is serious business in a world where recipes can often be discovered through reverse engineering or consulting a published cookbook (although chefs often omit little tricks and secret ingredients from their published recipes). One chef explained, "If another chef copies a recipe exactly, we are very furious: we will not talk to this chef anymore, and we won't communicate information to him in the future." These norms cross the French border, suggesting haute cuisine chefs everywhere follow the rules. The study's authors cite a globetrotting case in which an Australian chef tried to pass off recipes he learned in a Chicago restaurant as his own. He was severely criticized in online blogs, and the story spread to other news media. The co-owner of the Chicago restaurant publicly questioned the chef's "intellectual integrity" on eGullet, an online forum sponsored by the Society for Culinary Arts & Letters. The offending chef apologized and removed the dishes from his menu.

Simple rules are not, of course, the only way to coordinate activities in a community or society. Many interactions among members of a modern economy are governed by contractual agreements — such as mortgages, terms and conditions for on-line services, employment agreements, cell phone contracts, and leases — that are anything but simple. PayPal's terms and conditions contract, for example, is 36,275 words long — nearly five times the length of the U.S. Constitution (including all amendments). Formal contracts work particularly well to coordinate behavior when the number of parties to the agreement is small, so they can invest the time and effort to come to a shared understanding of what they are agreeing to. It also helps if each side is equally sophisticated and has the legal expertise to know what they are getting into. When two sophisticated parties, like Samsung and Google, for example, forge a very specific technology alliance, it makes sense that they rely on a detailed contract rather than simple rules. When many parties must work together, simple trumps complex. Property rights are noteworthy for their simplicity, dominated by simple rules like "No trespassing" and the principle that whoever owns the land owns the air above it and the soil beneath it. Simple and clear property rules draw a bright line around private property that is easily interpreted by anyone encountering it.

Simple rules work because they do three things well. First, they allow for flexibility in the pursuit of new opportunities, avoiding the rigidity of too many rules and the chaos of none at all. They are particularly effective when the situation is in flux, flexibility trumps consistency, and the benefits of seizing opportunities exceed the cost of making mistakes. Second, simple rules can produce decisions that match or outperform more sophisticated decision models across a wide variety of possible scenarios, and do so quickly, with limited data requirements, and when cause and effect are imperfectly understood. Their simplicity, in addition, increases the odds that people will remember them, act on them, and stick with them over time. Finally, collective action, like the honeybees' choice of nest, can emerge from simple rules even when individuals' mental capacity is limited and no one member understands the situation in its entirety. By following a few simple rules, members of a community can produce results, like the choice of a safe nest or the protection of intellectual property, far better than what individuals could do on their own.

A striking feature of simple rules is their variety. The rules of the early Jesuits are nothing like those for healthy eating or finding a new nest. After years of studying simple rules, however, we have learned that despite the diversity of specific rules, they share an underlying structure, falling into six broad categories. In the next two chapters, we introduce the six types of rules, and describe what they do and when they are most effective. Chapter 2 looks at rules for decisions, and chapter 3 covers rules for actions.

2

Making Better Decisions

IN MOST COURTROOM DRAMAS, the climactic scene occurs when the jury returns with the verdict. But this is just one of several crucial decisions that influence whether justice will be served. In most countries, judges decide whether defendants must stay in prison awaiting their trial or whether they can post bail, a sum of money they pledge to ensure they will return for later court dates. In the United States, approximately five hundred thousand prisoners are in jail pending trial on any given day, a number that equates to 20 percent of the total American prison population. Worldwide, approximately three million people at any given time are sitting in prison without having been tried or found guilty.

The bail decision matters. On the one hand, freeing defendants on bail can pose risks to innocent victims and society. They may commit another crime, fail to return for their court dates, or intimidate witnesses against them. On the other hand, requiring defendants to stay in jail before trial can impose costs for defendants and society as a whole. Globally, the average length of pretrial detention is nearly six months, and can range up to a few years in some countries. Defendants held in pretrial detention cannot fulfill their family, community, or work responsibilities. A study in England found that one-half of men and two-thirds of women who were employed at the time of their arrest lost their jobs if they were imprisoned prior to their trial. Prison is often a recruiting and training ground for young criminals, and studies have shown that detained juvenile offenders are more likely to commit crimes later than those who are granted bail. Defendants who are held for their entire pretrial period are three to four times more likely to be sentenced to jail compared to defendants with similar backgrounds who were released on bail. They also serve sentences that are two to three times as long as comparable defendants who received bail. Prison is no picnic anywhere, but in many countries, defendants denied bail are exposed to violence, disease, and torture.

Choosing between bail and release is a complex decision for judges. To assess the risks involved, judges could consider multiple factors, including the circumstances of the defendant's current charge, prior arrests and convictions, outstanding warrants, past failure to appear in court, history of violence, stability of employment and residence, community and family ties, financial resources, mental health status, substance abuse issues, and character. In many jurisdictions around the world, the precise factors that should be considered are laid out in statutes or in detailed risk-assessment models designed to guide a judge's decision.

At least that is how these decisions are, in theory, supposed to be made. In practice, judges often rely on a handful of simple rules to decide whether to imprison or free a suspect pending trial. One study found that approximately 95 percent of bail decisions could be explained by three simple rules: Did the prosecution either request conditional bail or oppose bail altogether? Were conditions imposed on the bail by a judge earlier in the process? Did a previous court insist on keeping the defendant in custody? If the answer to any of these questions was yes, then the judge would almost certainly set a high bail or deny bail altogether. Judges clearly rely on simple rules.

The rules for judges deciding bail appear vastly different from the rules of bees seeking new nests and Jesuits pursuing new missions. But despite this apparent variety, we've found that effective simple rules always fall into one of six distinct categories. These types of rules vary with regard to what they do and when they work best, and some are easier to learn than others. In this chapter we'll be focusing on the three types of rules that improve decision making by structuring choices and centering on what to do (and what not to do). These rules work because they are easy to use and can lead to quick, accurate decision making across a wide array of situations.

We'll start with *boundary rules,* the most basic variety of decision rules. Boundary rules can help you decide between two mutually exclusive alternatives, like whether bail should be granted or denied. Boundary rules also help you to pick which opportunities to pursue and which to reject when faced with a large number of alternatives. The other types of decision rules — prioritizing and stopping rules — are less common and typically harder to learn than boundary rules. *Prioritizing rules* rank options to decide which alternatives will receive limited resources, such as medical care during battle or cash in a startup. Prioritizing rules are particularly useful when you lack sufficient resources or time to do everything, or when people hold conflicting views about what to do. *Stopping rules* dictate when to reverse a decision. They provide guidance, for example, on when to sell a stock, end the search for a mate, or descend from a treacherous mountaintop.

BOUNDARY RULES

Judges' boundary rules guide the yes-or-no decision of whether to grant bail. Doctors use boundary rules to decide whether or not a patient is suffering from a particular disease. Police officers use them to determine whether a suicide note is authentic. Even female hyenas apply them when deciding on a mate. Because these rules define the boundaries of inclusion or exclusion, they sometimes take the form of negative prohibitions, like the "thou shalt nots" of the Ten Commandments. Employees at Kickstarter, the crowdfunding website, for example, had rules to screen every potential project and reject those that did not fit one of its categories, like movies, art, or books.

Although they live on the wrong side of the law, professional burglars, like judges, also rely on boundary rules. The choice of which house to enter is a high-stakes decision for burglars. If they break into an occupied home, they risk capture, prison, or worse if the homeowner is also a gun owner. In one study, Texas burglars were asked what kind of residence they would attempt to rob. A full 90 percent said they would never deliberately enter an occupied residence. Hollywood versions of burglars may rely on complicated formulas to plan their crimes — perhaps a twenty-six-variable equation, where a is the duration of the local police officer's coffee break, x is the length of time it takes Brad Pitt to charm the nosy neighbor, and z is the velocity of a nearby guard dog. But most real-life burglars rely on only a few simple rules to decide if a house is unoccupied, and hence a good candidate for breaking and entering.

In a recent study, researchers contacted residents of Newfoundland, Canada, with an unusual request. Homeowners were asked if they would let the researchers take photographs of the outside of their houses at unexpected times. The researchers would then show these photographs to convicted felons at the local prison and ask them to determine which residences would make attractive burglary targets. Surprisingly, a sizable number of homeowners agreed to have the photographs taken and shown to the felons. The burglars ignored many factors, like the presence of a security system in the house, landscaping that might provide cover, and deadbolt locks on doors. Instead, in determining targets, they employed simple rules to assess whether a house was occupied, ignoring all other considerations. The burglars significantly outperformed chance in identifying occupied houses, and two-thirds of the time they used a single rule to pick their target: "Avoid houses with a vehicle parked outside." This simple rule is unlikely to dazzle fans of heist films like *Ocean's Eleven*, but it works. The presence of a vehicle was indeed the single most reliable predictor of occupancy in the homes that the researchers photographed.

The above example illustrates an important benefit of boundary rules — they narrow down the alternatives, helping people decide which opportunities to pursue in the face of an overwhelming number of choices. Professional housebreakers face hundreds or thousands of possible candidates for burglary and lack the time to painstakingly case each one. Boundary rules provide a quick screen to select the most promising targets based on readily available information (is there a car parked outside?), which is highly correlated with what makes an opportunity attractive — in this case, an unoccupied house.

Just as boundary rules can help pick the most promising opportunities when time is scarce, they're also useful when money is the binding constraint. Founded in 1958 in the wake of the Soviet Union's stunning *Sputnik* launch, the Defense Advanced Research Projects Agency (DARPA) is the U.S. Defense Department's research lab, charged with preventing strategic surprises by adversaries while developing surprises of its own. The agency's ongoing projects employ cutting-edge technology with results that can seem right out of science fiction. The One Shot XG, for example, mounts onto a rifle and enables snipers to hit their targets with one round, day or night, at distances sometimes exceeding a mile, even in high winds. Another program, called Z-Man and inspired by the biology of geckos, aims to develop climbing aids that allow soldiers with full combat loads to scale vertical walls without the use of ropes or ladders. Brain-controlled prosthetics? DARPA is on it. A robotic horse that can move with troops and carry four hundred pounds of equipment? DARPA is developing it. Plan X? Don't ask — it's highly classified. But DARPA is on it.

DARPA's accomplishments are as extensive as they are mind-blowing. They are all the more impressive when viewed in light of the organization's limited resources. DARPA is not the military behemoth that one might think. Its permanent personnel number 120, about half the size of the Pentagon's cafeteria staff. Its annual budget of $3 billion is not particularly impressive, especially since it is spread among roughly two hundred programs at any given time. Until DARPA develops a groundbreaking alchemy program, it will continue to have a limited number of dollars to throw at projects, and thus must carefully select the ones that will deliver the most bang for the buck.

Considering the jaw-gaping complexity of DARPA's initiatives, it is perhaps surprising that the organization uses two simple boundary rules to decide which projects to fund. First, the project must further the quest for fundamental scientific understanding, and second, it must have a practical use. DARPA favors projects that meet both of these criteria, allowing them to avoid highly theoretical projects with few practical applications, and projects that may have practical applications but offer few scientific benefits. The model for DARPA's rules is Louis Pasteur, who advanced basic science while tackling real-world problems, like preservation of food and the prevention of tuberculosis.

Boundary rules are also used to diagnose a wide range of medical conditions, from HIV and celiac disease to dangerous infections in infants, among others. Boundary rules can help medical staff make rapid decisions when delay can result in death. There are, for example, over 2.5 million emergency room visits in the United States each year by patients suffering from acute dizziness. A small fraction of these patients are suffering from a rare type of stroke whose symptoms mirror a common viral infection. Time is of the essence in distinguishing between a stroke and a viral infection. An MRI scan can spot the difference, but can require hours or even days of waiting time.

A recently developed test, in contrast, consists of three simple rules that doctors can administer at the patient's bedside. These rules are too technical for laypeople — for instance, one involves measuring the specific way in which a patient's eyeballs move together — but are immediately comprehensible to a doctor. The simple rules are as accurate as an MRI and yet take only about one minute to apply. Boundary rules are also cheap to employ — an important selling point in many situations, such as managing health care costs. This particular set of simple rules, for example, allows doctors to avoid an MRI scan, which can cost $1,000 or more in many U.S. hospitals.

Boundary rules are also easy to use. Consider the case of clinical depression, which afflicts an estimated 350 million people per year worldwide — a United States or Indonesia of sufferers — and accounts for a million suicides annually. Despite its prevalence, depression is a shape-shifting disease that can be fiendishly difficult to diagnose because it has so many manifestations. Symptoms can be as subtle and varied as overeating (or undereating), persistent aches and pains, oversleeping (or undersleeping), digestive problems, and chronic indecisiveness. Depression can be difficult to diagnose, even for mental health professionals, who rely on lengthy structured interviews or detailed guidelines to spot the disease. These complicated protocols can prove daunting to use for people like school nurses or Army chaplains whose charges might be suffering from the disease. A recently developed diagnostic tool for depression relies on four simple rules, expressed as questions that can be asked in under a minute: Have you cried more than usual within the last week? Have you been disappointed in yourself or hated yourself within the last week? Have you felt discouraged about the future within the last week? Have you felt that you failed in your life within the last week? Patients who answer yes to all four questions are likely to be clinically depressed, and the rules correctly classified depressed patients over 97 percent of the time.

Boundary rules are also easier to understand and communicate than the results of complicated statistical studies. Physicians are among the most highly trained professionals in the world, but few are trained as statisticians. In one study, 160 gynecologists were asked the following question:

> A breast cancer mammogram has a sensitivity of 90% (meaning it will detect 9 out of 10 cases of breast cancer). It has a false-positive rate of 9% (meaning that, for 9% of women who do not have breast cancer, the test will say that they do), and there is a prevalence of 1% (meaning that 1% of the population is expected to actually have breast cancer). As a physician, what would you tell a woman who tested positive about her chances of having breast cancer?

If you are like most people, you probably had difficulty figuring out the probability that this woman has cancer. Even if you got the right answer in the end, it required some calculation and consumed valuable time. And the correct answer — the woman has more than a 90 percent chance of *not* having breast cancer — is hard to determine even for doctors. Over half of the gynecologists in the study believed that at least eight out of ten women who tested positive would have cancer — not a helpful message for a patient who is overwhelmingly likely to be cancer-free. Doctors are smart, but they are still human. Complex models, which make simple statistical problems like the one above look like child's play, are difficult to understand and explain, leading to dangerous misunderstandings. Boundary rules can translate statistical findings into easy-to-use decision aids.

Boundary rules can also translate broad policies into practical guidelines. Consider the case of military drones, where a computer screen can register a bird's-eye view of even the most remote village, with small figures scrambling to and fro. The human operating a drone has one of the most stressful office jobs imaginable. Deciding whether to pull the trigger on a drone strike is an extremely difficult call, based on imperfect information and often made under extreme time pressure. Every case is a life-or-death situation. Fire and you risk killing innocent civilians, but refrain and you might let a terrorist live to kill others. And even when the target is almost certainly the enemy, every drone strike has geopolitical ramifications, particularly when it encroaches on a foreign government's sovereignty. There are many factors to consider before pulling that trigger, every one of them momentous, and the person making that decision may only have a split second to decide what to do. After all, the events are unfolding on the screen in real time.

In a 2013 speech, President Barack Obama laid out three rules for deciding whether to launch a drone strike against a specific target. The starting point was the national security, geopolitical, and civilian-safety objectives the president hoped to achieve. Three simple rules translated these broad goals into more concrete guidelines: Does the target pose a continuing and imminent threat to the American people? Are there no other governments capable of effectively addressing the threat? Is there near certainty that no civilians will be killed or injured? Only if the answer to all three of these questions was yes would a drone strike be authorized.

The American drone program is shrouded in secrecy, and it is unclear exactly how these simple rules have been used within the chain of decision making. By virtue of their simplicity and directness, however, they could provide a useful framework to structure discussions about these very tough decisions. And there is some evidence that they are working. In 2013, the year Obama articulated these simple rules, there was a sharp decline in confirmed civilian casualties by drone strikes. The concreteness of these rules also makes communicating them, both to U.S. citizens and the international community, straightforward. The United States has enjoyed a virtual monopoly on military drones, but that will not last forever. The U.K., China, Israel, and Iran had operational military drones in 2014, while other countries, including India, Pakistan, and Turkey, have advanced development programs. By articulating and adhering to a set of principles governing the use of drones, the United States has an opportunity to shape the international standards that other countries will use to guide their decisions in the future.

Boundary rules guide the choice of what to do (and not do) without requiring a lot of time, analysis, or information. Boundary rules work well for categorical choices, like a judge's yes-or-no decision on a defendant's bail, and decisions requiring many potential opportunities to be screened quickly. These rules also come in handy when time, convenience, and cost matter. Boundary rules cover the basics of *what* to do, while the next two types of decision rules cover two particular challenges: how to prioritize and when to stop doing something.

PRIORITIZING RULES

Prioritizing rules can help you rank a group of alternatives competing for scarce money, time, or attention. These rules are harder to learn than boundary rules, as we'll discuss in chapter 7, but they can be very effective. For example, corporations use them to rank customers, geographic markets, or alliance partners. One Silicon Valley tech giant uses a simple prioritizing rule in deciding between two equally qualified candidates: all else equal, hire recruits referred by a current employee. Another company allocated its scarce manufacturing capacity among different products by prioritizing gross margin. The simple rules of medical triage are another example of prioritization: prioritize for care those wounded soldiers who can be saved but only if treated immediately. Prioritizing rules are also relevant in our personal lives for guiding everything from deciding how we spend our limited free time to ranking home-improvement projects. Prioritizing rules are useful when a large number of opportunities meet the threshold of the boundary rules, but resources are limited.

Prioritizing rules are often used in business to allocate cash when money is tight. In the late 1990s the Brazilian government privatized the country's freight rail system. After decades of government underinvestment, the rail infrastructure was literally falling apart — half of the bridges needed repair and one in five was on the verge of collapse. Venomous pit vipers that could exceed five feet in length hid in the overgrown grass blanketing freight terminals, regularly biting unwary employees. The system still deployed two-dozen steam-powered locomotives, a throw-back to the nineteenth century.

A prominent Brazilian private equity firm bought the portion of the rail network that ran through southern Brazil, and installed Alex Behring as CEO of the new railway, América Latina Logística (ALL). Behring, then all of thirty-one years old, walked into a tough situation. The railway generated cash only a few months each year, when Brazil's soybean farmers harvested their crops and shipped them to market. Unfortunately, insufficient capacity and damaged tracks forced the company to turn down business during the peak harvest season, leaving crops literally rotting in the fields. The railway could not expand services to current customers without upgrading its tracks and trains. Yet the company had only $15 million available for capital spending, less than one-tenth the total funding requested by managers. The company had been starved for investment capital for years, so nearly all of the projects had merit, but there wasn't enough cash to go around. Which were the high-priority projects that should be tackled first? Which projects could wait?

The textbook answer for how to prioritize projects for investment is to create detailed cash-flow projections for each proposal, adjust them for inflation and the cost of capital, and then rank the projects by economic value. There is no question that Behring understood cash-flow models — he was the top finance student in his MBA class. But he did not take that route. Instead, Behring assembled a team of managers from different departments and charged them with developing simple rules to rank the worthwhile proposals that had cleared the bar for capital spending. The team came up with a handful of prioritizing rules, ranking projects according to whether they (1) removed bottlenecks to growing revenues, (2) provided benefits immediately (rather than paying off in the long term), (3) minimized up-front expenditures, and (4) reused existing resources.

The simplicity of the rules made it straightforward for employees at many levels to understand and support the company's investment strategy. While competitors spent lavishly on new equipment, ALL recovered decommissioned engines from its "dead fleet" of idle trains, bought used locomotives from African railways, and replaced damaged sections of the main line with dismantled tracks from abandoned stations. The simplicity of the prioritizing rules also enabled employees at every level to propose better projects. A frontline supervisor, for example, suggested increasing the size of fuel tanks to extend the distances that engines could operate without refueling. This would sharply reduce downtime during the peak harvest season and increase revenue immediately, moving his proposal to the top of the rankings. The simple rules provided sufficient structure for the company to stay on track (so to speak) in terms of using their capital well, while leaving ample room for creative solutions from every employee.

Within three years, ALL increased revenues 50 percent and tripled its operating cash flow, while maintaining the best safety record of all freight lines in Brazil. When the company went public in 2004, it had grown into Latin America's largest independent logistics company, controlled the most extensive rail network in Latin America, was listed among the best employers in Brazil, and was noted for its performance-oriented culture. Behring himself went on to lead 3G Capital, which acquired Burger King and H. J. Heinz, with Warren Buffet's Berkshire Hathaway as a co-investor.

Prioritizing rules are hardly a modern invention. The ancient Romans used them to reconcile the overwhelming number of conflicting laws and legal interpretations in the Roman Empire.

At its founding, Rome was a city, not an empire. In its early years, a panel of patricians codified ancestral customs into the "Twelve Tables," a constitution consisting of just over one hundred laws. In the ensuing centuries, successive emperors issued new edicts that increased the body of Roman law dramatically. Leading jurists layered interpretations and opinions on top of these decrees. These opinions assumed the force of law, but they often conflicted with one another on the same legal question. How was a judge to make sense of this conflicting morass and make valid legal decisions?

In 426 AD, Valentinian III, emperor of the western empire, issued a law to help judges prioritize incompatible edicts and legal opinions. (Actually, it was the emperor's mother who issued the law, as Valentinian was only seven years old at the time.) The Law of Citations first specified a rule that limited the use of historical opinions to those written by five jurists widely acknowledged to be the greatest legal thinkers that Rome had ever produced. The law then laid out four prioritizing rules that further clarified what judges should do: (1) when the jurists unanimously agreed on the issue, the judge was to follow their opinion; (2) if there was disagreement, the judge should follow the majority; (3) if the historical opinions were divided evenly, the judge should follow the opinion of Papinian, who was considered the greatest legal mind; and (4) if there was a tie among jurists and Papinian did not express an opinion, the judge could rely on his own discretion to decide the matter before the court. The Law of Citations guided Roman jurisprudence for more than a century. It provided judges with guidance on how to prioritize past legal interpretations while leaving some scope for judicial discretion.

Prioritizing rules are not just for corporations and societies; individuals can use them as well. Consider the question of how to rank investments across asset classes, such as domestic stocks, international equities, real estate, and bonds. More than sixty years ago, a young economist named Harry Markowitz published a paper in the *Journal of Finance* that offered would-be investors a way to maximize returns on their investment for any given level of risk. Although only fifteen pages long, the paper was hardly a light read. A typical sentence reads, "Thus the slope of the isomean line associated with $E = E_0$ is $-(\mu_1-\mu_3)/(\mu_2-\mu_3)$ its intercept is $(E_0-\mu_3)/(\mu_2-\mu_3)$." Markowitz went on to win a Nobel Prize for his pioneering work, and his model remains influential to this day.

For all its theoretical elegance and widespread adoption, however, the Markowitz model has a problem: it cannot outperform a simple rule that originated in the Babylonian Talmud, written about fifteen hundred years ago. According to this rule of thumb, "a man should always place his money, one third in land, a third into merchandise, and keep a third in hand." The general extension of this Talmudic advice is the $1/N$ principle, whereby total available funds are prioritized with equal ranking across the total number of asset classes. The $1/N$ rule ignores a lot of data and relationships that the Markowitz model captures, such as each asset's historical returns, risk, and correlation with other asset classes. In fact, the $1/N$ rule ignores everything except for the number of investment alternatives under consideration. It is hard to imagine a simpler investment rule.

And yet it works. One recent study of alternative investment approaches pitted the Markowitz model and three extensions of his approach against the $1/N$ rule, testing them on seven samples of data from the real world. This research ran a total of twenty-eight horseraces between the four state-of-the-art statistical models and the $1/N$ rule. With ten years of historical data to estimate risk, returns, and correlations, the $1/N$ rule outperformed the Markowitz equation and its extensions 79 percent of the time. The $1/N$ rule earned a positive return in every test, while the more complicated models lost money for investors more than half the time. Other studies have run similar tests and come to the same conclusions. The returns from the complicated models, unimpressive as they are, still overstate the returns investors could expect in the real world, because they exclude the fees that asset managers might charge for active management.

One surprising follower of the $1/N$ rule is Markowitz himself. While working at the Rand Corporation, Markowitz had to allocate his retirement fund across investment opportunities. According to his own theory, he should have calculated the correlations between different asset classes to draw an efficient frontier and rank the asset classes accordingly. Instead, as he later confessed to a financial journalist, he allocated his retirement funds evenly between stocks and bonds and called it a day.

Prioritizing rules are particularly common in business settings, as we will discuss in chapter 5. They are especially powerful when applied to a bottleneck, an activity or decision that keeps individuals or organizations from reaching their objectives. Bottlenecks represent pinch-points in companies, where the number of opportunities swamps available resources, and prioritizing rules can ensure that these resources are deployed where they can have the greatest impact. In business settings, prioritizing rules can be used to assign engineers to new-product-development projects, focus sales representatives on the most promising customers, and allocate advertising expenditure across multiple products, to name only a few possibilities.

STOPPING RULES

When choosing a mate, female field crickets face a universal romantic dilemma: when to stop searching and settle down with a partner. There are pros and cons to both committing and continuing to play the field. From a female cricket's perspective, looking for Mr. Right costs time and energy, and if the search extends too long, it increases the risk that she will pass up her best option. But if she stops the search too early, she might settle for a suboptimal partner, when a little more patience might have resulted in a superior mate.

Male crickets chirp as rapidly as they can to woo their stick-like paramours. Females directly benefit from mating with faster-singing males, as products in their seminal fluid can increase female fertility and perhaps even lifespan: a compelling pickup line if ever there was one. In order to study how females stop searching and settle on a mate, biologists constructed a bizarre cricket-sex playpen bathed in dim red light, with a video camera recording all the action. Crickets were held in captivity and fed Purina cat mix. The corners of the pen were fitted with loudspeakers, and in front of each, a male cricket was secured with string, its wings glued together with beeswax so that it was unable to produce sound. A female cricket was then released into the center of the square pen as the loudspeakers behind the males blared out prerecorded cricket chirps set to various frequencies. The scientists then observed which loudspeaker (and male) the confused female approached, thus revealing her chirp-rate preference.

Female crickets favored chirp rates above three chirps per second, but they did not distinguish among chirp rates beyond this threshold. In deciding to stop searching and choose a mate, female crickets followed a simple rule: If a chirp rate exceeds the frequency of three chirps per second, then mate. The researchers also found evidence to suggest that female crickets used another simple rule: Lower your standards if you have not come across an attractive male in a while. If a female cricket went twenty-four hours without hearing a fast chirp rate, she would settle for a less virile singer.

Biologists have observed several different rules that insects use to decide when to end their search and settle on a mate. These rules include "Choose a mate who meets your quality threshold," which is known as the *fixed-threshold* strategy. In contrast, the female crickets that lower the bar if they do not run across enough high-quality males adhere to what is known as the *variable-threshold* strategy. Studies of cockroaches, midwife toads, and guppies have found that females of those species adopt a variation of this strategy, becoming less picky in their choice of mates as they age, independent of the number of attractive males they encounter. Another simple rule for ending a mate search is to visit a fixed number of potential mates and then return to the highest-quality mate within that sample. And anyone who has stayed until last call at a singles bar will recognize the "fixed threshold with last chance option" rule, where the seeker maintains his or her threshold until a set time, and then mates with the next potential partner regardless of quality.

The field cricket's decision of when to quit looking for love and mate exemplifies a common problem. Whenever alternatives present themselves sequentially (as opposed to appearing all at once), the question of when to stop searching and make a choice arises. Think of an employer interviewing candidates for a job, a driver scanning through radio stations in search of the perfect song, or a teenager shopping for shoes. Knowing when to stop searching is a thorny problem. Continuing the quest costs time, effort, and opportunity—you forgo listening to a good song while trying to find a great one. But the next tune might be worth the wait. You just don't know.

An insect's rule for when to halt the search for a mate is an example of a *stopping rule*, which provides guidance on the decision to call it quits. Nobel Prize–winning economist Herbert A. Simon argued that individuals lack the information, time, and brainpower to determine the single best option when faced with a sequence of alternatives. Instead, like crickets, they rely on a rule of thumb to stop searching when they find an alternative that is good enough. Simon called this rule *satisficing,* an inelegant but descriptive combination of the words *satisfy* and *suffice.*

While ending a search is hard, it is even tougher for people to reverse a significant investment that they have already made. Yet when it comes to investments of time, energy, or resources, "you've got to know when to hold 'em," as Kenny Rogers sang, and "know when to fold 'em." A well-documented tendency among human decision makers, known as the *status quo bias,* leads individuals to hold 'em when they should fold 'em across a range of decisions. Aging professional athletes are susceptible to this when deciding whether to play another season, as are venture capitalists considering whether to pull the plug on a startup, musicians thinking about breaking up their bands, and nations deciding when to pull out of a foreign conflict.

These stay-versus-go decisions are particularly important for investors. Stopping rules can help investors by providing some guidance on when to sell their assets. And, if there was ever a good time to know when to sell a stock, it was right before the Great Depression. While images of financiers plummeting to their deaths from Wall Street windows spring mainly from urban legend, there is no doubt that market conditions caused widespread despair among financiers, along with the rest of the country. Out of the rubble of the 1929 crash, one banker rose up stronger than ever. Gerald Loeb, the son of a French wine merchant, sniffed out the crash of 1929 before it happened and helped his clients avoid heavy stock market losses. Loeb was hailed as a Wall Street sage, and a nation of skittish investors subsequently followed his advice. The first edition of Loeb's 1935 book, *The Battle for Investment Survival,* sold over 250,000 copies, and *Forbes* magazine called him "the most quoted man on Wall Street."

The secret weapon of Loeb's investing strategy was a simple but powerful stopping rule: "If an investment loses 10 percent of its initial value, sell it." This rule ensures that the investor does not stick with a loser over the long term. While it may be tempting to wait for a pet stock to regain its value, Loeb's 10 percent rule recognizes that it is often best to cut your losses and move your money elsewhere. "It is a great mistake to think that what comes down must come back up," he wrote. "The most important single thing I learned is that accepting losses promptly is the first key to success."

Loeb did not intend his rule to be applied mindlessly. "If there is anything I detest," he wrote, "it's a mechanistic formula for anything." He hoped that people would exercise their judgment, using his rule as a guide for intelligent action. Nevertheless, Loeb was such a strong believer in this particular rule that he was tempted to elevate it to an unwavering principle. "If you make an investment of $10,000 and the market value shrinks to $9,000," he wrote, "I'm almost inclined to say, dogmatically, sell it out and try again."

Stopping rules can also help people desist from mindless behavior. Consider overeating. For years, researchers have puzzled over the so-called French paradox, the observation that French citizens enjoy a low incidence of heart disease and obesity, which is surprising when you consider how much of French cuisine is drenched in butter. Between the éclairs, crêpes, and mayonnaise-dipped *pommes frites*, the French are hardly culinary puritans. Indeed, they enjoy one of the most decadent cuisines in the world. When Chicago's civic leaders drew up a plan for their city's future in 1909, they called it "Paris on the Prairie." But walking through the midwestern city is a very different experience than strolling along the Rive Gauche. Americans are twice as likely to be obese as their counterparts in France.

One study suggests that the rules diners use to stop eating, rather than those they use to decide what to eat, play a crucial role in thwarting obesity. A cross-continental team of researchers matched 145 Chicagoans with demographically similar Parisians. Both the Chicagoans and Parisians used stopping rules to decide when to finish eating, but the rules themselves were very different. The Parisians employed rules like "Stop eating when I start feeling full," linking their decision to internal cues about satiation. The Chicagoans, in contrast, were more likely to follow rules linked to external factors, such as "Stop eating when I run out of a beverage," or "Stop eating when the TV show I'm watching is over." Stopping rules that rely on internal cues — like when the food stops tasting good or you feel full — decrease the odds that people eat more than their body needs or even wants.

Stopping rules are particularly critical in situations when people tend to double down on a losing hand. A well-documented decision error occurs when people embark on a course of action, receive negative feedback, and then up the ante rather than stop. Escalating commitment to a failed course of action is a well-documented error, with over 150 studies of cases as diverse as NBA teams overplaying draft-pick busts, rogue traders doubling down on their money-losing investments, construction projects becoming money pits, and failing military campaigns where success is always described as just around the corner (the Vietnam War is often used as the poster child of escalating commitment to a failed course of action). Several factors increase the odds of this error, such as proximity to completion, the desire to save face, reluctance to write off sunk costs, and the fear of living with the regret of not trying. All of these factors played a role in the most deadly year of climbing in Mount Everest's history.

Two dozen mountaineers lost their lives trying to scale Mount Everest before 1953, when Sir Edmund Hillary and Tenzing Norgay ascended the world's tallest mountain. Within a few decades, climbing Everest had transformed from the domain of a few intrepid adventurers into a multimillion-dollar industry. By 1996, 846 climbers had reached the summit of Everest, paying up to $65,000 for the privilege. The founder of one tour company claimed that the professional guides had "built a yellow brick road to the summit."

Against this apparently benign commercial backdrop, the deadliest climb in the mountain's history unfolded. Just after midnight on May 10, 1996, sixteen mountaineers, led by two world-renowned climbers and accompanied by several Sherpa guides, set off to reach the summit of the world's highest mountain. The climbers included several doctors, a New York socialite, the journalist Jon Krakauer, and a sixty-eight-year-old mountaineer who was attempting to become the oldest person to reach Everest's summit. The final ascent — from Base Camp IV to the summit — was expected to take eighteen hours, mostly in the Death Zone — an altitude beginning about five miles above sea level, where the human body cannot acclimatize due to a lack of oxygen in the atmosphere. There is no room for error.

To ensure everyone made it up and down the mountain safely, Scott Fischer, the leader of one of the expeditions, explained to all of his climbers that they would stick to a stopping rule he had devised — If you aren't on top by two o'clock, it's time to turn around. Fischer's two o'clock rule ensured that the climbers would avoid descending at nightfall, and that they would have enough energy and bottled oxygen to descend safely. When the climbers began their final ascent to the summit around midnight, things went wrong quickly. They discovered that the ropes they had expected to be fixed for the final sixteen hundred feet of the climb were not in place, causing a delay.

As the group ascended the final stretch of the mountain behind schedule, the two o'clock rule became more and more tempting to break. The climbers had spent tens of thousands of their own dollars, dedicated months to training, and endured weeks of discomfort, all for a fleeting moment on top of the world. To be deprived of that lifetime achievement when the summit was within reach would be torture. One member of the group had come within three hundred feet of the summit on an earlier expedition and spent the previous year agonizing over his failure to reach his goal. Deciding whether to proceed or turn back would be a tough decision in the best of conditions, but it is hard to think straight in the Death Zone. In subzero temperatures, after more than a dozen exhausting hours of hiking with scarce oxygen, the climbers' judgment was impaired. One of the appeals of the two o'clock rule is its simplicity — it could easily be remembered and followed, no matter how disoriented or oxygen-depleted the climbers were.

In the end, the temptation to reach the peak proved too much. By 2:00 PM, most of Fischer's clients had not yet arrived at the summit. Fischer himself did not reach the summit until 3:45, nearly two full hours after his own stopping rule dictated he turn around. As the mountaineers began to descend the slope in fragmented groups, the weather took a turn for the worse — with winds picking up, snowfall reducing visibility to zero, and the temperature, with wind-chill, falling to 100° below zero Fahrenheit. Exhausted and disoriented, the climbers struggled on, but only one made it back to camp before darkness fell. Five climbers from the group died that night, including the two guides. Sherpas tried to rescue Fischer where he collapsed, but found him beyond saving. His body still lies on Mount Everest, a frozen reminder to climbers to turn around before it is too late.

Decision rules — boundary, prioritizing, and stopping — provide clear guidelines for making better decisions across many situations and in the most challenging circumstances. They help answer the question of what to do — what is acceptable to do, what is more important to do, and what to stop doing. In the next chapter we turn to process rules, which provide guidance on how to do things better.

3

Doing Things Better

Until it burned to the ground in 1987, Jack's was a popular bar midway between Harvard and MIT on Massachusetts Avenue. Given its location between two storied institutions of higher learning, you might envision a cozy pub, decorated with ferns, where tweed-clad scholars would debate the nuances of T. S. Eliot's *Four Quartets*. But Jack's was less *Dead Poet's Society* and more *Sons of Anarchy*. Instead of wood-paneled walls, Jack's had plate glass windows facing the street, which allowed the members of the Rum Pot Rustlers motorcycle club to keep an eye on their Harleys while drinking. The bikers and their entourage scared off most of the students. The bar's policy of featuring live rock bands every night, including local legends like the Bosstones, 'Til Tuesday, and Sleepy LaBeef, attracted rockers from all over Boston. On the occasional Monday night, a jazz ensemble or an art band might sneak onto the bill (They Might Be Giants raised some eyebrows when they played). But most nights, Jack's was a hard-rocking place.

The club's owner, a Harvard alum from the 1970s, recruited

bouncers from Harvard's hockey team and boxing club to keep the peace. This is how one of us (Don) came to work the door at one of Cambridge's rowdiest bars. As a part-time job, being a bouncer at Jack's had much to recommend it: the base pay was good, with tips even better. The doormen and their friends drank for free, most of the bands were entertaining, and you met a lot of colorful characters. The one drawback, especially for a 175-pound light heavyweight, was that Jack's attracted more than its fair share of barroom brawlers from higher weight classes. You could count on a scuffle pretty much any night of the week. Friday and Saturday consistently produced a few brawls, some of which escalated into full-out donnybrooks.

One particularly rough month required Don to take two late-night trips to the emergency room (one caused by a drunk who reacted to a full nelson by thrusting himself backward from his barstool, crashing himself and Don through a half-inch-thick wooden counter). Sheer brute force was not a winning strategy for a light heavyweight bouncer, so Don instead reflected on his experience to date and formulated a set of simple rules for keeping the peace. The first was "Don't let trouble in the door." There were several local toughs who had started fights in the past, and experience proved it was much easier to keep them from coming in than to kick them out when fists were flying. Not surprisingly, most barroom fights are started by guys who have had too much to drink. The rule to "Stay sober until the last patron leaves" (which might have been the club's official policy anyway) provided an edge that was critical in a lot of situations. Certain types of music attracted a disproportionate share of knuckleheads, which led to another rule: "Double up for heavy metal, ska, and punk bands." Don persuaded the manager to throw an extra guy on the door when these types of bands played.

The final rule — "Keep the bikers on your side" — was the

most important. Common sense dictated avoiding the Rum Pot Rustlers' bad side, but Don went out of his way to stay on their good side—letting their friends in for free, grabbing them a pizza when he got one for himself, and keeping an eye on their choppers if they had to leave the bar. In exchange he sought from the bikers only one small favor. Whenever a situation looked like it could get out of control, he'd ask one or two of them—typically Man Mountain and Shotgun (who despite their ominous nicknames were the most amiable of the lot)—to accompany him when he approached the troublemakers. Don would then calmly explain to these patrons that they had two choices: either leave the bar now or take it up with the bikers. It never failed. Looking up at Man Mountain, whose tattooed arms were bigger than most men's legs, even the most testosterone-addled troublemaker would leave meekly, often apologizing for causing a fuss.

The boundary, prioritizing, and stopping rules discussed in the last chapter provide a framework for making better decisions, and center on what to do, what is most important to do, and what to stop doing. In contrast, *process rules*, the focus of this chapter, are more about how to do things better, and center on getting the job at hand done. Process rules work because they steer a middle path between the chaos of too few rules that can result in confusion and mistakes, and the rigidity of so many rules that there is little ability to adapt to the unexpected or take advantage of new opportunities. Simply put, process rules are useful whenever flexibility trumps consistency.

The most widely used process rule is the *how-to rule*. How-to rules guide the basics of executing tasks, from playing golf to designing new products. The other process rules, coordination and timing, are special cases of how-to rules that apply in particular situations. *Coordination rules* center on getting something done when multiple actors—people, organizations, or nations—have to work together. These rules orchestrate the behaviors of, for example, schooling fish, Zipcar members, and content contributors at Wikipedia. In contrast, *timing rules* center on getting things done in situations where temporal factors such as rhythms, sequences, and deadlines are relevant. These rules set the timing of, for example, when to get up every day and when dragonflies migrate.

HOW-TO RULES

In many ways, announcers are as important as the athletes they cover in modern sports. The early radio (and later television) broadcasts allowed fans to follow the action of their favorite teams without having to attend the game, transforming sporting events from local attractions into international spectacles. Sports commentary is a central part of games today. Superstar sportscasters like Bob Costas and Al Michaels have eclipsed the fame of many of the athletes they cover, and John Madden, rather than John Elway or Tom Brady, has his name on the NFL's premier video game franchise. ESPN, whose flagship employees are sportscasters, is worth more than the world's twenty-five most valuable sports franchises combined.

In the early days of radio announcing, sports commentators had little guidance, and one early announcer recalled that "people just talked and hoped for the best." Into this vacuum strode Seymour Joly de Lotbiniere, a pioneer in radio and later television announcing, whom one contemporary referred to as the "Lenin of the commentary revolution."

The son of an English general, de Lotbiniere (universally known by his nickname, Lobby) stood at six feet eight inches tall, towering over his classmates at Eton and Cambridge before he joined the BBC. Over the following two decades, Lobby transformed the BBC's new and decidedly amateurish commentary into a polished art form that was emulated by sportscasters around the globe. Despite his old-world view of Americans (he derided one commentator, declaring, "His rather overpowering American voice, all on one note, bores into one's head with the persistence of a pneumatic drill"), Lobby's approach to commentating has had an enduring influence on sports announcing on both sides of the Atlantic.

Distilling a decade of experience commentating and training other sportscasters, Lobby wrote a memorandum in which he codified his insights into six how-to rules. A good commentator, he explained, should:

1. set the scene;
2. describe the action;
3. give the score or results, regularly and succinctly;
4. explain, without interrupting, the stadium's reaction to the game's event;
5. share "homework," such as historical facts and figures or personal information; and
6. assess the significance of the occasion and key moments.

These rules provided robust guidance for commentators across diverse events, including the Summer Olympics, Wimbledon, the English Football Association Challenge Cup, and cricket tests everywhere. To gauge their potential, prospective hires for Lobby's commentary teams were often asked to climb to the seventh story of the BBC office building and provide running commentary on the busy West End street below. On one occasion, an applicant was asked to commentate on a table tennis game between BBC employees in the corporate cafeteria. Using Lobby's how-to rules of commentating, the BBC produced a number of multiskilled broadcasters who could fluidly cover any given sport.

How-to rules are particularly helpful when there is extreme pressure and severe time constraint. Consider the Mann Gulch tragedy, perhaps the best-known forest fire in U.S. history. On August 5, 1949, fifteen young Forest Service smokejumpers parachuted from a Douglas dual-prop transport plane into the outskirts of Helena National Forest in Montana to battle what looked to be a routine fire. To be safe, the smokejumpers landed on the northern side of the gulch opposite the slope where the fire was burning. Shortly after they landed, the winds gusted, fanning the fire, which jumped the ravine. It quickly grew into a wall of fire a hundred feet high, burning at over 500° Fahrenheit and advancing at twelve miles per hour.

The smokejumpers, many of them young and relatively inexperienced, panicked and ran from the flames in all directions. R. Wagner (Wag) Dodge, the seasoned foreman, stopped in his tracks and lit an escape fire to deprive the approaching fire of fuel, and instructed the others to join him in lying down atop the burnt-out grass. With a raging wall of fire closing on them fast, the inexperienced team continued sprinting. But they could not outrun the fire, which sucked the oxygen out of the air and scorched their lungs. All but Dodge and two others died immediately or suffered fatal wounds. It would ultimately take 450 firefighters five days to extinguish the Mann Gulch fire, one of the deadliest forest fires ever.

At the time of the Mann Gulch fire, the U.S. Forest Service had four simple rules for how to deal with out-of-control fires:

1. Start an escape fire in the path of the advancing fire if possible.
2. Go to where the fuel is thinner.
3. Turn toward the fire and try to work through it.
4. Don't let the fire choose the spot where it hits you.

Facing a wall of fire, the foreman Dodge did exactly as the rules guided: he ran to the high ground where the grass was sparse, burned an escape fire, and lay on its ashes. Later investigations attributed the disaster, in large part, to the crew's unfamiliarity with the smokejumpers' rules for dealing with dangerous fires. The crew was young — most were in their teens or early twenties and fighting fire as a summer job. Absent time to think through what to do, their ignorance of the rules cost them their lives.

How-to rules can also foster artistic creativity. At first glance, this seems counterintuitive, because following the rules and being creative are often viewed as antithetical. The reality is, however, that a blank canvas and no rules on how to fill it can overwhelm an artist with too many degrees of freedom. A recent study experimented with approaches for sparking creativity among 180 Chinese high-school students. The students were assigned two tasks — to complete a story and design a collage from stickers — and divided into three groups. The first group was simply given the assignment, while the second group received the additional exhortation "Please try to be creative." The third group received the assignment and simple rules on how to complete the activity, such as "Fold or tear the stickers to vary the shape and size of the materials." Four independent judges assessed creativity (and agreed 75 percent of the time for stories and 86 percent of the time for collages). The group that received the simple rules was deemed the most creative — the concrete guidance on *how* to be creative gave the students an effective starting point and channeled their creativity. In contrast, the group that was encouraged to be creative without any simple rules performed no better than the group that was simply given the assignment.

Simple rules are not just for beginners, but rather can also stimulate the creativity of master artists. Patricia Stokes, a painter and psychologist at Columbia University, studied how influential artists like Claude Monet, William Motherwell, and Piet Mondrian produced their groundbreaking work. She argues that truly original artists work by imposing constraints on themselves, in terms of the subjects they paint, materials they use, and artists they draw upon for inspiration. Monet, for example, purposefully limited his subjects, repeatedly painting pictures, by the dozens, of subjects like grain stacks and water lilies. This self-imposed constraint allowed him to focus on exploring how light changes, and his exploration helped spark a transition in the art world from representation to impressionism, setting the stage for twentieth-century artists such as Picasso. By constraining infinite possibilities, simple rules allow creativity to flourish, less from thinking outside the box and more from deciding how to draw the box in the first place.

How-to rules can also accelerate creativity. In the span of two years, the White Stripes produced two albums that are widely considered among the best of the 2000s, and the British newspaper the *Guardian* called the rock duo "the key band of their time." "The whole point of the White Stripes," according to founder and frontman Jack White, "is the liberation of limiting yourself." Their breakout album, 2001's *White Blood Cells*, which is featured on many lists of the decade's best albums, follows five simple rules: (1) no blues; (2) no guitar solos; (3) no slide guitar; (4) no covers; and (5) no bass. These rules constrained the band to a box—but it was their box, and staying in that box helped enable their rapid-fire creativity. "I'm disgusted by artists or songwriters who pretend there are no rules," Jack White said in a *New York Times* interview. "There's nothing guiding them in their creativity. We could've spent six months making our last album. We could have recorded 600 tracks. Instead, we went and made the whole album, 18 songs, in 10 days." By restricting their creative process, how-to rules freed the White Stripes to follow a short, clear path to their favorite patch of creativity.

For creative products with multiple iterations, like the Grand Theft Auto series of video games or a long-running TV show, simple rules can help balance novelty and continuity and add a dash of efficiency to the creative process. Elmore Leonard was working on his forty-sixth novel when he died at the age of eighty-seven. Leonard's work spanned multiple genres and formats. He wrote westerns, crime fiction, and suspense thrillers, and churned out novels, short stories, and screenplays. Many of Leonard's most popular works were adapted for the screen, including *Get Shorty, Out of Sight, Jackie Brown,* and *3:10 to Yuma.*

At the prodding of the *New York Times,* Leonard published his simple rules of writing, which include "Avoid prologues," "Never use a verb other than 'said' to carry dialogue," and "Try to leave out the part that readers tend to skip." These are not universal rules that apply to all writers. If you cut out the boring bits of Nathaniel Hawthorne's *House of the Seven Gables,* as many high-school students might suggest, you would be left with about three pages of text. These are the rules of how to write like Elmore Leonard, a spare style moved forward by dialogue. These how-to rules embody the essence of Leonard's distinctive voice, which he maintained over six decades without ever slipping into formulaic writing.

Balancing novelty and consistency, it turns out, is especially important for individuals and organizations that want to grow.

Kathy teamed up with her former PhD student Shona Brown to study why some firms had repeated success with new products and others did not. Based on their global study of computer firms, they discovered that the most successful firms were poised between too much and too little structure, creating an edge of chaos. Small tips either way — too little or too much structure — caused serious blips in the new-product pipeline in this very volatile industry. The firms that eschewed rules altogether were soon overcome by complexity, dissipating their scarce time, attention, and cash in the pursuit of any opportunity that passed their way. But the firms that followed many rules were too slow and stodgy. The environment of these technology-based companies was far too complex for a structured solution, enumerated in a fat rule book, to ever make sense.

Kathy and Don saw the same edge-of-chaos phenomenon when they compared the top firms that emerged from the late-1990s Internet boom to the biggest flops. The more successful firms, including then-fledgling startups like Yahoo and eBay, did things very differently from firms that failed. The winners selected a critical process — such as new-product development, acquisitions, or geographic expansion — that put the company in the flow of growth opportunities. They developed a short playbook of simple rules with enough structure to scale up that process and fuel expansion. For Cisco, a key bottleneck process was new technical ideas, and the firm focused on simple rules for how to acquire those ideas from small and often local firms. With Yahoo, growth depended on adding new services, and the bottleneck process was alliance formation, shaped with only a few how-to rules like "no exclusive deals" and "basic service is always free." With Amazon, the rules shaped how to add product categories. More recently, Airbnb began using simple rules like "focus on hosts" to decide which cities to add.

One of the best examples of growth at the edge of chaos is Google, where Kathy's coauthor Shona became senior VP of business operations (her informal title was Chief Chaos Officer). Google's senior executives were passionate about staying on the edge of chaos. One journalist commented that the multibillion-dollar company felt like a freshman mixer, with an anything-goes spirit. But the company also lived by simple rules. Early on, Google formulated a playbook of simple rules to hire top talent, especially computer scientists, the recruitment of whom was a critical bottleneck to growth. Here Google had simple rules for acquiring small companies (ten to fifteen employees) primarily for talent, and hiring individuals: "Look for eccentricity," because it often correlates with creativity; "Look for strong referrals from other Google employees," because top people want to work with other top people and are always looking for that kind of talent; and "Avoid anyone with even the smallest inaccuracy on their resumé," to help ensure only high-integrity employees. Google used these rules and a few others to hire the right talent. One of Google's most intriguing how-to rules for innovation was to re-create grad student offices. Although Googlers could decorate their offices as they liked and name their own conference rooms, their offices were open-plan and sized like cramped grad-student cubicles. On the surface, this rule saved money because the offices required less space, important in pricey Silicon Valley. But Googlers followed the rule even when they had extra space. The cramped quarters heightened communication and creative exchanges and helped keep even Google's millionaire employees in hungry, underdog-startup mode.

How-to rules address the basics of getting things done without prescribing every detail of what to do. They work well in situations where the unexpected is the expected, like Jack's bar, where every night the crowd and vibe were different, and sportscasting, where no match is ever quite the same. They can stimulate creativity, shape action when there is no time to plan, and create structure that allows entrepreneurs to grow their company. The next two types of process rules address particular aspects of getting things done: coordination and timing.

COORDINATION RULES

As dusk falls in Rome between the months of November and February, tourists gather at the entrance to the Eternal City's Termini train station. They're clustering, not to catch the Inter-City to Florence but to observe flocks of starlings in flight. Flocks of birds are known by different names, depending on the species — a charm of finches, for example, or an unkindness of ravens. Starlings in flight are known as a *murmuration*. The English poet Samuel Taylor Coleridge described the murmuration he observed through the window of a carriage bound for London, a scene that stayed with him for the rest of his life:

> Starlings in vast flights drove along like smoke, mist, or anything misty without volition — now a circular area inclined in an Arc — now a Globe — now a complete Orb into an Elipse & Oblong — now a balloon with the car suspended, now a concaved Semicircle — & still it expands & condenses, some moments glimmering & shivering, dim & shadowy, now thickening, deepening, blackening!

While poets can capture a murmuration on paper, scientists have struggled to explain this flocking behavior. Edmund Selous, an English naturalist, published his first book on bird watching in 1901 and devoted the rest of his life to ornithology, with a particular interest in how flocking birds coordinate their behavior.

After three decades of close observation, Selous wrote a book in which he proposed to explain how hundreds or thousands of birds could fly in close formation, darting and dodging in unison. He dismissed as ridiculous the possibility that a single bird leader could dictate the behavior of an entire flock. Instead, he postulated that birds could synchronize their actions through "thought-transference," a form of avian telepathy that allowed the birds to send mental impulses to other members of the flock instantaneously.

It is easy to dismiss thought-transference as the crackpot theory of an eccentric Englishman who perhaps spent too much time alone in the glades. Although he was reclusive, Selous was not a foolish man. He studied at Cambridge, practiced as a barrister, published twenty books on nature, and is acknowledged as a pioneer of ethology (the study of animals in their natural habitats). Instead, his telepathy theory is a testament to how mysterious bird flocking is, even to someone who studies it carefully. (A YouTube search of "starling murmuration" will give you a sense of the mystery of synchronized flight.) Fellow ornithologists wisely dismissed thought-transference but could not come up with a better explanation of flocking behavior. For fifty years after Selous published his book, the question of how starlings orchestrated a murmuration remained unanswered.

The solution to how starlings flock came unexpectedly from a software engineer working in a computer lab, not from an ornithologist traipsing around a field. Craig Reynolds studied at MIT, where he wrote his bachelor's and master's theses on computer animation. While designing computer-graphics software, Reynolds grew interested in how to simulate coordinated activity in animals, such as the flocking of birds. Reynolds created avian avatars, which he dubbed "boids," and wrote a software program in which each boid followed three simple rules based on the position and behavior of nearby flock mates. The three rules are: (1) avoid collisions, (2) head in the same direction as your nearest neighbors, and (3) stay close to your nearest neighbors. These three rules are all that boids need to coordinate with one another and produce their amazing group-level flocking behavior, closely matching that of real birds. Behavioral biologists, who tested Reynolds's rules in the wild, found that they could explain collective behavior in a wide range of settings, including how mosquitofish shoal, starlings flock, and pedestrians self-organize into orderly lines on busy streets.

The flocking rules are an example of *coordination rules* — rules that guide interactions among members who intermingle in a complex system. Coordination rules work by clarifying what to do in relation to others. Starlings in a murmuration know to avoid colliding with their neighbors, and can dart and turn confidently knowing that their flock mates will avoid rear-ending them. In fact, coordination rules only make sense in a social context. A bird cannot stay close to its neighbors if it is flying alone.

Collectives can attain objectives that are impossible for individuals to achieve alone. A predator can easily pick off a single bird when the group is flying in uncoordinated fashion. In flocks, however, individual birds minimize their risk of predation by coordinating their motion and evasive maneuvers to confuse predators. Predators can benefit from collective behavior as well. A solitary locust is nothing special. But as a swarm, locusts constitute a pestilence of, well, biblical proportions. Even today, locusts threaten the sustenance of one in every ten people on earth. A swarm can contain millions of locusts, blacken the sky over several kilometers, and travel the length of a continent, devastating crops and livestock along the way. Yet most of the time locusts live a solitary existence, avoiding contact with one another, and only occasionally mobilize into a hellish army. The difference between locusts in their solitary versus their collective state is so massive that biologists at one time classified them as separate species. The trigger for the transition from one locust state to another remained a mystery.

It turns out that coordination rules, of a particularly grisly sort, explain locusts' transition from reclusive loners to deadly horde. When the density of locusts exceeds a threshold, they begin to sneak up behind others to bite them. A locust that fails to escape is quickly devoured, often in midflight, by its attackers. Locusts can avoid cannibalism most of the time by steering clear of one another. But when they are forced into tight quarters, they follow two simple rules: (1) flee from the locusts chasing you from behind and (2) try to eat the locust in front of you if it gets too close. Locusts that ignore these rules are devoured. But when millions of locusts individually follow these rules, they collectively stabilize into a pestilent conga line that can devastate wide swaths of farmland.

When individuals follow coordination rules, collective behavior emerges. Birds flock, wildebeests migrate, fish school, and locusts swarm. But people are smarter than birds and boids, and so their emergent behavior can be both more unpredictable and more innovative than that of animals. Consider the case of improvisational comedy, an art form that traces its origins to the Compass, a bar near the University of Chicago. In 1955 a group of young comedians began acting out scenarios suggested by patrons. Members of the group went on to found The Second City, the improvisational comedy troupe whose alumni read like a who's who of comedy, including Tina Fey, Mike Myers, Bill Murray, Gilda Radner, Steve Carell, Stephen Colbert, and Amy Poehler. The form of improvisation pioneered at The Second City inspired influential U.S. television shows including *Saturday Night Live, Whose Line Is It Anyway?, Curb Your Enthusiasm,* and too many movies to mention.

In contrast to standup comedians, who succeed or bomb alone onstage, improvisation is a team effort where it is hard to look good unless everyone else does. Few tasks are as daunting as getting onstage with a group of actors whom you may barely know and making up a performance as you go along, with the proviso that your performance must be hilarious. As a team, improvisers must incorporate unexpected twists, reuse earlier material, and weave disparate themes into a fluid narrative. Moreover, they must coordinate their interactions in real time without a script to dictate what happens next, a rehearsal to work out the kinks, or even a director to guide the action. All of this is done in front of a live and potentially hostile audience. When you think about what is required, it is a miracle that improvisation ever succeeds.

In the six decades since its founding, the community of improvisational comedians has experimented with countless practices, abandoned those that bombed, and informally codified the ones that work into rules of thumb to coordinate actions onstage. While comedians may have their own idiosyncratic principles, a handful of widely shared rules have emerged through collective trial and error. The best-known rule is to build on whatever is said or done just beforehand by saying, "Yes, and . . ." Another rule is "Don't tell jokes," because they often stifle an emerging storyline by imposing an artificial punch line onto an organic situation. The rule to make others look good underscores the importance of helping other players shine. In improv, prima donnas just make everyone, including themselves, look second-rate. Instead, you help yourself by helping the group.

While coordination rules work well for groups like improvisational comedians, jazz bands, and basketball teams that are all interacting in plain view, they are also helpful in situations where coordination must take place over space and time. In these situations, no one can see the big picture. Coordination rules can be followed using only local information. No single starling can see the entire flock, but every starling can see the half-dozen or so birds that are nearby and use them to follow the flocking rules. Coordination rules also allow for adaptation to local conditions while still recognizing the group objectives. So by following the rules, starlings can adapt to local surprises (like power lines blocking their path) then quickly rejoin the group.

Battle is one domain that requires a mix of local and global rules. Coordinated behaviors are crucial for victory, but the "fog of war" often obscures the big picture. To foster battlefield coordination, Napoleon is reputed to have issued a standing order to "march toward the sound of gunfire," a simple rule that enabled his officers to coordinate their activities without knowing exactly what was happening. Generals and soldiers could locally adapt to the facts on the ground, such as deteriorating weather, a gap in enemy defenses, or unexpectedly intense resistance, which were impossible to anticipate. But the rule also helped ensure that the fighting force would arrive where it was most needed and would have the most impact. In contrast, a detailed coordination plan would likely not work well because the units could not adapt to changing local circumstances. At the other extreme, if every Napoleonic general relied solely on his own initiative, there would be no coherence and the battlefield would degenerate into disconnected firefights.

Simple rules for coordination address how to accomplish activities that require multiple actors, such as people, animals, and nations, to work together. Coordination rules delineate what to do, and likewise what others should do, so that collective objectives like winning battles and flying safely can be achieved. Coordination rules, however, do not deal with *when* to do things. For that, we turn now to the third process rule, timing, which addresses when to act.

TIMING RULES

Insomnia affects one-third of all adults, and is a condition that can severely reduce one's quality of life and create major hazards for others. The Exxon Valdez oil spill, the *Challenger* space shuttle explosion, and the Chernobyl nuclear meltdown have all been attributed to sleep-deprived humans making errors. Insomnia particularly affects older adults, who have greater difficulty sleeping than younger people and are also more likely to experience the adverse side effects of common sleep medications. Thankfully, recent research shows that relief can be provided with the use of simple guidelines that even the most exhausted brains can follow. Researchers from the Sleep Medicine Institute at the University of Pittsburgh recently tested a drug-free treatment on a group of seventy-nine senior citizens, all of whom suffered from chronic insomnia. The results are encouraging. Two-thirds of the participants reported an improvement in sleep quality, and over half experienced no symptoms of insomnia at all. Of those who slept better, three-quarters had sustained their improvements for at least six months — all without drugs, side effects, or even a trip to the doctor.

Insomniacs can get a good night's rest by following four simple rules for when to sleep. The first is "Get up at the same time every morning," which turns out to be more crucial than a regular bedtime for establishing a restful sleep pattern. The second is "Avoid going to bed until you feel sleepy," even if this means hitting the hay later than you would ideally like. The third rule is "Do not stay in bed if you are not sleeping," and the final rule, which follows from the others, is "Reduce the time spent in bed." Following these rules keeps troubled sleepers from spending ten or twelve hours in bed in order to snag a few hours of sleep — a common pattern in older adults. In the short run, these rules may lead to people feeling tired or sleep deprived as they adjust. But over the long term, patients who follow these rules usually enjoy a deeper, more restful sleep that comes on more quickly.

The simple rules for sleeping are examples of *timing rules* — rules that guide when to take actions. Timing rules sometimes specify taking action when some triggering event happens. Known as *event pacing*, this kind of rule links actions to events, such as getting drowsy in the insomniacs' rule of going to bed when tired. Other timing rules call for action at a particular time on the clock or calendar. Known as *time pacing*, these timing rules create deadlines and rhythms, like the morning drumbeat of the insomniacs' rule to get up at the same time every day. Regardless of type, timing rules clarify when to do something and work best when temporal considerations like deadlines, rhythms, and sequences are relevant. Going to bed only when tired, getting up at the same time every day, and limiting the time spent in bed are all rules about how to sleep better by paying attention to time.

Dragonflies provide a clear example of timing rules that rely on event pacing. There are more than five thousand known species of dragonflies. Approximately fifty of them migrate, like birds, in the autumn and spring, sometimes covering more than four hundred miles (the distance between Boston and Washington, D.C.) over two months. When migrating, dragonflies spend varying amounts of time in flight each day. They cover more than sixty miles on some days, but they also have stopover days when they fly less than a mile. While scientists know the overall migration pattern of dragonflies, they have long puzzled over how exactly the insects decide to fly on any particular day.

A team of scientists led by researchers from Princeton Univer-

sity decided to solve the mystery by studying the timing of dragonfly migration. They captured green darner dragonflies in New
Jersey in the autumn, and used a mixture of Krazy Glue and eye-
lash adhesive to fix a tiny transmitter to each insect's midsection.
Dragonflies are remarkably strong flyers (they mate in the air,
with the male carrying the female on his back), so the additional
weight of the electronic gear would not slow them down. The
scientists then used an airplane and ground vehicles equipped
with tracking devices to track the insects' movements.

The scientists followed the dragonflies as they flew south for
the winter, carefully observing the insects' behavior. They learned
that green darners avoid headwinds and instead surf the prevail-
ing breezes, which explained their mystifying zigzag flight paths.
The scientists also discovered that a few timing rules explained
when the insects fly and when they stay put. One rule is to fly
only when the nighttime temperature falls for two consecutive
nights. Falling nocturnal temperatures are highly correlated with
frigid northern winds that carry the green darners south and
remind the dragonflies to get going. While some wind is ideal,
extreme gusts are dangerous regardless of which way the wind
is blowing. So the second timing rule is to stay put on windy
days — that is, when the wind blows more than fifteen miles per
hour. Together, these timing rules specify the events that trigger
when green darners start flying.

In contrast, time-pacing rules dictate acting at a particular
time on the clock or the calendar, and thereby create rhythms and
deadlines. The insomniacs' rule for getting up at the same time
every day, for example, sets the pace for starting each day. The
green darners' annual pattern of migration also follows a rhythmic time-pacing rule — fly south in autumn, fly north in spring.
In fact, nature is full of examples of time-pacing rules, with the
rhythms often synchronized with some external rhythm. Exam-

ples include our bodies' circadian clock adjusting to sunup and sundown, the tendency of adjacent pendulum clocks to converge on the same rhythm, and the seasonal hibernation of brown bears.

Time-pacing rules can make sense outside nature, too. Take Pixar, the computer-animation studio that marches to rhythmic rules for when to release movies. Pixar's first full-length movie was *Toy Story*. The Oscar-winning film was a huge success, but the studio unfortunately needed about four years to create a movie like *Toy Story* that could meet Pixar's lofty quality bar. And yet, releasing a movie every four years is not much of a business, and might not attract the best storytellers to the studio. As it turns out, part of Pixar's solution was to put in place timing rules. One rule called for releasing a new movie every year in order to create the critical mass required to run a viable business. A second rule was to release movies at Thanksgiving, and so synchronize the studio with the kickoff of the holiday season — one of the two annual peaks of family movie-going when box-office revenues and product tie-ins soar.

Following these timing rules, in practice, was no easy task. To release a movie every year, Pixar needed to have four films in production at any one time, and yet the company barely had staff for one when *Toy Story* was made. Pixar had to ease into its timing rules because of a shortage of animators, and it took the studio several years to hire and train enough people in the Pixar way of telling stories. Ultimately, Pixar established a pipeline of movies, with one set of people working on a given movie in its first year of development, another set in the second year, and so on. Every year, a movie would ideally move to a new development stage with a fresh set of people, until it was released four years later. It took a while and there were blips, but Pixar created something close to a hit moviemaking factory. By getting the right people on a given movie at the right stage every year and then annually rotating them to the next movie, Pixar was able to consistently turn out creative successes, from *Monsters, Inc., Finding Nemo, The Incredibles,* and *Ratatouille* to *Wall-E* and *Up.*

The one-movie-per-year rule worked because, like all time-pacing rules, it gave people a rhythm with a goal and a sense of urgency to achieve it. The rule also proved efficient because it kept everyone continuously busy and not sitting around waiting for their next job — a very costly proposition. Pixar's leaders could choreograph movie projects, keeping employees engaged from film to film while still providing time for creativity. Pixar's artistic types could also develop personal rhythms for their own tasks, consistent with the annual cycle. A surprising benefit of the rule was its unforgiving deadlines, since many creative people simply cannot resist fine-tuning their art without hard stops.

Timing rules are particularly relevant in competitive situations when rivals go out of their way to disrupt their opponents. This is common in sports like basketball, where quick teams attempt to play up-tempo while less athletic teams try to slow the game, and baseball, where pitchers try to upset the timing of hitters by mixing up the speeds of their pitches.

An intriguing timing rule in competitive situations is to stay out of sync. Stanford engineering professor Riitta Katila has studied the global robotics industry, looking at product rivalry and firm success, using over thirty years of data. She finds that the best firms purposefully stay out of sync with their rivals. They stay ahead by introducing their newest products, those utilizing the latest technology, before their competitors. But more surprising, the best firms also stay behind by exploiting well-known technology to the fullest, and avoid releasing products when their rivals do.

The nineteenth-century financier Nathan Mayer Rothschild would agree. One well-known investing rule attributed to Rothschild is "Buy when there is blood on the streets." This may sound like the heartless advice of a distant, unfathomably wealthy man, but it is actually Rothschild's highly successful out-of-sync investing rule. Nathan Rothschild was very rich (owning 0.6 percent of British GDP), but he was not born that way. The full rule attributed to Rothschild is "Buy when there is blood on the streets, *even if that blood is your own.*" As a young boy living in the cramped Jewish ghetto of Frankfurt, Germany, Rothschild was well acquainted with suffering. French Revolutionary troops laid seige to the ghetto in 1796, when he was eighteen, causing widespread destruction. Rather than the rule of an aloof aristocrat, "Buy when there is blood on the streets" is more like the hard-won wisdom of a tough street kid. According to the rule, when there is a crisis — and precisely when everyone else is most likely to freeze, panic, and give up hope on an asset — do the opposite and invest.

Timing rules can also guide activities that follow predictable patterns or sequences. A terrific example is Start-Up Chile, where Kathy sits on the advisory board. Start-Up Chile (SUP) is the brainchild of Nicolás Shea, a fourth-generation Irish Chilean, and the Chilean government. Initially, SUP's idea seemed crazy: give $40,000 to foreign entrepreneurs to come to geographically remote Chile and bootstrap their startups. The Chilean government would hand out free office space and a one-year visa. There were no strings attached, and the entrepreneurs could leave Chile right after participating in the program. The dream was to attract high-potential entrepreneurs to set up shop in Chile, and transform the national mindset and entrepreneurial ecosystem. By "importing" entrepreneurs, Chileans could learn from these leaders, and Chile might then become an innovation hub like Singapore or Israel. The fear was that no one but South Americans from poor countries would apply, and that ordinary Chileans would vociferously complain about giving away taxpayer money to foreigners.

To make SUP work, its founders came up with timing rules for hosting entrepreneurs. The first required that the entrepreneurs live and work in Chile for six months. This rule struck a balance. Six months should be enough time for the entrepreneurs to make a difference in Chile and be tempted to stay, but not so long that they would be reluctant to commit to the program in the first place. A second rule mandated that the entrepreneurs' performance be reviewed at two months. This rule came about because a small minority of entrepreneurs simply did not work out, and this was usually apparent quickly. It was best for both parties to take swift corrective action. A third rule came later, and set the four-month timing for "Demo Day," when entrepreneurs would present their progress to outsiders. Together, the rules drove a relentless two-month cadence with momentum-inducing milestones, but the rules didn't spell out exactly what each entrepreneur should do.

SUP illustrates another major point. The six types of rules—boundary, prioritizing, stopping, how-to, coordination, and timing—are often used in combination. SUP combined boundary (what to do), prioritizing (what is important to do), and stopping (what to cease doing) rules to structure the choice of entrepreneurs. "Select teams with business experience and personal networks," for example, is a boundary rule which acknowledges that the quality of talent and connections matters as much as or more than the initial idea for the entrepreneurial ecosystem, and that experienced entrepreneurs are the best role models for Chileans. By contrast, there was no rule about fitting in with Chile's core industries like copper, agriculture, winemaking, and fishing. A prioritizing rule gave the top 20 percent of the entrepreneurs in a cohort (determined at the two-month review) preferential access to scarce resources like meetings with VIP visitors. A stopping rule called for the removal of slackers, who were easy to spot by the number of tourist junkets they took. An unusual how-to rule ensured that entrepreneurs contributed to Chile's entrepreneurial ecosystem: activities such as attending meet-ups or giving a talk at a local university earned them a number of points toward the four thousand they were asked to accumulate during their six-month stay. Collectively, these rules helped SUP lure top-notch talent from abroad and achieve its aims of improving Chile's business environment.

In 2010 the first cohort of twenty-two startups from fourteen countries arrived in Santiago. From there the numbers grew. In 2013 there were over four thousand applications from ninety-four countries, for 285 slots. The SUP startups have raised about $50 million in venture capital financing from investors in South America, the United States, and Europe, and initial evidence indicates that SUP is changing the mindset and behaviors of its Chilean participants. It is still too early to measure the definitive value for Chile, but Santiago is now buzzing with entrepreneurs — foreign and domestic — who are sharing their knowledge in sectors from social media to biotech.

By now you should have a good idea of what simple rules look like and how they work. But where do these rules come from in the first place? Understanding how simple rules are formed is the next step in figuring out how to create your own rules. That's where we'll turn in the next chapter.

4

Where Simple Rules Come From

A T FIRST GLANCE, IT is an idyllic vista. A green hilltop surrounded by vibrant butterflies, so numerous that they bump into backpackers hiking to the summit. *Hilltopping*, the term for when some butterflies congregate, is just a few woodland critters short of a scene from a Disney movie. But to the butterflies, it is more of an X-rated feature. Males and virgin females ascend their local hilltops to mate en masse, wings entwined with one another, male claspers embracing female abdomens.

You might think that a butterfly orgy requires no coordination, that masses of randy butterflies colliding into one another at random will be enough to produce scores of offspring. In reality, relying on random collisions doesn't work. Butterflies have a lot of space to cover, and very little time to do it. If butterflies were the size of humans, their population density would be one-tenth that of Alaska. Butterflies live, on average, just one month, so time is of the essence. The butterflies need to find each other, and quickly. From an evolutionary perspective, the stakes are high, since romantics who fail to mate cannot pass their genes on to the next generation.

How do butterflies know where to go to maximize their chances of finding a suitable mate? Hilltopping is a complicated operation. Butterflies must navigate vast terrain to find the spots where potential mates are most likely to congregate, particularly those from other populations who can mix up the gene pool. They must avoid settling too quickly on a hill, when higher ground, and better mating opportunities, may be within range. These are complex optimization problems for humans to calculate, but butterflies are working with much less processing capacity (2.5 million butterfly brains could fit inside one human brain).

Biologists have established that animals like butterflies, salamanders, and wild goats use simple rules to navigate complex terrain. To see whether butterflies relied on simple rules, a multinational team of scientists studied the *Melitaea trivia,* a butterfly with a wingspan of one inch, native to the Mediterranean and Middle East. The team released one hundred adult butterflies in Israel's Lahav hills — an area noteworthy for its complex terrain and proximity to the ancient city of Beersheba. The butterflies were released from different starting points including hilltops, dry streambeds, and slopes. An observer tracked each butterfly on foot, carefully maintaining a distance of one meter to avoid casting a shadow on the insect's path, and planting flags to mark the flight path.

The scientists found that a handful of simple rules guided how male and female butterflies search for one another. First, "Fly uphill most of the time." Second, "Fly toward the highest slope in sight" (within the butterfly's range of vision of about 165 feet). Third, "Pause to check out local peaks, even if they are not the highest, but leave if you do not get lucky right away." Fourth, "Periodically make a random movement" to avoid getting trapped on a summit that is the highest peak in the nearby vicinity, but not the highest overall. The same team later used computer models to test how well these rules would predict butterflies' behavior over a dozen maps of real landscapes. They found that the rules explained real-life butterfly hilltopping behavior over a wide range of terrains.

Hilltopping works. It is a clever way for butterflies to reproduce, bringing males and females from disparate regions together to create one big, healthy gene pool. But how did such a sophisticated system of coordinated behavior emerge among these beautiful insects? Throughout this book, we have described how simple rules are ubiquitous in nature, business, medicine, sports, creative arts, and elsewhere. Where do they come from?

NATURAL SELECTION

The simple rules that govern hilltopping evolved over hundreds of millions of butterfly generations (the species first arose approximately 150 million years ago, when Jurassic-period dinosaurs ruled the earth). Random variation hardwired the rules into a few lucky butterflies, which were more likely to mate and pass the relevant genetic code for hilltopping to a larger number of offspring. Butterflies without the adaptive mutations fluttered gracefully into extinction.

The Nobel Prize–winning economist Friedrich Hayek believed the rules that guide human society emerged through an evolutionary process much like that which produced hilltopping rules among butterflies. As people went about their day-to-day lives, they encountered the same problems over and over again. Travelers dragging carts in different directions along the same path, for example, would reach an impasse if both stayed in the middle of the road. People presumably tried alternative ways of resolving the resulting conflicts — one imagines that cudgels and cursing played a prominent role in these early experiments. Ultimately, people stumbled on simple rules, like "Stick to one side of the road," that worked well for everyone and won widespread adoption.

Simple rules evolve in communities much as they do in societies as a whole. Consider the case of standup comedians, a community governed by the simple rule "Don't steal jokes," and where the punishment for violating the rule is no laughing matter. In one 2005 incident at the Laugh Factory comedy club in Los Angeles, George Lopez grabbed fellow comic Carlos Mencia, slammed him against a wall, and punched him. Mencia's alleged crime? Plagiarizing Lopez's material. Joke stealing is the cardinal sin in standup comedy today, but it was not always so. For much of the twentieth century, stealing jokes was no big deal. In the vaudeville era, performers would repeat other comedians' material verbatim without attributing the source. Later comedians, such as Milton Berle and Bob Hope, drew on vast stores of generic jokes. Expert delivery and timing, rather than originality, mattered most. Hope was widely accused of joke stealing, and Berle was so notorious for it that he once quipped that the prior act "was so funny I dropped my pencil."

In contrast, the current generation of comedians, including Jerry Seinfeld and Louis C.K., rely on distinctive routines that mirror their individual personalities, rather than standalone one-liners. Modern comedy is driven by unique material rather than expert delivery, and today's comedians have worked out rules to protect their intellectual property and sanctions to enforce these rules. The "Don't steal jokes" rule emerged, like the rules of the road, out of ongoing interactions among community members, without any particular guiding hand, and is strictly enforced by the community itself (recall the haute cuisine chefs in chapter 1).

Rules evolve to address the most pressing issues in communities. In the case of standup comedy, the resolution of who "owns" a joke is both an essential and nonobvious issue. For example, comedians often formulate material collaboratively. In this instance, the rule gives ownership of the joke to the person who came up with the premise, rather than the punch line. This rule arose through discussions among comedians and spread. When two performers come up with similar jokes, the rule is that the first person to perform the joke on television owns it, giving authorship to the comedian who can prove he or she told the joke first. Another ownership issue, what to do when one comic sells a joke to another, or writes the joke as the comic's employee, is resolved by the rule that the person who paid for a joke owns it, and the originator cannot publicly identify herself as the joke's writer.

While evolved rules benefit from legitimacy and relevance, they also have weaknesses. Evolved rules are often implicit and deeply entrenched, making it difficult to examine them critically when circumstances change, or abandon them when they become dysfunctional. Entrenched rules may prevent people from imagining alternative ways of behaving. New comedians, for example, are likely to imitate the rules of famous comedians without thinking much about why they're doing so. Without a guiding hand, rules often take on a life of their own.

The hilltopping rules of butterflies are elegant and effective, but their formulation required tens of millions of years and billions of evolutionary dead ends. The community of comedians developed its rules for joke ownership faster, but the rules still took time to evolve. An unguided evolutionary process can lead to effective rules. But those rules are often implicit and deeply ingrained, qualities which do not allow for easy adaptation.

Luckily, people aren't butterflies. We can take a more active role in forming our own simple rules. Over more than a decade of studying simple rules and working with individuals and organizations to develop them, we have identified four approaches that people commonly use to formulate rules. People can develop their rules through thoughtful engagement with their own experience, a particularly effective approach for those with lots of relevant history. People can also develop their rules by adopting the experiences of others, as conveyed through firsthand advice, books, and analogies. This approach works especially well when there is a close match between the borrowed experience and the situation at hand. When high-quality scientific evidence exists, distilling it into simple rules can be the best approach. Finally, simple rules can arise through negotiation, when diverse stakeholders have divergent aims and views of what to do.

CODIFYING PERSONAL EXPERIENCE

In a comedy hall of fame, Tina Fey would be a first-ballot inductee. Her stats — eight Emmy Awards, two Golden Globe Awards, four Screen Actors Guild Awards — speak for themselves. After starting her career as an improvisational comedian at The Second City, Fey took a job writing, and then performing, for *Saturday Night Live.* There, she became the first female head writer in a profession dominated by men. She went on to produce and star in the highly acclaimed *30 Rock,* a show loosely based on her time as head writer. Fey is noteworthy not only for her successes, but for the variety in her career. In the span of two decades, she moved through a series of diverse roles including standup comedy, writing, leading a team of writers, producing a show, and starring in feature films.

Fey is an incredibly talented comic, yet simple rules also play a role in her success. In an insightful article, Fey distilled what she learned from her experience with Lorne Michaels, the legendary producer of *Saturday Night Live*. She articulates nine rules for managing a comedy show, five of which deal with handling extremely creative people. Rule number 4 states, "When hiring, mix Harvard nerds with Chicago improvisers and stir." The *Harvard Lampoon* alumni bring logic and sophistication to the humor, while veterans of improvisation know what will work in front of a live audience. Rule 9 is "Never tell a crazy person he's crazy," which recognizes that the most creative people are often the most eccentric.

Values are another source of rules that often arise from personal experience. Personal values can dictate what is correct and even essential to do. The rules of the late Steve Jobs, for example, dictated the clean, intuitive designs of Apple products for decades and reflect his personal aesthetic. Those who value energy conservation may adopt rules to buy only locally grown organic produce because of its lower transportation costs and avoidance of energy-intensive chemical fertilizers. The rules of the crowd-funding site Indiegogo require that any project be legal and not promote hate or violence, but after that anything goes. Indiegogo's rules reflect its founders' values that everyone has the right to go after their dreams on the Internet — from getting a root canal funded to making a movie. Parenting is another domain where values often shape the rules. Some parents prize independence and self-confidence in their children. Consistent with these values are the parenting rules of noted child psychologist Debbie Glasser, which call for paying attention to your child's positive behavior and entrusting him or her with household chores. Some parents have values that favor education and collective effort, and their parenting rules often call for close involvement with their children's activities and an emphasis on academic achievement.

It's common for people to derive their simple rules from experience. And this makes sense. By drawing on their own experience, people are more likely to create relevant rules and to understand where the rules came from and why they matter. When people develop rules themselves and base them on values that matter to them, they also feel a greater sense of ownership over their rules. People are more likely to use rules devised by themselves, reflecting their own values, rather than those imposed on them by someone else. Moreover, when people invest the time to reflect on their experience and codify it into rules, they typically do so to achieve some goal that matters deeply to them, like producing a winning comedy show or successfully raising a child. If they believe the rules will help them to do a better job on something that really matters, they will use them.

People also draw on their experience to solve specific problems. In a study she conducted while a professor at the University of Michigan, Leslie Perlow looked at a team of forty-five employees who were designing a new laser printer at a Fortune 500 company. The printer was to sell for one-tenth the price of the previous product, a challenge made even more difficult when senior executives slashed the timeline from a leisurely four years to a meager nine months. The division was bleeding cash, and the new product — code-named PEARL — was the hoped-for salvation.

To develop the printer, the engineers needed long stretches of uninterrupted time to work on their own parts of the design, but they also needed to talk with each other to coordinate the overall plan. The project's tight schedule led to endless minor crises, which in turn created constant interruptions that delayed individual work. Some engineers compensated by working nights and weekends to catch up, leading to heightened stress and even burnout. Others felt obligated to prioritize their own work, and skimped on the necessary coordination, creating snags later on.

Perlow spotted the downward spiral as the engineers struggled to balance solo work and cooperation under a tight timeline. Based on her experience, she suggested that the team adopt a simple rule to establish quiet times for individual work. After some experimentation, the team settled on a rule: "Tuesday, Thursday, and Friday mornings are quiet times." This rule ensured that engineers could focus without interruption at these times, but also left the rest of the week available for collaboration. After the quiet-time rule was implemented, two-thirds of the engineers reported that their productivity increased. Despite the aggressively tight schedule, the printer shipped on time (only the second time that had happened in the division's history), a result that the team leader attributed to the quiet-time rule.

This approach to developing rules works especially well when it draws on a deep pool of experience. Based on many years in the entertainment industry, Tina Fey could derive insightful rules from her vast experience. Her rule "Never tell a crazy person he's crazy," for example, embodies a rich understanding of the close link between creativity and eccentricity. But when people lack sufficient firsthand experience to create such rules, it makes sense to look to other sources, such as the experience of others.

DRAWING ON THE EXPERIENCE OF OTHERS

The experience of others can be as valuable as one's own experience in shaping people's simple rules. Advice from experienced people about how to parent, play poker, or manage people, for example, whether given directly or conveyed through a book or magazine article, can prove useful in formulating one's own approach. Personal observation is another effective way to learn what works for others. We also use analogies, finding similarities between our own experience and others', which can streamline the process of devising our rules.

When people face an unfamiliar situation, they often recall a similar situation that they have heard about or seen, draw lessons from it, and apply those lessons to their current situation. When they do so, they are using an analogy. When applied to crafting simple rules, analogies involve three elements: a new situation, a prior example that is similar in important respects to the new situation, and rules that can be transferred from the prior example to the current situation. A useful analogy can help people save time and effort in formulating their rules.

Analogies to existing companies and other competitive domains like sports and battle are a favorite approach of entrepreneurs looking for guidance in attacking new opportunities. Netflix is an example. In 1997 Reed Hastings was annoyed by a $40 late fee on his rental of the video *Apollo 13* from Blockbuster. As an already successful entrepreneur, he recognized a golden opportunity to create better customer service than that delivered by video rental stores by exploiting the emergence of DVDs and the rise of the Internet. He launched Netflix as a service that let consumers order DVD movie rentals online and receive them at home by mail.

Hastings initially conceptualized Netflix as the online version of the offline giant, Blockbuster. This early analogy helped to shape the template of simple rules that guided how Netflix structured its activities, such as rental decisions: to charge $4 per rental, for example, and set a return deadline with late fees. Since analogies are holistic solutions, they do well in complex situations, providing a ready-made framework for a new endeavor. In the case of Netflix, Blockbuster had already refined a set of rules that worked well, some of which Netflix just copied. The Blockbuster analogy also clarified what Netflix, as the online Blockbuster, was trying to do for customers and investors. Since analogies are rarely a perfect fit, they are often most useful as a starting point for simple rules, not an endpoint. Hastings later upgraded these initial rules to better ones, switching to monthly subscription pricing and dropping the deadline rule, but the Blockbuster rules helped Netflix get started.

Analogies can be a powerful source of rules even when the comparison involves two very different domains. A cross-disciplinary team of scientists in Japan, for example, studied the optimal way to design a commuter-rail network for Tokyo and its surrounding communities. Designing a commuter-rail system is a complex proposition that demands hard tradeoffs between the costs of building and maintaining a network to transport passengers efficiently from one location to another, and the costs of creating redundant pathways to counter possible disruptions. Trial and error may be the single worst way to develop a city's transportation network. Knocking down a rail line that did not work out and then building another one at random would enrage taxpayers and commuters. The team needed some rules for designing rail networks without actually building them.

To tackle this problem, the researchers drew an analogy to *Physarum polycephalum* (commonly known as the many-headed slime mold), notable for its propensity to seek out decaying leaves and logs, avoid light, and not much else. Slime mold is not an obvious source of inspiration for designing transportation in Tokyo, one of the most technologically advanced cities in the world. For one thing, the slime mold has no brain. But this organism happens to be particularly adept at resolving its constant battle against starvation with an efficient yet resilient network of sprawling probes, precisely the tradeoff at the heart of designing rail systems. Slime molds act by sending out tube-like probes in multiple directions to search out food and transport nutrients. Scientific experiments show that the many-headed slime effectively lurches through complex terrain in search of food by mostly following efficient paths that are the shortest distance between one food source and the next. Yet occasionally the slime oozes along to its next meal via redundant routes that can work in a pinch, creating alternatives if paths to food sources are disrupted.

To model the complexity of Tokyo's rail system, the Japanese scientists placed oat flakes on pieces of glass, with each food source representing Tokyo or one of its thirty-six surrounding towns. The amount of food was proportional to the municipality's population. The scientists then watched as the slime mold figured out its food network. It grew from Tokyo outward, creating a network of interconnecting tubes that looked much like the existing rail system. The researchers then added lights, which slime molds avoid, to stand in for physical features like mountains and lakes where rail systems cannot go. From their observations, the team codified the how-to and stopping rules for the slime's expansion, which included: (1) begin by searching randomly in many directions for food; (2) when you find food, thicken the tube; and (3) when you don't find food, shrink the tube.

The scientists used these rules to build a computer simulation to determine the optimal rail network. By experimenting with variables, such as the amount of food per city or the size of tubes, the scientists could try out various designs to find the optimal network — all without laying a single kilometer of track. By studying organisms that evolved over millions of generations and codifying their simple rules, scientists could incorporate the wisdom of millennia into cutting-edge design.

Designing a railway using slime mold might seem like an esoteric illustration of learning simple rules from the experience of others, but drawing inspiration for simple rules from the animal world is not so rare. Termites, bees, and other social insects provide a particularly fertile source of simple rules. They have enough collective intelligence to accomplish complex tasks like finding nests or migrating long distances, but since each animal has little brainpower and few physical skills, their actions can often be captured by simple rules. The results of simple rules learned from ants, for example, are seen by many people every day in their own homes. Roomba, a vacuum cleaner that resembles a Frisbee on wheels, is the world's most widely owned robot. Rather than attempting complicated calculations, such as mapping the floor to be vacuumed, Roomba is programmed to follow simple rules that its creators learned from watching how ants forage for food. The precise rules that guide Roomba are proprietary, but observing the robot in action suggests the following: (1) turn when you hit an object; (2) spiral when caught in a corner; and (3) return to the docking station when power is about to run out. By copying the actions of cognitively limited insects alive since prehistoric times, engineers are bringing futuristic helpers into our living rooms.

Learning from another's experience can be helpful in crafting our own simple rules when the essential features of that experience correlate with our own. But it's possible to be misled by superficial features when deciding whether an analogy works. In one study, two groups of international-relations students were asked to recommend a political strategy for a complex (fictitious) border conflict between a small democratic country and a large totalitarian one. While both groups received identical scenarios, the first group also received superficial details, like the involvement of a U.S. president from New York and the presence of refugees leaving in boxcars. Without being asked to draw historical comparisons, these participants nonetheless often advocated aggressive military action consistent with the Second World War. The second group received the identical situation except that their superficial details included a U.S. president from Texas and refugees fleeing in small boats. These participants were significantly more likely to advocate passive, nonmilitary action consistent with the lessons often drawn from the Vietnam War. The superficial details the groups received were not relevant to the choice of political strategy, and yet the participants were easily swayed by these details to draw an unhelpful analogy.

Analogies and other forms of vicarious experience can provide a useful starting point in formulating simple rules when the two situations share important features. There are, however, cases in which the experience of others takes the form of disciplined scientific evidence. When this evidence is high-quality and substantial, it may be possible to create simple rules by distilling it.

DISTILLING SCIENTIFIC EVIDENCE

Throughout this book, we have used examples of simple rules derived from scientific evidence — think of the four rules to beat insomnia and the simple rules for diagnosing depression. Scientific knowledge accumulates over time as researchers conduct diverse studies looking at complex phenomena from unique vantage points and with distinctive methodologies. Scientific evidence, however, is not inherently simple. The resulting knowledge is often full of qualifications and contingencies that hold under some circumstances, but not others. One way to develop simple rules is to review a body of scientific research, sort through to determine the most consistent findings across studies, and distill these findings into a few simple rules. Doctors, for example, often rely on just such a distillation process to develop the rules of thumb to diagnose specific illnesses.

A significant issue in medicine is how to diagnosis children with serious infections. Such infections are rare. Well under 1 percent of all children seen by pediatricians are suffering from them. But when serious infections do occur, they pose a mortal threat to children, particularly those under the age of four, and account for 20 percent of childhood deaths in some developed countries. Identifying these deadly infections is tricky, both because they are very rare and because many children visit the doctor before their symptoms are sufficiently severe to signal serious problems.

A European research team recently reviewed the scientific evidence on diagnosing serious infections in children with the goal of developing a handful of simple boundary rules that general practitioners could use to identify or rule out serious infections. They scanned medical databases and identified 1,860 possible studies for inclusion. They then selected the articles that were relevant to their specific question. They looked for studies that included explicit rules for diagnosing serious infections, focused on children as the patients, and were conducted in developed countries by general practitioners, because they wanted only rules that primary care providers could use. These criteria winnowed the relevant articles from 1,860 to 255. The authors then screened these for the quality of their research design and chose 36 articles of sufficient merit to include in their final analysis. They then analyzed each diagnostic rule to see how accurately the rule either spotted a serious infection or ruled it out.

This systematic distillation allowed the research team to boil down a vast body of scientific evidence into a handful of high-quality rules to help primary care doctors identify (or exclude) specific serious infections on the spot. Convulsions, reduced consciousness, rapid breathing, and slow capillary refill turned out to be highly reliable signals of serious infection, and formed the basis of the rules. In contrast, whether a child is smiling, for example, or has unusual skin color were rejected as signals despite their widespread use by many doctors. These indicators were just too unreliable. The resulting handful of rules let primary care doctors quickly detect the life-threatening illnesses of children before it is too late.

Distilling scientific evidence into simple rules is particularly helpful when nonspecialists are the intended users. California passed a law in 1999 to create a network of marine protected areas to safeguard ocean wildlife. Five groups composed of scientists and laypeople were chosen to design this network along their own stretch of the state's eleven-hundred-mile coastline. The designs were to be based on the best available science, but translating that science into guidelines for nonspecialists was not easy. Marine ecosystems are complex — interactions among species are poorly understood, and key variables, such as the number of fish, are hard to measure. The relevant ecological and biological science consisted of diverse studies. One study, for example, examined the effects of marine protected areas on eight fish species with differences like travel patterns and longevity. The study considered three habitats (i.e., drop-offs, reefs, and gradual slopes), used data collected by scuba divers, and found significant predator-prey interactions.

Distilling scientific evidence from complex studies like this one into design guidelines for nonspecialists put the emphasis on the most consistent findings, supported by multiple studies. Numerous studies, for example, found that mature female fish produce exponentially more offspring than smaller females. The scientists translated this research into a simple rule that took into account the travel patterns of these fertile females: "Marine protected areas should be nine to eighteen square miles," a rule that gave clear guidance on the optimal size of marine protected areas.

Translating scientific evidence into simple rules has another benefit. It prevents scientists and laypeople from speaking past one another. Marine ecologists, like all scientists, prefer to acknowledge the limits of their findings and qualify their recommendations. But to the layperson unfamiliar with scientific discourse, these uncertain statements sound like so much waffling. By focusing on the most consistent findings, scientists can be more comfortable advocating them, without qualification, as practical advice. Nonscientists receive what they want — clear guidance on action.

Distilling the evidence works well when there is sufficient, high-quality evidence and when stakeholders view the situation in similar ways. There are, however, situations in which different people and organizations have their own distinct goals and even conflicting values, and there is no one right answer. In these situations, it is often necessary to develop simple rules by negotiating an agreement.

NEGOTIATING AN AGREEMENT

When one of us (Don) took responsibility for overseeing Executive Education at the London Business School in 2008, it provided a serendipitous opportunity to develop a set of simple rules. At $50 million in revenues, Executive Education was tiny compared to most public companies, but it provided half of the school's cash flow. Despite its small size, Executive Education faced big problems when Don took over. Its ranking among competitive programs, as determined by the *Financial Times*, had dropped from eighth to nineteenth in three years, and the team forecast a significant budget shortfall.

Half of the revenues came from fifty programs, typically one week long, which were open to anyone. These programs competed for scarce faculty, lecture rooms, and marketing attention. A quick analysis revealed that the top ten programs provided 94 percent of all profits, the bottom ten lost money, and thirty programs in the middle broke even. Many programs had substantial overlap, and several earned mediocre participant evaluations. It did not take a business school professor to figure out what to do — prune the portfolio. The issue was how. Faculty members often viewed their own programs with all the objectivity of proud parents gazing at their firstborn child. As a fellow professor, Don lacked the carrots (bonus or stock options) and sticks (demotion) that a CEO might employ.

The key to moving past the political impasse was shifting the debate from "Which programs should we run?" to "What simple rules should we use to decide which programs to run?" The Executive Education team met with faculty members, explaining the financial situation and drop in rankings, and asked the professors what guidelines they would suggest to manage the program portfolio. The team emphasized that they were aiming for a general set of rules that would apply to every program. The professors argued with one another, but ultimately converged on a handful of robust rules that would work across many situations: A program had to: (1) meet an annual profit threshold, (2) fill two weeklong programs per year, (3) achieve a target level of participant satisfaction, and (4) avoid overlap with other programs in the portfolio.

The team used these four rules to decide which programs

to add, grow, and cut. Within two years, revenues grew by 25 percent, and net profit increased by 72 percent despite a much smaller program portfolio. When Don stepped down in 2012, the open enrollment programs had regained their eighth-place ranking in the *Financial Times*. Of course, individual professors were not pleased when their own programs were cut. But since they had actively participated in negotiating the rules, they were much less likely to oppose the change.

As the Executive Education example suggests, negotiating simple rules works particularly well when it is cumbersome or impossible to resolve conflicts by escalating them to a higher authority. James Buchanan, a Nobel Prize–winning economist, argued that when there are competing interests, it is critical for stakeholders to negotiate decision rules (like the Executive Education ones) before haggling over specific decisions (e.g., Should we cut this specific program?). An agreed set of rules provides a clear framework for settling contentious issues. When negotiating rules to guide future decisions, stakeholders cannot anticipate every situation or what their interests might be in every case. Since they cannot forecast every contingency, they are more likely to converge on general rules that a wide range of stakeholders can live with and consider fair across a broad set of choices.

Negotiation can be a helpful approach even if there is a higher authority, when multiple interest groups are involved, their values conflict, and some facts are hard to come by. This was the situation faced by the National Oceanic and Atmospheric Agency (NOAA) in determining the whale-watching rules for southern resident killer whales. Killer whales are the largest species in the dolphin family, and one of the world's most powerful predators. They often travel in pods, led by a female, and patrol the cold-water oceans off places like Iceland and Antarctica. The southern resident killer whales are a distinct group that live in the Salish

Sea — the island-studded waters between Vancouver Island and Washington State. They are cultural icons, mainstays of a flourishing tourist industry, and were declared an endangered species in 2005.

In theory, NOAA could dictate the whale-watching rules, but there were two problems. First, the economics and science were contentious — general causes of the whales' decline were identified, but the specifics were not. The southern residents' favorite meal, Chinook salmon, was declining in numbers, but it was not clear if the whales were undernourished. The southern residents are highly contaminated, yet it was unknown how much damage pollution was causing to their health. Boating also takes a toll. On a typical summer afternoon, up to sixty commercial whale-watch boats and private boaters plus hordes of kayakers track the whales, hoping to catch a glimpse of these impressive animals. The on-water melee and underwater engine noise disrupts the whales' hunting, but how much traffic can they tolerate?

Second, NOAA needed to engage divergent stakeholders. The owners of the roughly eighty commercial whale-watch boats from the United States and Canada were a vocal group. The independent-minded owners had diverse opinions, but they coalesced around the belief that salmon decline was the real problem. Some private boaters vociferously opposed any regulation that would impinge on where they could fish, and kayakers wondered why regulations should even apply to them. In contrast, an environmental organization advocated an outright ban on whale watching from any watercraft. To complicate matters, the southern residents freely travel between the United States and Canada without paying attention to passport control.

NOAA followed a negotiation approach to create whale-watching rules. After determining the need for regulation, the agency issued proposed regulations. NOAA had to weigh both the southern residents' health and economic concerns (NOAA is in the Department of Commerce). The agency considered options, from banning vessels for a ten-mile stretch of coast to regulating boat speeds and kayaker access. The Whale Museum played a key role, as its Soundwatch program provided on-the-water information to boaters, analyzed boating and kayak data for NOAA, and supported the whale-watch industry as educators. NOAA gathered further citizen input and developed alternatives that crystallized tradeoffs between whale protection and public use.

NOAA settled on a single whale-protecting rule that was explicitly simple to understand, enforceable, and accomplished the goal of helping the whales: all boats must stay two hundred yards away from the whales and four hundred yards out of their path. The science and economic analyses underlying these rules were not perfect, and no stakeholder got dream rules, but the negotiated process made the rule more likely to be followed.

Now that we've seen the various ways people create simple rules, we're going to walk through the process for systematically crafting better simple rules. We'll start by looking at how this process works for businesses before translating the rule-creation steps to everyday personal challenges.

5

Strategy as Simple Rules

Y ONI ASSIA WAS ONLY twenty-four years old when he
founded eToro with his brother and a college friend,
but software was in his blood. Yoni's father, David, was
a cofounder of the first Israeli software company to list on the
NASDAQ. In 2007 eToro raised $1.7 million and launched a web-
based platform that depicted currency trades as games, such
as a tug-of-war between the U.S. dollar and the euro, with the
stronger currency pulling the weaker one closer. eToro's founders discovered that the game-like interface was attractive for neophytes, but lacked the functions that more experienced traders
demanded. Two years later, they upgraded their platform, but
still failed to attract many experienced traders, who saw it as a
"me too" product.

Undaunted, the founders searched for ways to differentiate
eToro from competitive offerings, and found the answer where
they least expected it. eToro's trading platform included online
chat that allowed traders to swap tips and ask one another questions in real time. The founders had included chat because it was

easy to code, never imagining that traders would find much use for it. They were surprised by how popular chat was, even among users who did not trade actively.

Intrigued, Yoni decided to interview users who had registered for the site and chatted regularly but had not conducted any trades. He learned that many of these users were novices who lacked confidence and appreciated the opportunity to learn about currency markets from more seasoned traders. He also discovered that neophytes who chatted with seasoned traders were more likely to start trading and also more likely to stick with it. Building on this insight, Yoni decided to create a social network for traders, with a vision of becoming "the Facebook of trading."

To realize this vision, eToro launched OpenBook, a social investment network that allows users to explain their investment strategies, swap advice, enter trading competitions, and follow or even copy one another's trading activity in real time. Open-Book includes a league table where traders are ranked by their total gains, win ratio (percentage of trades that made money), and number of users copying their trades. eToro also launched a one-click function that lets users imitate, in real time, the investment decisions made by the traders they want to copy. Traders who have a positive trading record for the prior three months and have attracted at least ten "copiers" can apply to become one of eToro's Popular Investors, and if they are approved, they can earn cash bonuses based on their performance and the number of copiers they attract.

By late 2011, Yoni had several million dollars in the bank, two hundred employees, and over one million registered users. He also had a lot of questions that would be challenging for an experienced executive, but were particularly daunting for an entrepreneur a few years out of college. For help, Yoni turned to his fellow members of the Young Presidents' Organization (YPO), a network of business leaders who have run a significant organization by the age of forty-five. The YPO calls itself "the most powerful network in the world for business leaders," and it is easy to see why. In 2014 the YPO had over twenty thousand members operating in 120 countries, and as a group YPO members oversee combined revenues of more than $6 trillion and employ more than fifteen million people. The core of the YPO experience is the Forum, a monthly meeting where eight to ten members convene to discuss their most pressing business and personal challenges with a group of peers.

STUDYING SIMPLE RULES IN ACTION

In 2011 Yoni and ten other YPO members attended a program on simple rules at the London Business School. The simple rules program, which Don designed and ran with a team of his students, combined learning with action research, an approach that generates knowledge while solving real-world problems. Kurt Lewin, an MIT academic who pioneered action research, once observed that the best way to understand something is to try to change it. Researchers don't stand on the sidelines, but jump into the fray, solve a real problem, and pause periodically to reflect and learn along the way. The YPOers brought members of their management team to meet in London for three classroom sessions, which each lasted a day or two. In the classroom, the YPOers learned the theory behind simple rules and discussed how to apply it in their own companies. Between the lectures, the teams returned home to develop simple rules, working with an MBA student who helped keep the process on track.

The problem that Yoni and the other YPOers tackled was fundamental: how to translate their broad objectives into a strategy that would shape employees' behavior on a day-to-day basis. It is one thing to aspire to be the Facebook of trading, but quite another to make sure that hundreds of employees spread around the world consistently take the steps necessary to achieve that goal. The YPOers are not alone in struggling to define and implement their strategy. In a recent survey of over four hundred global CEOs, executing strategy topped the list of challenges, ahead of eighty-three other issues including innovation and geopolitical instability. A separate survey of one thousand organizations in over fifty countries found that nearly two-thirds struggled to execute their strategy. Developing a strategy and implementing it are often viewed as two distinct activities — first you come up with the perfect plan and then you worry about how to make it happen. This approach, common though it is, creates a disconnect between what a company is trying to accomplish and what employees do on a day-to-day basis.

Strategy and execution, in our view, cannot be separated, because they represent two sides of the same coin. Our 2001 *Harvard Business Review* article "Strategy as Simple Rules" argued that companies can close the gap between strategic intent and day-to-day action by adopting a strategy of simple rules, applying a handful of guidelines to a critical activity or decision within the organization. A strategy of simple rules provides the flexibility to seize opportunities, produce good decisions when data and time are scarce, and help the various parts of an organization coordinate their activities to achieve common objectives. The YPO program was designed to help executives and entrepreneurs develop a strategy of simple rules for their own companies.

More than three dozen companies participated over four iterations of the simple rules program between 2011 and 2014. The diversity of YPO members allowed Don to test strategy as simple rules in companies that varied widely in terms of industry, age, ownership structure, geography, and just about any other dimension you can imagine. Half the companies were European, one quarter were North American, and the remainder from elsewhere around the world. They ranged in age from seven to nearly four hundred years old, in revenues from $10 million to over $2 billion, and in number of employees from under a hundred to ten thousand. The companies included technology-intensive startups like eToro, midsized German manufacturing firms, a spinoff of a major airline, a private equity firm based in London, and a multinational serving the global oil industry. The research supported the main hypothesis that a strategy of simple rules can improve results across diverse organizations. Companies consistently increased their performance, often achieving dramatic results within a few months.

With each successive cohort of YPO members, Don learned more about what worked and what did not when it comes to putting a strategy of simple rules in place, and he codified these insights into a process that consists of three steps:

1. Figure out what will move the needles.
2. Choose a bottleneck.
3. Craft the rules.

When working with a company, we begin by gaining clarity about how management plans to increase profits into the future. We advise people to visualize corporate profits as the gap between two parallel needles — an upper needle that corresponds to revenues and a lower needle that tracks costs.

The first step is to identify the critical choices that will drive a wedge between revenues and costs to increase profits and sustain them over time. The second step is to identify a bottleneck, a decision or activity that is preventing the company from improving profitability. The final step is to craft a set of simple rules that, when applied to the bottleneck, improves profitability.

Managers are tempted to jump right in and begin crafting the rules, but by working through the first two steps they can ensure that the simple rules they develop are truly strategic and will help them achieve profitable growth. Along the way, we also learned how to streamline the process. In the most recent edition, the YPOers moved from figuring out what would move the needles to testing their simple rules in twelve action-packed weeks. In addition to describing the three steps, this chapter will share practical tips on how to implement a strategy of simple rules in your own organization.

FIGURE OUT WHAT WILL MOVE THE NEEDLES

When Don ran the first iteration of the program, he believed that the YPO members would have a clear idea of what their company was trying to achieve and could dive right into developing their strategy of simple rules. That was wrong. In nearly every case, the company's goals were imperfectly understood, and top executives disagreed on what mattered most for the company's success. One YPO member, who runs a professional-services firm in London, met with her management team once a month and began every meeting by repeating the firm's key priorities. When she surveyed her staff, over 80 percent of her managers claimed they knew the firm's top objectives, but when we asked these same managers to list those priorities, fewer than one-third of them could name even two of their company's top five objectives. Her experience was typical. Don and his colleague Rebecca

Homkes conducted a survey of managers in over 250 companies around the world. When asked to list their company's top priorities for the next few years, only half of the managers could name even their company's single most important objective.

Without a clear understanding of what their company is trying to achieve, executives struggle to identify where to apply simple rules, let alone what the rules should be. To help the YPOers identify what mattered most, Don taught an introductory session — a sort of Strategy 101 — that laid out the fundamentals and explained where a strategy of simple rules fits in. The field of strategy is based on a precise point of view of what a company's ultimate objective should be — to create economic value over time and capture it as profits. Economic value is defined as the difference between what a customer is willing to pay for a product and the cost of all the inputs required to produce it. Willingness to pay works better than alternative measures, such as revenues or price, because it anchors the analysis in the customer's point of view and forces managers to consider what customers value and what alternatives they have. If a company succeeds in generating economic value (and protecting it from competitors), it will generate profits and cash flow into the future — the ultimate goal of a company's strategy. Other measures of success, such as market share, revenue growth, and customer satisfaction, serve as useful markers along the road to profitable growth.

Economic-value creation is a powerful lens for focusing managers on what matters most, but the concept can be a bit abstract. A practical way to visualize value creation is to picture two horizontal needles running parallel to one another. The upper needle marks how much a company's customers are willing to pay for its goods — so it will be much higher for Audi than it will be for Hyundai. The bottom needle indicates the costs of producing a product (including the risk-adjusted cost of capital). Ikea, by selling its furniture unassembled out of cavernous warehouses, keeps its cost needle lower than most of its competitors. The gap between the needles represents economic value created.

This image tees up a critical question — what will move the needles? Countless tactical moves can cause the needles to twitch — an advertising campaign may briefly boost customers' willingness to pay, for example, while switching to lower-quality materials may reduce costs a bit. Only a handful of choices, however, will significantly increase willingness to pay or decrease costs and sustain those improvements over time. Focusing on how managers can move the needles cuts through peripheral considerations to hone in on the underlying drivers of value creation. When Yoni and his team talked through what would move the needles at eToro, for example, they quickly converged on the importance of increasing the number of Popular Investors. The successful traders not only traded themselves, but also increased their followers' and copiers' willingness to trade (and pay the associated transaction fees). Tapping eToro's existing members to share their insights was cheaper than hiring outside gurus to provide investment advice.

For another example of figuring out what will move the needles, consider the case of Janis Oslejs, a YPOer who is trying to revolutionize one of the oldest products in the world — concrete. In 1997 Janis founded Primekss (pronounced PREEM-ex), a construction company that specialized in laying floors in large buildings (such as Volvo factories or Ikea stores). Within a decade he had operations throughout northern Europe. As he was expanding his business, Janis grew dissatisfied with the concrete currently in use, which was prone to cracking, required a thick layer to provide the required strength, and was very environmentally unfriendly. The production of cement, the ingredient that causes concrete to harden, is the third-largest producer of manmade carbon dioxide in the world. When Janis looked for better alternatives, he learned that concrete was ancient (the early Egyptians invented it) and ubiquitous, second only to water in terms of per capita consumption. What cement was not, however, was a hotbed of innovation. When Janis could not find any alternatives to the traditional product, he set about trying to improve concrete himself, hiring a team of researchers and partnering with universities. In his quest for ideas, Janis scoured ancient texts, where he learned that Roman engineers added horsehair to strengthen their concrete and blood to withstand freezing temperatures. By embedding steel fibers (the modern equivalent of horsehair) within a fortified concrete matrix, Primekss developed a proprietary concrete that allowed customers to use less cement, avoid cracking, and cut carbon dioxide emissions by half.

When Janis joined the simple rules program, he worried that top executives diverged on the direction the company should pursue, and their disagreement created what he described as "a constant source of mild frustration." One camp believed the company should serve its current customers in Scandinavia, leverage the company's existing labor force and reputation for excellent service, and grow by offering existing clients a wider range of products. Another faction argued that Primekss should focus on licensing its innovative concrete globally, perhaps getting out of the company's legacy contracting business altogether. Both alternatives had strong proponents within the company, who competed for scarce cash, talent, and management attention. As a result, the two camps were pulling Primekss in different directions at the same time. Several of the YPO companies struggled with fundamental disagreements about what the company should be doing, confusing employees and dissipating scarce resources. These disagreements were particularly common in companies, like Primekss, where an innovative product opened up new possibilities, or when changes in the market rendered old ways of competing less viable.

To figure out what would move the needles, Janis convened a group of eighteen stakeholders, including senior managers, board members, investors, and managers of the country subsidiaries. The group concluded that existing customers would not pay a premium for additional construction services and Primekss could not serve these customers at lower cost than competitors. In contrast, there were potential buyers around the world who would pay more for Primekss's innovative concrete. Janis and the team settled on a strategy of selling the company's proprietary concrete to customers anywhere in the world by partnering with local construction companies. Everyone in Primekss understood the new direction, but that didn't mean everyone agreed with it. Two members of the sales force felt strongly that the new approach took Primekss in the wrong direction and ended up leaving the company. Those who remained, however, were clear on what the company was trying to achieve and committed to making it happen.

Through the first four years of the simple rules program, Don experimented with various ways to help the YPO companies figure out what would move the needles. One exercise proved particularly productive. He had the company's management team work as a group to answer three questions that are fundamental to any company's ability to create economic value:

1. Who will we target as customers?
2. What product or service will we offer?
3. How will we provide this product at a profit?

Not all customers will be willing (or able) to pay a premium — many construction contracts, for example, go to the low-cost bidder regardless of the concrete's quality or carbon footprint. Some customers, moreover, are costlier to serve than others — the cost of delivering concrete to remote locations with poor infrastructure is very high. The same logic applies to products. Not every product a company sells will command a premium price or be cheaper to make than competitors' offerings. Equally important are the choices on who *not* to serve and what *not* to offer. In their quest to grow revenues, companies are constantly tempted to chase unattractive customers or sell unprofitable products. Clearly stating their *who* and *what* helps managers resist the temptation to pursue unprofitable business and focus on the combination of product and customer that will create the most value. The third question addresses *how* a company will provide its product and defend its position from competitors. By locking in the best franchise partners in key markets, Primekss could sell its concrete globally and also make it harder for potential rivals to enter those markets.

The who, what, how framework is a general-purpose tool that works across a wide variety of different settings. Consider, for example, the case of the Zatisi Group, a fine-dining and catering business headquartered in Prague. When Sanjiv Suri opened the V Zatisi wine bar in 1991, it was one of the first fine-dining restaurants in Prague after the collapse of Czechoslovakia's Communist regime. Sanjiv went on to start other restaurants (the group runs three of the top ten ranked restaurants in Prague), and later expanded into catering and cafeterias. Sanjiv believed that the group's cafeteria business offered the most promising opportunity for profitable growth, and assembled a team of chefs and cafeteria managers to develop a strategy of simple rules. The Zatisi team began by identifying which customers would pay a premium for their services. In terms of the who, they decided to target large, progressive companies (Google is a customer in Prague, for example) and schools, which wanted to nourish, versus simply feed, their employees and students. Working through the exercise, the team defined the *what* as food that promotes balanced, healthy eating and the *how* as preparing tasty meals onsite from fresh, natural ingredients.

Clarity on what will move the needles is a necessary prelude to developing a strategy of simple rules. Crystallizing your who, what, and how defines which game you are going to play. Janis, for example, decided to sell innovative concrete through global partners rather than remain a contractor in northern Europe, while Sanjiv opted to differentiate Zatisi by providing healthful meal options using fresh ingredients. Once you know what game you are playing, you still need a strategy to win. This is where simple rules come in. Simple rules applied to a critical bottleneck embed insights about value creation into the heart of the organization and shape a company's most important activities on a day-to-day basis.

IDENTIFY A BOTTLENECK

When it comes to implementing a strategy of simple rules, pinpointing the precise decision or activity where rules will have the most impact is half the battle. We use the term *bottleneck* to describe a specific activity or decision that hinders a company from moving the needles. At eToro, for example, the key bottleneck was the scarcity of Popular Investors who could attract lots of followers and copiers. The term *bottleneck* comes from engineering and refers to a component that limits the performance of the larger system. The slowest step in an automobile assembly line, for example, is the bottleneck that sets the pace for the overall manufacturing process.

The best bottlenecks to focus on share three characteristics. First, they have a direct and significant impact on value creation. What moves the needles will vary from company to company and so should the chosen bottleneck. For example, Coller Capital, a private equity firm in London, chose the process for screening job applicants, while Filigran Trägersysteme, which manufactures steel girders in Germany and Poland, selected its monthly steel-purchasing decisions. Second, chosen bottlenecks should represent recurrent decisions (rather than one-off choices), so the rules can be tested, refined, and used many times. At Primekss, the choice of licensing partners was a good candidate for simple rules (in fact it is what they chose), while the one-time decision to shift from contracting to licensing their innovative product did not lend itself to simple rules. Finally, bottlenecks, as their name implies, arise when opportunities exceed available resources. Typical examples include mergers and acquisitions, new-product development, capital budgeting, and new-market entry.

In any organization there will be dozens of activities or decisions that could be improved by simple rules, but it is essential to select a single bottleneck that simple rules will guide. One German manufacturing firm decided that higher product quality would increase customers' willingness to pay. Disregarding our advice, the company developed a set of broad principles meant to cover any activity, anywhere in the organization, that might impact quality. The resulting rules — such as "Recognize and reward good practices in improving quality" and "Don't make promises that cannot be kept" — were too abstract to provide useful guidance on any specific activity or decision, and they were largely ignored by employees. Focusing on a critical bottleneck, in contrast, can pay off. By honing in on the process to cultivate Popular Investors, eToro nearly tripled their number in two years, while increasing the number of followers for the most popular traders fiftyfold.

The choice of bottleneck may seem obvious after the fact, but selecting one activity among many is a daunting task for most managers. The *how* from a who, what, how analysis is a good place to start, and often points in the right direction. The Zatisi team, for example, defined their how as preparing tasty meals on-site from fresh, natural ingredients, which pointed toward meal selection as the bottleneck. In the past, the chef at each cafeteria had complete autonomy to decide which dishes to include and when to set the menus. When the team reviewed the menus for the previous year they were surprised to learn that the number of recipes used by the chefs approached one thousand in total.

Chefs would often choose dishes requiring ingredients that were out of season or not available locally. Tomatoes, for example, were used mostly during the winter, when they were at their most expensive and least fresh. The chefs typically set their menu weeks in advance, which kept them from incorporating ingredients that were fresh and on sale. Each chef, moreover, selected dishes without conferring with colleagues at other cafeterias, which prevented the company from buying fresh ingredients in bulk. Finally, the chefs valued novelty, offering even the most popular dishes only a few times a year.

Based on their analysis, the team developed a set of rules to guide menu selection: The menu must be fixed by noon on Wednesday for the following week; three of the five dishes every day must have been bestsellers in the past; the chefs had to ensure that at least two dishes are offered across all cafeterias the same day; and 90 percent of the fruits and vegetables must be seasonal or sourced locally. Within a few months of adopting the new rules, revenues increased by one-third and profits doubled. The strategy of simple rules also provided a platform for future growth, and Zatisi tripled the number of cafeterias it served in eighteen months.

A company's *how* will often point to a broad process, such as marketing and sales or new-product development, crucial to creating economic value. These overarching processes consist of several discrete steps, each of which is a candidate for simple rules. Several of the YPO companies used a flow chart to break a process down into its distinct steps. By plotting key activities and decisions in the process, it is easier to pinpoint the precise spot where simple rules can work their magic. This was the approach taken by Grupo Multimedia, Mexico's leading provider of installed multimedia systems, such as in-home cinemas and corporate videoconferencing facilities. Federico Bausone and his team quickly focused on the sales process, which they broke down into four distinct steps: (1) discover and qualify opportunities; (2) develop a pre-proposal; (3) design a solution; and (4) conduct pre-sales planning. Next they analyzed, for the first time, the distribution of projects by step in the sales process.

They were shocked to learn that more than 70 percent of the projects were stuck in the design stage, waiting for engineers to create proposals, most of which were customized for each customer. Federico knew that his design engineers were busy, but so was everyone else in the company. This analysis revealed that design was the key bottleneck limiting profitable growth. Not only were the design engineers stretched thin, their win ratio wasn't great either — only one in six of their proposals resulted in a sale. The team decided to develop simple rules to determine when to invest the time and effort to design a solution and when to offer an off-the-shelf product instead.

When searching for the right bottleneck, it helps to look for a critical activity where the number of opportunities exceeds the available resources, such as when sales opportunities outstrip a company's ability to meet demand. Consider Weima Maschinenbau, a German company that produces machines for processing plastics, wood, and metal to make these materials easier to recycle. In a typical year, Weima receives approximately ten thousand requests from customers, but only has the capacity to sell around a thousand products. Weima's managers had tried using a detailed checklist of more than forty criteria to prioritize customer requests. The sales representatives and distributors balked at the checklist, which they viewed as too complex and time consuming to use, and passed most proposals on to headquarters for review. As a result, Weima's top management spent hours each week sifting through stacks of proposals.

Inspired by the simple rules of battlefield triage, Martin Friz, Weima's managing director, decided to apply a similar approach to quickly sort sales opportunities. He convened a team, which developed four boundary rules to screen customer requests for any product that required customization: (1) Weima must collect at least 70 percent of the price before the unit leaves the factory; (2) any product discount can be no more than a set percent; (3) there can be no "hidden costs" of installing and servicing the machine (e.g., extreme climate, dangerous political environment); and (4) Weima must have sold and tested a similar product in the past twelve months. If a customer request cleared these hurdles, it was fast-tracked for immediate production. Any request that failed to clear more than two hurdles was rejected. If a customer request violated one or two rules, it was forwarded to top management for review.

Choosing external partners is another bottleneck where opportunities often exceed a firm's capacity to pursue them. After Primekss won an industry award for innovation at a Las Vegas trade conference, over one hundred contractors approached Janis about a potential partnership. The time required to select, train, and support partners meant that Primekss could enter into only a handful of new relationships every year. How to choose? In the past, Primekss had selected partners without any guidelines, and more than half of these partnerships failed. Janis convened a team to develop the rules to pick partners. To avoid cannibalizing the company's existing operations, they adopted a rule that no partners would be sought in countries with existing Primekss subsidiaries. Another boundary rule specified that potential partners must have a Laser Screed machine (a machine that lays concrete using lasers to ensure precision). Ownership of this state-of-the-art piece of equipment served as a reliable proxy for a potential partner's size, technical expertise, and commitment to quality. The team also formulated two timing rules. To ensure that the Primekss relationship was a high priority for the partner, they had to start a project within three months of signing a contract. To ensure Primekss did not have too many new relationships at once in its first year, the team developed a rule that the company would maintain a gap of at least three months between adding new partners. Using simple rules, Primekss increased the success rate of partnerships to over 80 percent, and quadrupled its licensing exports within a year.

Decisions that require coordination across different departments or teams are another good place to look for bottlenecks. A company's most important activities — like developing new products or providing customers with integrated solutions — require different parts of the business to work together. Specialized functions, like finance or sales, however, have their own objectives and distinctive ways of working. As a result, department managers often end up arguing or talking past one another, rather than getting things done. Simple rules can provide a framework that helps managers from different departments make decisions, even difficult ones, more quickly and effectively.

Consider, as an example, the VLS-Group, a European provider of logistics to the chemical industry, which traces its origins back to 1616 as a storage facility for the Dutch East India Company. When Sandrine Montsma became the CEO in 2010, she joined a company that had been hit hard by the global economic crisis. To return the VLS-Group to profitability, Sandrine worked with leaders throughout the company to identify major projects that could improve operations and generate cash. Sandrine estimated that VLS could complete no more than six major projects and do them well in her first year.

There was no lack of options as the company's managers generated twenty-eight proposals for major projects. The problem arose when it came to deciding which initiatives to pursue. Different parts of the business favored different projects — the finance department was looking to cut costs, while sales wanted to sell more products — and managers ended up pushing their pet projects and opposing other departments' proposals. As a bottleneck, Sandrine and the team decided on the decision of which turnaround initiatives to pursue immediately, which to put on the back burner, and which to postpone indefinitely. She then assembled a team, drawn from different divisions and functions, that negotiated rules to prioritize major projects.

When it comes to deciding where to apply simple rules, the most obvious activity is not always the right answer. Consider the case of Mercado Eletrônico, a Brazilian firm that connects the purchasing departments of large companies, such as Caterpillar and Avon, with over sixty thousand suppliers through an online platform. It's like an eBay for big corporations and their suppliers. But unlike eBay's interface, which looks and functions the same for every customer, Mercado Eletrônico offers each of its largest buyers a customized interface to manage its purchases. Eduardo Nader initially planned to apply simple rules to his company's process, located within marketing, to develop new features for users. After discussions with his team, however, he discovered an even more productive source of new product ideas. When customers wanted to change their customized interface, they sent the request to Mercado Eletrônico's engineering team, which was overwhelmed by the sheer volume and struggled to clear the backlog of unfulfilled requests. Eduardo's team recognized that some of these change requests would appeal more broadly to other customers. Nestlé, for example, might request a change that would also appeal to PepsiCo or Walmart. So the team developed a set of simple rules to identify and fast-track requests for technical changes made by one client that could be offered to other customers. Applying a few simple rules, such as "A feature is requested by two or more customers and it does not duplicate existing functionality," doubled the hit rate of Mercado Eletrônico's new-product-development process within a year.

CRAFT THE SIMPLE RULES

The first instinct of many leaders in formulating simple rules is to go to their office, close the door, write down their ideas, and then emerge, like Moses coming down from the mountain, with their rules etched in stone. The temptation to dictate rules is particularly strong among entrepreneurs who founded and built their companies from the ground up. Among the YPOers we worked with, several thought that the "right" answer would be obvious and could be predicted beforehand, and that assembling a team to formulate the simple rules would be a waste of time. They were wrong. Before developing simple rules, we asked YPOers to write down what they thought the ultimate rules would be. They almost never got them right.

Developing rules from the top down is a big mistake. When leaders rely on their gut instincts, they overemphasize recent events, build in their personal biases, and ignore data that doesn't fit with their preconceived notions. It is much better to involve a team, typically ranging in size from four to eight members, and use a structured process to harness members' diverse insights and points of view. When drafting the dream team to develop simple rules, it is critical to include some of the people who will be using them on a day-to-day basis. At eToro, Yoni picked a few account managers responsible for cultivating Popular Investors to help develop the rules, while Martin asked Weima's sales representatives to help develop the rules for screening customer requests.

Having users make the rules confers several advantages. First, they are closest to the facts on the ground and best positioned to codify experience into usable rules. Because they will make decisions based on the rules, they can strike the right balance between guidance and discretion, avoiding rules that are overly vague or restrictive. Users can also phrase the rules in language that resonates for them, rather than relying on business jargon. By actively participating in the process, users are more likely to buy into the final rules and therefore apply them in practice. Firsthand knowledge also makes it easier to explain the rules, and their underlying rationale, to colleagues who did not participate in the process.

A close look at Herkimer Corporation reveals how companies can craft simple rules. In 2011 Victor Belmondo took over the Middle East and Africa business of Herkimer, a global supplier of specialized products to the oil industry, with over ten thousand employees and $2 billion in revenues. Victor was responsible for the operational and financial performance of a unit that encompassed eighty-one countries. More than four hundred people reported directly to him, and Victor also needed to coordinate his team's efforts with colleagues in corporate functions — such as finance and the legal department — that did not report directly to him.

"When I joined the company, people talked a lot about strategy," Victor recalled, "but nobody could tell me how we made money — we were trying to be all things to all people, and it wasn't working." Victor worked with his management team to group Herkimer's customers into three buckets based on the country where they operated. Seven countries were designated as strategic and would be the focus of Herkimer's efforts, three were put on a watch list for possible upgrading in the future, and the remaining seventy-one countries were designated as opportunistic, where sales could only be made under very favorable terms. The team also identified those products where Herkimer could charge a premium, and labeled these the company's "product sweet spot." After clarifying the *who* and *what,* Victor and his management team chose the decision of whether to bid on projects as their bottleneck. Preparing a proposal involved substantial pre-engineering and compliance work, often required site visits to remote locations, and typically cost tens of thousands of dollars. The sheer volume of work overwhelmed the proposal team and produced a win rate of less than 10 percent.

Deciding on whether to bid or not involved users from five different departments, and Victor included representatives from each unit on the team that would develop the simple rules. Rather than dictating from on high, in devising simple rules senior executives should ensure that everyone is onboard, maintain momentum, and keep the process on track. Victor handpicked the team and spoke to each member in person to explain the process and answer any questions in advance. Stefano Turconi, a lecturer at the London Business School, interviewed each team member before the simple rules workshop, and asked them to generate a handful of rules that they believed the company should use when deciding whether to bid on a project. To come up with their rules, each team member walked through examples of projects where Herkimer's bid had proved particularly successful or unsuccessful. The interviews generated a list of fifty-seven rules, which provided the raw material for developing the final simple rules.

The team met for a full-day workshop to distill the fifty-seven rules down to a handful agreed upon by the team as a whole. Victor kicked off the meeting by reviewing which customers and products were most profitable, explaining why the bidding process had been selected as a bottleneck, and outlining the process they would follow to develop and test the rules. Stefano, who facilitated the workshop, then guided a discussion where the team used Post-it notes to group similar rules. Within an hour, they identified several overarching categories of rules, such as "type of equipment," "strength of relationship with customer," and "potential for aftermarket sales." They then proceeded to discuss and negotiate with one another which rules were most important, and by the end of the day had agreed upon seven boundary rules for selecting which projects warranted a bid.

Testing the first-cut rules is critical to ensure that they work. After the workshop, three of the Herkimer team members agreed to test the rules against twenty historical deals to see whether the initial rules would have selected promising requests and screened out unattractive ones. At the same time, the team tested the rules as guidelines to evaluate current customer requests. The rules on technical and commercial complexity proved to be overly open-ended, requiring a significant amount of additional data collection and analysis, which did not add much insight. Team members also found that seven rules was too many when it came to maintaining focus on the most important factors. Victor convened a second workshop to further refine the rules.

The team decided to drop two rules, and tweaked the wording of the remaining five. The company considers its precise rules proprietary, but they focus on whether the opportunity fell into the product sweet spot, whether it was in a strategic country, whether Herkimer had previous experience with that type of project, the strength of the relationship with the customer, and the resources required to complete the project. A project that conformed to all of the rules was put on the fast track. If a project violated the country and product criteria, the company declined to bid. The remaining bids were forwarded to senior management for further consideration. Within a year of implementing the rules, Victor's unit won half of the projects it bid on (up from under 10 percent before the rules were implemented), sales were up over 20 percent, and profits more than doubled. Victor was promoted, and he extended the strategy of simple rules to other operations in the company.

It is critical to test your first-cut rules in a rigorous fashion, and refine them in light of your findings. Unfortunately, many managers shortchange this critical step. Frontier Dental Laboratories, in contrast, is an example of a company that did a good job of testing and refining its preliminary rules. Paolo Kalaw, a microbiologist turned entrepreneur, started acquiring dental laboratories at the age of twenty-nine, and sold his company nine years later. When he joined the YPO simple rules program, Paolo had purchased Frontier Dental Laboratories, which produces crowns, inlays, and veneers to restore damaged teeth. Frontier's twelve sales representatives covered the entire North American market, with nearly two hundred thousand dentists. Members of the sales force spent their days trying to talk to potential customers. This is a tough job, because the typical dentist may have two or three patients sitting in a chair at any point in time, and a receptionist whose life's work is making sure no one disturbs the dentist. The sales representatives were always busy, but not particularly productive. In a typical day, a rep would contact twenty dental offices, talk to one or two dentists by phone, and arrange a second meeting with under 5 percent of the dentists they reached. In the end, they had to approach a few hundred dentists to land a single sale.

To increase the company's profits, Paolo wanted the sales force to focus its efforts on the best prospects, and assembled a team to develop simple rules to prioritize potential customers. They began by analyzing their database of current and past customers and discovered that 10 percent of their customers accounted for over half of the company's revenues. The team was charged with developing a set of simple rules to identify the "ideal dentist." Following a process like Herkimer's, the team developed an initial list of nine rules, which identified dentists who owned their own practice, were between thirty-five and fifty-five years old (younger dentists were still building their practices, while older dentists often scaled back their hours), had less than 5 percent in finance charges (a measure of whether the dentist paid bills on time), provided at least $10,000 in business every year (a measure of steady volume), and had attended a Frontier training program (a proxy for the dentist's familiarity with Frontier's products).

To refine the rules, Paolo divided the group into three teams, which tested the provisional rules against a sample of Frontier's customer database to see how well they identified promising clients. The teams reconvened a few weeks later to discuss their results. All the teams agreed that a few of the rules worked well as they were. For other rules, like whether a dentist owned the practice or how old they were, necessary data were hard to find and they scrapped these rules. Independent testing by separate teams produced diverse insights into the preliminary rules. The first team, for instance, thought the $10,000 threshold of business in a year was too high, and by experimenting with different levels found that a lower threshold of $5,000 still identified attractive leads. The second team discovered that dentists who had a website tended to practice more cosmetic dentistry, so "dentist has a website" was added to the rules. Most important, they refined some of the existing rules to make them easier to use and more robust. "Less than 5 percent in finance charges," for example, was cumbersome to calculate, and thus was changed to "has fewer than four finance charges in a year."

After testing and refining the rules, Frontier used them to identify which dentists to target. The sales force shifted its approach from trying to squeeze in as many visits per day as possible to investing the time to build a relationship with the dentists who were most likely to buy Frontier's products. The results were dramatic. Using the rules to prioritize potential customers, Frontier was able to sell to two out of every three dentists they targeted. Within a year of implementing the rules, the company had increased sales 42 percent despite a declining overall market. More impressive, they achieved these results with two sales representatives, versus the twelve required to generate lower revenues before the simple rules were adopted.

Where does strategy live in a company? Too often, a company's strategy sits on a shelf, gathering dust. A strategy that doesn't influence critical decisions on a day-to-day basis, however, is not a strategy — it is a book report. Strategy as simple rules provides a vital alternative. Strategy, in our view, lives in the simple rules that guide an organization's most important activities. They allow employees to make on-the-spot decisions and seize unexpected opportunities without losing sight of the big picture.

The process you use to develop simple rules matters as much as the rules themselves. Involving a broad cross-section of employees, for example, injects more points of view into the discussion, produces a shared understanding of what matters for value creation, and increases buy-in to the simple rules. Investing the time up front to clarify what will move the needles dramatically increases the odds that simple rules will be applied where they can have the greatest impact.

Don developed the process to implement a strategy of simple rules across a diverse range of companies, and it has proven to be remarkably robust in other settings as well. We have used it successfully with companies outside the YPO, early-stage startups, not-for-profits, and universities. Most surprisingly, people were so excited about the approach that they brought it home with them to develop simple rules for their personal lives. The next chapter describes how you, too, can use the three-stage process described in this chapter as a structured approach to develop simple rules to achieve your own most pressing objectives.

6

Getting Personal

WE ORIGINALLY DESIGNED THE three-step process for developing simple rules to help businesses increase their profits. The same approach can, however, be applied at the individual level to address personal challenges. The power of simple rules in personal life became clear to us in an unexpected place, a Chinese restaurant near London's Baker Street, where Don was hosting a group of Young Presidents' Organization members at the end of the simple rules program. By the second course, the conversation had turned from business to how the participants applied lessons from the program to their personal lives. As we went around the table, one YPOer described how she developed rules to help her son with his math homework, another for selecting movies that he and his wife would both enjoy, and a recently divorced YPOer explained how he crafted rules to decide whether to go on a second date with someone. It turns out that the process outlined in the last chapter works as well at home as it does in the office.

In a subsequent iteration of the program, Don introduced a session on making simple rules personal, which turned out to be a great hit. The process of developing personal rules, like its professional counterpart, consists of three steps: (1) decide what will move your personal needles and increase the gap between what energizes you and what stresses you out, (2) identify a bottleneck that keeps you from creating personal value, and (3) develop simple rules that work for you. We developed a set of questions to guide people through the process, and looked at common challenges and practical tips for overcoming them. In this chapter, we will walk you through the process and tell the stories of how three people developed simple rules for very different situations — dating online, managing depression, and becoming more charismatic. (Their names and certain identifying details have been changed to ensure their anonymity.)

DETERMINE WHAT WILL MOVE THE NEEDLES FOR YOU

In companies, economic value is clearly defined (the gap between customers' willingness to pay and costs) and relatively straightforward to measure through cash flow and market capitalization. Defining and measuring personal value, in contrast, is a notoriously difficult task, and one that has occupied philosophers for centuries. While characterizing the meaning of life is difficult in the abstract, identifying concrete areas that will add personal value is quite manageable from a practical perspective. In many cases, people have a clear idea of which aspect of their lives they would like to improve. If not, there are a few tricks for helping you to hone in on the areas of your life that could benefit most from simple rules.

We've found it helpful to use the imagery of moving the needles introduced in the last chapter. "Strategic" improvements can come from two sources. You can raise the top needle by doing more of what makes life worth living, such as spending time with your children, for example, or contributing to your community. Increasing these activities will enhance your sense of well-being, happiness, and self-esteem. You can also create personal value by lowering the bottom needle, which represents problematic areas, such as money worries or poor health, that prevent you from getting the most out of life. Mitigating these negative aspects of life can reduce stress, anxiety, or fear. Personal value consists of the gap between those activities that bring you the most happiness and those that keep you from enjoying life to the fullest. As with business, there are many small steps that can cause the needles to twitch, but relatively few strategic changes that can drive a wedge between the needles of joy and suffering and hold them apart for a sustained period of time.

It is pretty straightforward for most people to identify strategic improvements in their lives, which range from diet to dating, from work-life balance to getting rich, from enjoying a more fulfilling social life to taking more "me" time. The only thing these choices have in common is that when selected they produce an "aha" moment of recognition that they could significantly increase happiness or decrease stress over an extended period of time. Strategic life areas resonate deeply with the user; you *want* to improve them. The questions below can help you decide where to start:

- What aspect of your life do you most want to improve? What are the first three things that come to mind?
- What activities bring you the greatest happiness and sense of well-being? How could you spend more time on these?
- Which aspects of your life cause you the most fear, stress, or anxiety? How could you decrease these?

- If you look back in five years, what will you regret not changing? What will you regret if you look back from your deathbed?
- How might a trusted friend, spouse, or loved one answer these questions for you? (It would be useful to ask them.)

It is helpful to list more than one area for improvement, as some will be more suitable for simple rules than others. Three to five is typically enough to get started. The first cut of this exercise often produces a list of very general values such as family, wealth, and health. This is a good start, but it is easier to identify a bottleneck if you can translate these broad areas into more concrete and measurable objectives that will move the needles for you. In this stage it is helpful to be as specific as you can on what you want to achieve. For instance, "eat better" might be refined into "lose twenty pounds," "increase energy," or "eat to manage blood sugar." These are very different objectives that will require, in all likelihood, different simple rules.

FIND THE RIGHT BOTTLENECK

After you have selected an area you would like to improve, it is time to choose the bottleneck where you will apply simple rules. Like their business counterparts, personal bottlenecks refer to a specific activity or decision where simple rules can exert the greatest impact in helping you move the needles. A bottleneck provides the focal point for the simple rules, and by managing the bottleneck the simple rules should create personal value. The best personal bottlenecks are strategic in the sense that addressing them will help you create and sustain personal value. Simple rules can be productively applied to dozens of personal activities, but it takes time and effort to develop, test, and refine them. This effort is best expended on an activity or decision that will produce the biggest bang, in terms of your personal happiness, for the buck. To help you identify promising candidates, ask yourself the following questions: Which activities or decisions keep you from achieving your objective? Where will rules have the greatest impact?

A productive bottleneck should not only create personal value; it should also lend itself to simple rules. The best candidates are recurrent activities (versus one-off decisions), so the investment in developing rules can be recouped over many applications of the rules. A good bottleneck might be how a couple handles disagreements over money or divvies up household chores, rather than the one-time choice of whom to marry in the first place. Activities and decisions that you repeat on a daily or weekly basis also yield data to measure how well your rules are working and refine them based on what you learn. Simple rules work particularly well in situations where the number of alternatives exceeds available resources, such as making investment decisions, deciding which home repairs to make, or choosing how to spend limited free time. Simple rules work best with activities that require flexibility, such as deciding what to eat, for example, or disciplining your toddler. If the problem stems from forgetting rote activities, like packing for a business trip, a checklist is a better alternative. Finally, simple rules work well in channeling willpower, so they are well suited for activities, like diet, exercise, and saving money, that require short-term sacrifices for long-term gains.

Bottlenecks do not have to satisfy all of these criteria, but the more they meet, the more likely they are to benefit from simple rules. As you search for a bottleneck, remember that you are looking for something that stands in the way of achieving one of your personal goals. Some key questions to consider when selecting a bottleneck include:

- Do you frequently make this decision or participate in this activity?
- Does the number of options exceed your available time, money, energy, or attention?
- Does this activity or decision require willpower?
- Does this activity or decision require some flexibility?
- Can you measure results to test and refine your rules?

After weighing the importance of potential activities and how suitable they are to simple rules, you should identify a single, specific bottleneck to tackle. When selecting a bottleneck, it is helpful to be as precise as possible. Data can play a vital role in nailing down which specific activity is standing in the way of moving the needles. Don, for example, had identified losing weight as a strategic goal, and his first instinct was to choose his exercise regimen as the bottleneck. At the advice of a friend, he tracked his diet and exercise for a week on a fitness app, and what he learned surprised him. He was working out about as much as his schedule (and aging knees) would permit, and more exercise seemed unlikely to produce significant gains.

Diet, in contrast, was a problem area. A review of one week's data showed him doing well most of the day, eating reasonable amounts of healthy foods through dinnertime. But post-dinner snacks were a problem, contributing as many calories as an extra lunch or breakfast every day on average. This insight allowed for a narrow definition of his bottleneck as after-dinner snacking. A very specific activity like late-night eating is a strong candidate for simple rules. Willpower is a reservoir, not a river, and when it runs out (as it often does at the end of a long day), rules can be effective tools for imposing limits on behavior. Narrow bottlenecks, in this case one restricted to a specific time period, have the advantage of limiting the amount of time you have to use the rules, thus focusing your attention and conserving your willpower.

CRAFTING SIMPLE RULES THAT WORK FOR YOU

As we saw in chapter 4, simple rules originate in various ways. Some are evolutionary. Some, like Tina Fey's rules of comedy, arise out of decades of personal experience. Others emerge from complex negotiations between various interested parties, as was the case with the rules to protect the killer whales. There is no single, tidy algorithm for developing such a wide, vibrant array of simple rules. The diversity of potential sources is not a limitation of simple rules, but one of their greatest strengths. By drawing on multiple sources, you increase the odds of finding rules that will work for you. When developing your own rules, it is best to spend sufficient time — a few days to a week typically works — pulling inspiration and insights from multiple sources, which provide the raw material that you can draw on and reshape to formulate your own simple rules. We list some particularly helpful sources of rules below to get you started.

If you turn to research for inspiration, we recommend looking for insights that have held up across multiple studies. Recall, as good examples, the rules for diagnosing serious infections in children, or Michael Pollan's rules for healthy eating ("Eat food. Not too much. Mostly plants."), which are consistent with extensive research findings. A single study can yield idiosyncratic results, but any finding that withstands repeated testing can be a robust starting point for your own simple rules. These days many researchers write popular books, blogs, or give interviews to bring their findings to a wider audience, and often provide diagnostic tools that can serve as a rich source of potential rules. In his book *Slim by Design*, for example, professor Brian Wansink includes a self-assessment focusing on factors such as plate size and serving options that can help people avoid mindless overeating, tips that constitute a great starting point in developing rules.

Role models are another excellent source of rules. If you are sitting down to pen your first western, for example, you might want to read Elmore Leonard's rules for good writing. On a personal level, if you know someone who is particularly good at managing the bottleneck you have decided to address, you would be wise to consult him or her. People are often flattered to be asked for their advice, and enjoy talking about activities in which they excel. Don't limit yourself to friends and family in seeking advice. You can diversify your pool of role models by casting your net widely and approaching, for example, members of your book club, sports team, church, country club, fantasy sports league, or volunteer organization. When talking with your role models, it's important to recognize that their simple rules will most likely be implicit, so asking for a list of rules may not be the best approach. A few tactics can help surface tacit rules. First, you can explain how you manage your identified bottleneck, and ask them what they do differently. It's also productive to tease out extremes, by asking if there are things that they always do or never do when managing the target activity. Another way to explore your role model's tacit rules is to ask them to walk you through a few recent decisions — what they did and why. People typically find it easier to describe their rules in the context of concrete examples rather than in abstract terms.

These same tips work well when drawing on your own experience to codify rules. A great starting point is to assemble comprehensive data on your recent experience. If you are developing simple rules for saving for retirement, for example, you might pull together your spending over the past year to identify potential areas for saving. Again, apps can help, as there are now several that consolidate all your bank accounts and credit cards into a single dashboard to make the analysis easier. In other cases, you may need to collect some quick and dirty data on your chosen bottleneck. If, for example, you wanted to come up with simple rules for divvying up chores in your family, you might keep a journal for a week or so to see who does what when. In general, it is better to get more comprehensive data for a shorter time period than relying on your imperfect recall of events for a longer period. If you rely too much on your memory alone, you are likely to overweigh vivid examples, ignore cases that don't jibe with your assumptions, or simply forget details. When it comes to gathering and reviewing data to craft simple rules, you typically want to take a few days to a week. If you skip the data collection altogether, you are likely to make false assumptions that will result in ineffective simple rules. If you go to the other extreme and stretch the data collection out for weeks, you will probably lose momentum.

Once you have some data to work from, you can divide the past examples into three categories — those that worked well in terms of moving the needles, those that worked poorly, and everything in between. Comparing the differences between the most and least successful cases is typically the quickest and most effective way to identify potential rules. It can also be helpful to ask people who observed your past experience to provide their assessment of what you did and how it went, since others may notice patterns that you missed. Typically a handful of successful examples and a similar number of unsuccessful ones will provide enough raw material to generate preliminary rules.

Negotiation is a particularly productive approach when more than one person needs to follow the rules in order for them to work. Common examples would be rules for couples' relationships, members of a condominium association, parents and children, or a book club. When more than one person is involved in formulating the rules it is critical for everyone to focus on the same bottleneck. If a family tries to develop rules to cover chores, use of the car, curfew, screen time, dinner, and pet care all at the same time, they will gravitate to broad platitudes — like "Work at being part of our family" or "Treat each other with respect" — that provide little concrete guidance for any specific activity. Ideally you would involve everyone in the first two steps of the process as well so they understand what the simple rules are intended to achieve.

Negotiation does not preclude other sources of rules. A family, for example, could walk through a week's worth of chore data together, provide their perspectives on what happened and why, and jointly develop the rules. Mom, Dad, or one of the kids could be charged with doing some quick research on rules that other families have used to stimulate ideas. It's also important to remember that negotiating rules does not mean everything is up for discussion. If a family is negotiating the rules for using a shared car, for example, the parents can of course impose non-negotiable rules like "No drinking and driving."

In the end, you will wind up with a pastiche of the best rules from all relevant sources. Don's rules for late-night snacking, for example, consisted of "Eat snacks from a small bowl, not the bag" (from Brian Wansink's book), "Don't stockpile snacks in the cupboard" (his wife), and "No dessert during the week" (his experience). The simple rules process is, at its heart, informed trial and error. By drawing on research, advice from friends, past data, and your own experience, you can make better choices of the bottleneck and first-cut rules. You want to make the rules as simple as possible to increase the odds that you will follow them. You can also limit your rules to two or three, as we have seen elsewhere in the book, to increase the odds that you will remember and follow them.

After crafting your preliminary rules, it is helpful to measure how well they are working. Measuring impact allows you to pinpoint what is and isn't working, and evidence of success also provides more motivation to stick with the rules. The best performance metrics are tightly linked to what will move the needles for you — pounds lost for a dieter, or dollars invested if you are trying to save for retirement. Apps have made collecting data and tracking progress easier than at any other time in history. Imagine what the legendary self-improver Benjamin Franklin could have accomplished if he'd had an iPhone.

To measure the impact of your simple rules, it helps to collect some data before you start using your rules. Last year's savings or last month's weight provide a baseline against which you can measure progress. The timeline for testing impact will depend on the bottleneck you choose. Pounds lost can be measured in weeks or months, but improving your son's math grades might take until the midterm of a semester to assess. Don't agonize about crafting the perfect rules right off the bat. Once you have gathered enough data to assess progress, you can step back and refine your rules.

The rest of this chapter describes how three people went through the process to make rules that worked for them.

THE SIMPLE RULES OF ATTRACTION

After graduating from college, Harry moved to Philadelphia to take a job in an architecture firm. His new position demanded long hours and frequent travel. Since he was new to Philadelphia,

Harry didn't know many people, and he did not relish going out to bars alone to try to meet women in his scarce free time. Harry was pretty clear on what would move the needles for him. He had recently ended a long-term relationship when he and his girlfriend moved to different coasts to pursue their careers. In terms of increasing happiness, Harry could think of nothing that would move the needles more than entering a stable relationship with someone he loved. The challenge was how to meet women in an unfamiliar city when he had limited time to socialize.

A friend from graduate school suggested that Harry give Internet dating a try. While he was initially dubious, he learned that a plethora of dating apps and websites had sprung up in the past few years. These ranged from Coffee Meets Bagel, an app that pairs users with one potential match per day, to Tinder, which has a reputation as a free-for-all lust fest but in reality is often used to set up perfectly wholesome dates. Online dating sounded like a good idea, but Harry soon realized that it was a lot of work. He could spend hours in front of a screen, clicking through profiles of potential dates, trying to find a good match, and then sending message after message to potential candidates. And this is what Harry did, at first: he spent hours online, but the return on investment was low. Many of the women he messaged did not reply, and when he did end up going on a date with someone, they often failed to make a real connection.

Harry initially considered his online profile as a potential bottleneck, since this provided the pictures and information that potential dates would use to make their decisions. He decided, however, that creating a profile was not a good candidate for simple rules, because it is more of a one-time creation than a repeated activity or decision. It was important to get his profile right, but simple rules could be more effectively applied elsewhere, Harry decided. In order to find a suitable bottleneck for online dating,

Harry went through each step of the process—from browsing profiles to sending initial messages, through exchanging followup messages, to going on the dates themselves—and analyzed what was and was not working at each stage.

For each step, Harry pulled together whatever data were easy to collect. He learned that the first step — sending the initial message to women—was much more time-consuming than he expected. Harry carefully read the profiles of potential dates, trying to discern common interests, and then wrote a thoughtful message. He knew he was not a fast writer, but still, he was shocked when he timed how long it took him to send one of these messages and discovered it could take more than twenty minutes per missive. And the results were lackluster. Reviewing his past messages, Harry found that only one woman in six responded to his online advances.

When women did respond to Harry, things tended to go better. They would exchange messages and, nearly half the time, exchange numbers. Still, the process of online flirting burned a lot of time. Harry tried to craft the perfect message but, when sent, it sometimes led to terse replies that then petered out into radio silence. This seemed like another black hole of time, but when Harry went back over his past few months of dating, he was surprised to learn that he ultimately went on a date with two-thirds of the women with whom he exchanged telephone numbers, a much higher percentage than he had thought. Finally, the dates themselves were a mixed bag. Reviewing his calendar, he realized that about half his first dates were enjoyable, but the rest were doomed from the start.

Reflecting on all of this, Harry decided that the biggest bottleneck in his dating life was the initial step of reading profiles and writing introductory emails. This was not only the most time-consuming stage of the process, it was also a stage where later problems — like spending too much time exchanging messages with unsuitable prospects and ultimately going on disappointing dates — might be nipped in the bud. Moreover, it was probably the least fun stage of online dating. Writing emails was less enjoyable than chatting with someone face to face, and repeated rejection was no fun either. Harry resolved to use simple rules to manage the bottleneck of initial messages.

In order to craft his simple rules for managing initial messages, Harry turned to a variety of sources. To start with, he looked at his outbox. What kinds of messages worked and what didn't? He noticed a counterintuitive pattern. The long, thoughtful introductory messages he was writing to potential dates — the kinds he spent a long time writing because he thought they would be more attractive to the women — were getting no higher response rates than his much shorter messages. Harry would rattle off these messages — often only two lines long — when he was tired, with little hope that they would elicit a response. He was surprised when they did. He had assumed that a long message would be more likely to pique the interest of potential dates. This was probably true in a few cases, he reasoned, but now he developed a new theory for how introductory messages worked — they flagged attention. No matter how long or short the message, potential dates would click on his profile. If they liked what they saw, they would respond. If not, they wouldn't. The length of the message did not matter very much, and longer messages might even be less attractive because they would make it seem like he had time on his hands. Harry glanced through his message exchanges and saw a similar pattern after the initial exchange; short messages were just as effective as long messages at prompting responses. All of this led Harry to develop his first rule: "Send feelers before essays." Sending short messages to establish interest, then following up with gradually longer ones, was a better course of action.

Next Harry turned to developing a simple rule to nip doomed dates in the bud. Reflecting on his recent dates, Harry realized they were least likely to work out when he went out with someone not because he thought they would click, but because his potential date responded enthusiastically to his initial overtures. Harry noted a common pattern to these dates. It seemed like a good idea when they agreed to go out, but on the way to the restaurant he realized he was not particularly excited about dinner. These dates were often pleasant enough, but they represented a significant opportunity cost, in Harry's view, because his work schedule meant he could only go out a few nights a week at most. This observation based on experience led to Harry's second rule: "Only pursue her if you would like to see her tonight." By making theoretical opportunities immediate, this rule helped Harry avoid approaching potential dates where they had little in common.

Another source of disappointing dates occurred when someone posted pictures and then didn't look anything like their photos when they arrived. Harry was not overly hung up on physical appearance, but he was bothered by the attempt at deception. He turned to his friend Will, who had been dating online for a while, for advice. Will explained that he had encountered the same problem early in his online dating career, but eventually learned a few tactics to detect misleading photographs. Will's tips centered around photographic variety: if there was none, especially if all the pictures were taken from the same angle, it raised a red flag. Will also cautioned against "beautiful outliers," which occurred when one picture was much more fetching than others. Harry added a third rule to "avoid photographic red flags" (and also checked his own profile to make sure he posted several recent and representative photographs).

Harry was pretty happy with his initial rules, but he also spent a bit of time online researching effective introductory emails. He found an analysis of dating messages that OkCupid had released a few years earlier. The study, entitled "Exactly What To Say In A First Message" was based on over five hundred thousand first messages, and even organized into six simple rules. Reading through the rules, Harry preferred his own simple rules, which were customized to his situation. Several of the generic rules, moreover, were pretty obvious. For instance, using "netspeak" like "wat," "ur," "ya," and "realy" was a big turnoff to potential dates, as was calling them "sexy" in the first message. However, one nugget struck Harry as useful. Less common greetings, like "What's up?," "Yo," "Howdy," and "Hola" had significantly higher response rates than staples like "Hey" or "Hello." Indeed, the most effective salutation, "How's it going?," was twice as likely to garner a response than the common "Hi." The rule the study advocated was "Use an unusual greeting," but Harry replaced that rule with "Ask her how it's going." After all, why use any but the most successful greeting?

Harry's story is a good example of how to pinpoint a specific bottleneck (in his case, sending an initial message to a prospective date) within a broad process (like online dating). He also did a good job of drawing his rules from multiple sources, in particular turning to his friend Will for advice, rather than trying to develop the rules all on his own. Next we turn to Susan, who used simple rules to address a very different challenge.

CRAFTING RULES TO MANAGE DEPRESSION

On the surface, Susan leads a storybook life. She is a successful lawyer in Saint Louis, a mother of three healthy children, and happily married to her college sweetheart. What most people do not know is that Susan has battled depression most of her adult life. She suffered her first major episode at the age of twenty-seven, when she was working as an associate at a prestigious law firm. She toughed out her first bout of clinical depression without seeking medical help, although she recalls it as the longest six months of her life.

Susan's second episode occurred six years later and lasted several months. She recalls playing hide-and-go-seek with her children on a beautiful fall day. "I was standing in the closet with tears running down my face. Our oldest daughter Cassie found me and asked why I was so sad. It was one of the worst moments in my life. Intellectually, I knew I should be happy, but all I felt was a sense of despair and hopelessness that was smothering me." This time, Susan went to a psychiatrist, who prescribed antidepressants. She tried them for a few months, but found that the side effects were worse than the disease itself: "I had disturbing nightmares, my libido disappeared, and I walked around like a zombie."

After she recovered from her second depressive episode and was feeling better again, Susan decided to research drug-free ways to manage depression. She began tracking how she felt when she woke up every morning on a scale of 1 to 10, where anything below a 5 was a depressed day. Over the years she experimented with a set of practices to help her avoid slipping into the void. She had been sporty as a girl, playing tennis and field hockey, but had fallen out of the habit of regular exercise after her children were born. She found that running helped to keep her mood stable, and worked a run into her routine three or four times per week. She also left her job at the law firm to pursue a portfolio career, working part-time as a tax attorney for a few clients, a career move that cut down on stress and gave her a more flexible schedule. When her sister died of breast cancer at the age of thirty-six, Susan suffered a third episode of depression, but it was neither as long nor as severe as the first two. Although she has not suffered an extended bout of deep depression since her sister died twelve years ago, Susan continues to experience periodic dips in her mood, which typically last two to five days. "I will be feeling fine one day, and then the next day it feels like a Dementor [a villain in the Harry Potter books] has sucked all the joy out of my life."

Susan was excited about simple rules because she felt like her progress in managing depression had stalled. "I read books and blogs about depression," she explained, "but I'm still not sure what to do next." For Susan, deciding what would add value was clear — she wanted to avoid the depressive spells that still plagued her, on average, once a month. Selecting a bottleneck was less clear. Through her research on depression, Susan had learned it is a complex condition influenced by diet, exercise, sleep, genetics, stress, social life, patterns of thought, weather, and personality (especially among perfectionists, like herself, who are prone to worry). Reading blogs written by other people who suffered from depression, she was a bit overwhelmed by the variety of possible bottlenecks: diet, herbal supplements, managing stress, exercise, sleep, and socializing, to name just a few. Where to begin?

Susan decided to focus on advice that was based on some scientific evidence and offered practical tips. She reviewed some of the more credible websites and books on depression, looking for approaches that met her criteria, and chose cognitive behavioral therapy (CBT), an approach that teaches people to challenge patterns of thought that distort reality and trigger anxiety and depression. Extensive evidence has established that CBT is effective in managing a wide range of psychological problems. Susan herself had tried the approach and found it helpful. She remembered one session in particular, when she was in the depths of depression and was convinced that she would never feel better. Her therapist pointed out that Susan's belief was a prediction about the future, and asked her to test her assumption against the evidence, including the fact that she had always recovered in the past and that depression is an episodic disease that comes and goes. Even in her depressed state, Susan's highly analytical mind had to concede that the evidence did not support her belief, and she felt a glimmer of hope for the first time in weeks.

CBT points to a clear bottleneck — challenging negative thoughts when they occur — and Susan decided to begin there. Having settled on a bottleneck, she turned to developing the rules. While Susan had found CBT helpful, she had also found it cumbersome, since the approach required her to interrupt whatever she was doing to complete detailed exercises that consisted of capturing her negative thoughts in a journal and challenging them in writing. Because of the time and hassle involved, Susan had fallen out of the habit of doing CBT exercises. She didn't want to go through a full-blown exercise to confront every negative thought that flitted through her brain. Reflecting on her past experience, she also realized that CBT didn't always work for her — sometimes it was great and other times it had little effect. Susan wanted to develop timing rules to decide when it was worthwhile to use the approach to challenge her negative thoughts.

She leafed through her previous CBT journal entries to try to spot patterns, and learned a few things. First, CBT seemed to work best when she had been feeling good and then suddenly felt her mood plummet. She could often identify a specific event that triggered a sharp drop in mood, and if she nipped the negative thoughts about that event in the bud, she could avoid slipping into a deeper funk. Once she was depressed, in contrast, CBT had less impact. When she was depressed, moreover, she had little faith that the approach would work and could not always muster the energy to walk through the exercise.

Susan also looked over the spreadsheet that she used to track her mood and found that she had experienced twelve dips over the past year, where her mood dropped below 5, her threshold for feeling depressed. Her downturns tended to follow the same pattern: she would be feeling good for weeks, and then wake up one morning after a poor night's sleep and feel depressed, a state that would last for two to five days. While her recoveries were gradual, her descent into depression was nearly always abrupt and began in the morning. Susan was also surprised to discover that half of her depressive spells began on Monday morning. It was a standing joke in her family that Susan hated Mondays, and for the first time she realized why.

Based on what she had learned, Susan took a first cut at her rules, which she planned to test and refine during the month of December before applying them in the new year. If she woke up and her mood had dropped more than one point from the previous day (a large change for her), she would identify troubling events, record her negative thoughts, and challenge each of them systematically. Second, every Monday she went through a CBT exercise, even if she felt okay when she woke up. She talked through what she was doing with her husband, and they agreed to juggle their schedules so that he could get the kids ready and to school on Mondays and any morning when her mood dipped. Susan wrote up a few more rules, but dropped them because they did not seem as promising. She was more confident that she would remember and act on two rules.

Susan didn't have long to wait: a week later she woke up feeling down. She spent forty-five minutes going through a workbook exercise to challenge her negative thoughts, which centered around her son, who was having trouble in school, and a particularly disagreeable client. She felt better immediately and didn't slip into a funk. Right before New Year's, she had another dip, this one steeper, and she tried CBT again, but it didn't have as much of an impact, and she spent four days down in the dumps. The weather didn't help, either, as they were entering the depths of winter in Saint Louis, which can be quite brutal. She also found the paper exercises a bit of a pain, especially on those Mondays when she woke up feeling okay.

In early January, Susan reevaluated her rules to see if she could make any refinements before adopting them (a topic we will discuss in greater detail in the next chapter). She decided it would be easier to replace the workbook exercise with an app. A quick search revealed several candidates, and Susan downloaded three before settling on iCBT as the best. She also tweaked her rules to incorporate two other tactics — using a blue light and going for a run — that sometimes helped to prevent her from slipping into a foul mood. Her new rules? First, if her mood dropped one point she would use the iCBT app while sitting in front of the blue light. She dropped the Monday writing exercise, reasoning that if her mood dropped that day she would pick it up with the first rule. Rule two: If she didn't feel her mood lift after using the iCBT app, she would run for at least an hour that morning. Susan was not, by her own admission, a morning person and preferred to run in the afternoon, but she hoped by "calling in the heavy artillery," as she termed it, she could keep the depression from spiraling downward. After following her rules for six months, Susan was pleased with the results. She'd had only three downturns between January and June, and those dips were shorter and less steep than the ones she'd experienced in the preceding six months. The results were even more impressive, she believed, since she had begun using the rules during some of the worst weather months of the year.

In formulating her simple rules, Susan did a few things very well. She drew on well-established research findings to identify a promising bottleneck, in her case stopping negative thoughts before they spiraled into depression. By collecting data on her daily mood, Susan was able to develop timing rules for when to apply CBT, and also measure the impact of her simple rules. Susan's story also illustrates how simple rules can be used to manage an ongoing challenge where progress has stalled.

RULES TO WIN FRIENDS AND INFLUENCE PEOPLE

After receiving his degree in mechanical engineering, Daniel accepted a job with a management consulting firm, where the majority of his coworkers had MBAs and years of work experience. To excel at this job, Daniel had to quickly build credibility with clients and senior colleagues. As an introvert, Daniel was used to tinkering with problems on his own rather than working with a team, particularly one that consisted of people he did not know well. Daniel's colleagues excelled at selling their ideas and projecting their authority, and he wanted to do the same.

Daniel searched Amazon.com for books that might offer guidance, experimenting with different search terms including *management, leadership,* and *communication* (all of which seemed too broad) before settling on *charisma* as the closest to what he was looking for, and selecting a book called *The Charisma Myth: How Anyone Can Master the Art and Science of Personal Magnetism,* by Olivia Fox Cabane. He was attracted to the book's promise, which, if it worked, would be just what he needed. Daniel was skeptical of self-help books, but his suspicion was tempered by the book's reviews, which averaged four and a half stars based on nearly 250 reviews. The author also seemed credible. She had lectured at prestigious universities, had published articles in several highly regarded publications, and came across as charismatic on her YouTube videos.

Daniel was pretty clear on what would move the needles for him — increasing his connection and credibility with senior colleagues and clients. He was less sure, however, about what specific decision or activity would be the best candidate for simple rules. Daniel dreaded formal presentations, and initially selected them as his bottleneck. When he reviewed his calendar over the past few months, however, he learned that scheduled presentations were relatively rare and, as a junior consultant, his role was limited. He was also pleasantly surprised to see that the presentations typically went well since he had ample time to prepare in advance.

As he read the book, Daniel kept a particular eye out for a better bottleneck, and eventually came to the realization that his more frequent challenge was informal business conversations, which occurred during breaks in meetings, while sharing a taxi with a colleague, and over meals. Daniel preferred to discuss topics that he had researched carefully and felt uncomfortable talking about business with coworkers and clients who had years or decades of experience. While he didn't love small talk in general, he was at ease discussing the weather or sports. Informal business conversations were another thing altogether, and he chose them as the bottleneck to tackle with simple rules.

Daniel read the book with a pen in his hand, underlining anything that struck him as important, seemed relevant to his bottleneck, or simply caught his fancy. Like many self-help books, *The Charisma Myth* does not offer a one-size-fits-all approach, but rather sets out a long list of useful insights, tips, and tools, only a fraction of which might apply to Daniel's specific situation. In sifting through the advice on offer, he began by thinking through what was most applicable to him personally. The author, for example, argued that there are four distinct types of charisma. Daniel thought that "focus charisma," which results from complete concentration on the other person, was a good fit with his personality. Introverts excel at listening attentively, so this type of charisma played to his strengths.

Daniel also focused on the exercises and practical tips that applied to informal business conversations, and identified five candidates for simple rules. In choosing his initial rules, he prioritized ones that would help him focus his attention on what the other person was saying. Five rules struck him as too many to remember on the fly, so he looked for opportunities to cut the number. He dropped two rules — to speak slowly, like a judge rendering a verdict, and to pause for two seconds before responding in a conversation — which struck him as awkward and stilted.

Daniel settled on three rules to develop the charisma that comes from focusing intensely on other people. First, "Imagine the person you are talking to is the sympathetic star in a film you are watching." Second, "Carry yourself like a king" — calm, comfortable, and without excessive nodding, "uh-huh"-ing, and fidgeting. Regal posture reduces the physical restlessness that can keep people from fully engaging in conversation. Finally, "Make and maintain soft eye contact," which means relaxing your eyes and face when you look at someone. By maintaining soft eye contact, Daniel learned, he could focus on what the other person was saying and build a stronger connection as they spoke.

Daniel's story illustrates an effective solution to a common problem: how to translate a self-help book into action. The simple rules process provides a framework for sifting through hundreds of pages and honing in on the nuggets of advice that are most likely to work for you.

· · ·

The last three chapters have provided how-to advice for developing simple rules that can be applied to professional or personal life. But crafting simple rules is not the end of the story (or the end of the book). Instead, simple rules often improve over time based on experience, a topic we will explore in the next two chapters.

7

Rules for Improvement

THIS CHAPTER EXPLORES HOW people can improve their initial simple rules. Although the systematic rule-creating process detailed in the last two chapters can help, first rules are often not very strategic or accurate. There is usually room for improvement, and specific learning approaches, not just gaining experience, stimulate that improvement. But before we get started on how to improve your simple rules, it makes sense to ask whether better rules really are better. After all, maybe just having some simple rules provides enough guidance.

To understand the importance of improving simple rules, Kathy teamed up with Professor Gerardo Okhuysen, then a graduate student at Stanford, to conduct a laboratory study that explored this very question. They randomly assigned participants into five-person groups given the task of solving the mystery of a food-poisoning incident at a fictitious restaurant. The five members of each group were given both unique and common information to solve the problem. The key to success was effectively combining the various pieces of information to see the whole context and, thus, the solution. Some groups were given the simple rule "Listen to others," while others were told "Share your information." A priori, Gerardo and Kathy believed that both of these rules would be helpful. Still other groups received the simple rule "Watch your time," which Gerardo and Kathy expected to be useless because the groups easily had sufficient time for the task. Still other groups were given no rules at all.

As expected, the groups with the task-relevant simple rule "Listen to others" were the highest performing. These groups took frequent breaks to reassess how they were doing and adjust their problem-solving direction. These adjustments helped the groups to find superior solutions. But, unexpectedly, groups with the irrelevant rule "Watch your time" finished second. The rule had seemed irrelevant because the groups had much more time than they needed to finish the task. The rule did, however, stimulate the groups to pause for time checks. When they did, they sometimes restrategized their problem-solving approach and redirected their subsequent efforts, just as the groups with the helpful rule "Listen to others" had done. So although the better rule "Listen to others" produced better results, an apparently irrelevant rule also stimulated some of the same beneficial behaviors.

There was also another surprise. The groups utilizing the simple rule "Share your information," which Gerardo and Kathy thought would be effective, actually finished last, tied with the groups given no rules at all. It turns out that advising people to share their information motivates people to talk a lot — the average length of a comment was significantly greater for the groups with this rule than for the other groups — but does not motivate people to listen to others or pause to reconsider their problem-solving approach. Rather, the rule centered people on their own information, not on working with others to solve the problem. The bottom line: better rules are better, and even apparently irrelevant rules can be reasonably effective if they happen to encourage helpful behavior. But rules that fail to stimulate effective behavior are as useless as no rules at all.

The prior chapters describe how people initially learn rules — by using common approaches such as personal experience, applying analogies, and negotiating, and in a systematic way by identifying what moves the needles and where the bottlenecks lie. In contrast, this chapter focuses on how people and organizations can improve their initial rules, and accelerate their process for doing so. The hero of our first example, Shannon Turley, did not have the benefit of this book to kick-start his initial simple rules, but he has been remarkably successful at fine-tuning them. As an innovator in his profession, Shannon demonstrates how people can successfully refine and enhance their rules.

CRAFTING BETTER SIMPLE RULES

Shannon Turley was a not-so-talented athlete at Virginia Tech, class of 2000. A self-described Appalachian American from West Virginia, Shannon was a walk-on track athlete who majored in the science of human nutrition, food, and exercise. His dream was to be a football strength coach. Strength coaches help athletes become faster, and more explosive. They rose to prominence after the 1970s, when their expertise helped the University of Nebraska Cornhuskers physically dominate their opponents on the football field. Strength coaches are quietly influential, spending more time with players than the football coaches do. The prototypical strength coach is a former football player, adept at creating rapport with young players and known for being a good guy.

Today, Shannon is the Kissick Family Director of Sports Performance for Stanford's often successful football team. When Shannon joined Stanford in 2007, the team was coming off a dismal 1–11 losing year, and most fans would have been happy with a break-even season. Yet only three years later, Stanford began its unlikely streak of top ten rankings, major bowl appearances (Orange, Rose, and Fiesta), and Pac-12 championships, all while accepting only top-notch students and maintaining a graduation rate of over 90 percent. While Stanford triumphed on the field, Shannon was twice voted the National Strength and Conditioning Coach of the Year. How did Shannon go from undergraduate assistant to the top of his profession in such a short time? And how did he accomplish this at a university known more for Nobel laureates than football wins?

When Shannon arrived at Virginia Tech, he had no hope of making the football team. Instead, he became a volunteer assistant in the strength program under a boss whom Shannon describes as "a great coach, and a legend in the profession who's still a mentor to me." The program's ethos was "Get stronger by lifting ever more weight." The walls of the weight room were decorated with a huge record board, and athletes wore personal-record T-shirts proclaiming their lifting prowess. Virginia Tech's strength-program rules were typical of strength programs around the country. They focused on weight-training exercises like the bench press, back squat, and power clean, and rewarded players for achieving personal and team weight records. As Shannon described it, "[Virginia Tech's strength program] was what everyone did. Chase personal records and get on the record board." Yet Shannon noticed that while the disciplined Virginia Tech process motivated athletes to become stronger, the players with the best weightlifting numbers were not necessarily the best players on the field. As Shannon put it, "The difference for me was that I didn't place that much value on the records because I didn't see that they correlated positively to success in the sport."

Armed with Virginia Tech's rules for building weight-room strength, Shannon's next stop was a summer job with the Wichita Wranglers, a minor-league baseball team in the Kansas City Royals organization. The team was packed with top major-league prospects. As Shannon recalled, "I was as green as I could be, and I thought my job was to push the players to get stronger." But he quickly realized that this was not what the Royals had in mind. Unlike his football experience, what mattered most to the Royals was health, not strength. The team wanted resilient and durable players — players who could perform on the field and remain injury-free during an entire 140-game minor-league season, and do so while enduring seemingly endless bus rides through small towns across Middle America. Also, unlike college football athletes, professional baseball players wanted to know exactly how his conditioning program would make them better at playing baseball, and why it would keep them healthy. This meant figuring out the logic behind his simple rules and tying that logic to on-field success. One player, for example, asked Shannon for help throwing a better fastball. Shannon recalls, "I had to start thinking about what exercises would do that and realized that the bench press from football would put way too much stress on the shoulder." Professional baseball players were different in another way, too. They expected to manage their own time. For example, if they had a particularly grueling night game, they expected to sleep late and delay their workouts the next day accordingly. Shannon could not just dictate. He had to be flexible.

After his baseball job, Shannon enrolled at the University of Missouri to study psychology. Here, he got his chance to be in charge of his own team in an entirely new domain: women's volleyball. Shannon recalls, "The volleyball coach made it clear that he wanted better volleyball players, not the football strength program." As Shannon soon recognized, football and women's volleyball are, at least on the surface, very different. Critical physical skills like jumping and footwork in transition between offense and defense, which matter in volleyball, are not essential for most football players. To figure out what makes an outstanding volleyball player, Shannon studied volleyball game film, went to practices, and worked with the volleyball coach.

Shannon also became the strength coach for the men's wrestling team. Wrestling is a pulling sport, and so the pushing exercises that dominate football don't work that well. As for the jumping skills of volleyball, Shannon said, "The wrestling coach told me that if a guy gets on the wrestling mat and jumps, I'll cut him from the team." Shannon reflected that the simple rules for strength coaching in one sport were not the same as those in other sports. In fact, there were more differences than similarities. About this time, Shannon's boss and one of his professors encouraged him to start creating his own system — not just implement someone else's. He made copious notes, reflecting on what worked and what did not, and started formulating his own rules.

As he accumulated ideas in his journal, Shannon started to think that maybe he had it all wrong. He realized that, in the abstract, the various sports were not so different. In every sport, avoiding injury is essential, often more so than brute strength. In every competitive sport, being functionally skillful is critical. Running a fast forty-yard sprint or bench-pressing hundreds of pounds is easy to measure, but irrelevant if it does not improve game-day performance. No individual can achieve peak performance in any sport without the right nutrition. Shannon's simple rules crystallized when he gave a talk at a local high school to explain the value of strength training. At that point, Shannon was ready to return to football. But who would take a chance on a young guy with no track record and untested, outside-of-the-box rules for strength coaching?

That somebody turned out to be Jim Harbaugh, the former quarterback of the Chicago Bears, at the time head football coach at the University of San Diego. When Shannon arrived at the Toreros' weight room, he saw the same weight records posted on the walls that were on the walls at Virginia Tech and Missouri. As Shannon recalls, "I told Harbaugh that he could have numbers or better football players, and I guaranteed Harbaugh better players when they came out for spring football if I could use my system during the winter." Harbaugh initially insisted on conventional rules emphasizing lots of weight-room time to build strength. But Shannon kept up the pressure, and Harbaugh eventually relented. Shannon switched the focus of strength training to being injury-free, and banished the almighty record board. When Harbaugh left a year later to become the head football coach at Stanford, he brought Shannon along.

When Shannon arrived at Stanford in 2007, he was only twenty-nine. Yet his rules had come a long way since his days at Virginia Tech. At the heart of Shannon's approach was his rule to choose physical activities to keep players injury-free. As he put it, "Your best players are the ones who are at the greatest risk of injury because they are in the game longer. And your opportunity to achieve and have success as a team is highly predicated on the performance of your best players." According to Shannon, activities should center on avoiding injuries, and so he put heavy emphasis on flexibility exercises, eccentrics, stretching, isometrics, yoga, and the correct use of equipment. A second rule emphasized activities that improve position functionality—in other words, that lead to becoming a better football player, not necessarily a stronger one. This led to prioritizing rules tailored to particular position groups, like defensive backs and linemen. Take all-American offensive lineman David Yankey: the key to success at his position is staying low and moving other giant men backwards. So activities to strengthen his lower core, balance, and shoulders are essential. The bench press, in which athletes lift weights while lying on their backs, a core aspect of most other football training programs, was not so important to Shannon. NFL scouts were stunned that Yankey could barely bench-press his own weight, but Shannon didn't see the point in emphasizing movements that don't matter in real games. As Shannon put it, "In football, if you're on your back, you've already lost."

Shannon also has another prioritizing rule: heal existing injuries first. When tight end Coby Fleener arrived as a freshman with a troublesome back, Shannon gave Fleener a specific exercise regimen to heal that injury. It worked. Fleener never missed a game in his career at Stanford and he ended up playing in the NFL after graduation. Shannon's rules give the players a striking amount of freedom. Players have flexibility in choosing some of their workouts and when they happen. In fact, the players develop their own annual plans for physical improvement. They can also choose their own meals as long as they follow Shannon's three rules for eating: (1) eat breakfast, (2) stay hydrated, and (3) eat as much as you want of anything that can be picked, plucked, or killed.

Stanford football was in shambles when Shannon arrived. The team had won only one game the prior season, and twenty-six players were facing season-ending or postseason surgeries. But since Shannon's arrival, injuries have dropped by a stunning 87 percent. In 2012 only two players required season-ending or postseason surgeries, and only one in 2013. And with Shannon's unorthodox simple rules, Stanford became the physically dominant Pac-12 bully, and one of the winningest college teams. From current standouts like Henry Anderson and Jordan Richards to pros like the Seahawks' outspoken All-Pro cornerback Richard Sherman and the Colts' budding superstar quarterback Andrew Luck, Stanford's "Nerd Nation" has thrived so far under Shannon's simple rules.

In earlier chapters, we focused on devising initial simple rules. In this chapter, we take the next step of making those rules better. It turns out that simple rules seem to improve in a predictable pattern. Although the systematic process laid out in the last two chapters can be a big help, initial rules are often automatic, obvious, and generally weak. Over time, three things happen. First, their content shifts from superficial and convenient rules to strategic and abstract ones that prove more effective over a broader range of activities and decisions. Second, the different types of rules are learned in a specific sequential order. Boundary and how-to rules usually come first, while the other rule types follow and are harder to learn. Third, the rules go through simplification cycling in which their number grows, and then shrinks and becomes constant. Over time, the rules may continue to shift as circumstances change, but the best rule users keep the number small. As we'll explain, learning processes accelerate this pattern and make better rules happen faster. In contrast, experience on its own does not necessarily improve simple rules — people and organizations have to do the right things. Key learning processes like consciously reflecting on past experience and engaging in varied but related experiences accelerate improvement, and combining multiple learning processes is the most potent approach to improvement of all.

Shannon Turley's initial simple rules for strength training, developed at Virginia Tech, called for posting raw numbers in the weight room and motivating players to lift increasingly heavier weights. Over time these first rules improved into his current simple rules at Stanford, which put a premium on staying injury-free and functionally effective on the field. Shannon's story follows a predictable pattern. His rules became strategic — related to winning football games — and abstract, fitting across many sports. Shannon's story also reveals his reliance on learning processes like reflecting on his experience through his journal and combining multiple ways of learning, like learning from others and trial and error. Shannon is a master of simple rules improvement. Even now, he is continuing to improve his rules in creative ways. He opens his gym to ex-Stanford NFL players, but only, as he says, "if they tell me what they've learned with their pro team." In the next sections, we'll probe more deeply into the learning processes that help people to improve, but first let's look closely at a pattern we've detected in the way simple rules improve.

HOW SIMPLE RULES IMPROVE

Chris Bingham, a professor at the University of North Carolina, and Kathy were curious about whether simple rules improved in a discernable pattern. They meticulously tracked what twelve entrepreneurial teams learned as they gained experience in internationalizing — that is, as they operated their new companies in different countries. The challenge for these teams was figuring out what, if anything, they learned in any particular country that could be generalized into rules for operating in other countries. For example, if the firm started operating in France and learned that the French close business deals over a bottle of wine, could that lesson be used as a rule when entering countries like Poland and Germany later on? Or was that lesson only relevant in France? The teams were from three very different countries. Some were from the United States. Others were from Singapore, a multicultural city-state at the crossroads of commerce in southern Asia. The remainder were from Finland, a Scandinavian country boasting a rich ecosystem of technology-based ventures. Despite this cultural and geographic diversity, Chris and Kathy observed an identical pattern for improving simple rules across the countries.

First off, Chris and Kathy found that people usually begin with poor rules or even no conscious rules at all. They lack the information and time to develop quality rules at the outset, so they engage in what Nobel Prize–winning psychologist Daniel Kahneman termed *fast thinking*—rather than expending conscious cognitive effort, they adopt innate universal heuristics that are cognitively easy, like representativeness ("Pick what is usual") and availability ("Pick what first comes to mind"). For example, every Finnish team began operating in Sweden as their first foreign country, although there was no particular reason for this choice beyond familiarity. Finland was ruled by Sweden for centuries; about 6 percent of Finland's citizens speak Swedish as their first language, and major road signs are often written in both Finnish and Swedish. As one entrepreneur said, "Sweden is nearby, it's familiar." The Singaporean teams were equally instinctual when they began operating outside Singapore. Most of them automatically followed the rules that worked for them in Singapore, even when those rules were unlikely to function elsewhere. The same was true of U.S. teams. For example, one U.S. team followed the simple rule to "target hospitals" in selling their expensive mammogram machines. This made sense in the United States, where hospitals make many of these purchases and compete to have the latest equipment. This same rule, however, did not work in countries like Sweden and Brazil, where health care systems are either nationalized, with centralized equipment purchases, or localized, with individual doctors making the purchases.

Second, Chris and Kathy observed that people improve their initial simple rules in characteristic ways. When the entrepreneurial teams had regular meetings to discuss how their companies were performing, they were able to make their rules more strategic (accurate and closely related to success) and abstract (applicable across multiple situations). For example, a Finnish team began with the rule "Target Nordic countries." Later they realized that choosing countries by their market size was a more strategically relevant selection rule than one focused simply on the similarity of being Nordic. The Nordic countries have small populations and lack the growth potential of major markets like France and England. Setting up in Sweden is almost as time-consuming as launching in England, but with a lot less potential for growth. The team switched to a more strategic rule that accelerated growth: "Enter the large European markets."

A Singaporean team illustrates how rules can become abstract. This team began by making it a rule to sell their advanced security software to government agencies. This initial simple rule, however, failed outside Singapore because governments rarely trust high-level security software from a foreign country. So when the team entered Malaysia, they switched to targeting insurance companies. In the financial center of Hong Kong, they shifted to major banks. Piecing together their experiences, the team realized that the best simple rule was an abstract one that covered many concrete situations: "Sell to organizations with large amounts of proprietary data and the ability to pay." They used this rule to focus on customers ranging from manufacturing giants in Japan and China to oil companies in Saudi Arabia.

The most surprising observation for Chris and Kathy was that people adopt their simple rules in a specific order, indicating that some types of rules are harder to learn than others. People begin with boundary and how-to rules. Next, they figure out prioritizing, timing, and coordination rules, and learn stopping rules last. A team from a U.S. semiconductor firm, Sunrise, provides an example. Arthur Hsu, a Chinese-American serial entrepreneur, founded the firm. Prior to entering their first foreign country, Hsu and his team developed several boundary and how-to rules that they expected to use going forward. One was the boundary rule to enter only Asian countries. The Chinese-American team believed that they would enjoy advantages in understanding the culture that their large multinational rivals could not match. Another was a how-to rule to emphasize their low-cost advantages when selling to customers. With these and a few other rules in mind, the team optimistically entered China, then Taiwan, and finally Korea. In each country, they fine-tuned their boundary and how-to rules. For instance, they specified a new rule, "Emphasize Arthur's successful track record," to assuage customers' concerns about doing business with a startup.

Once in Korea, the team had enough experience in foreign countries (i.e., China, Taiwan, and Korea) to see patterns. They realized it was easiest to introduce new products in Taiwan and hardest in China. That's when the team stipulated their first timing rule — "Introduce new products in the order of market difficulty" — which let the team focus on one country at a time and get their new products into the hands of the most receptive customers quickly. In their fourth country, Japan, the team figured out their first prioritizing rule: "Give preference to meeting automotive-industry customers," because these customers were most likely to buy.

Finally, Chris and Kathy observed that people add rules, cut back, and then maintain a roughly fixed and small number of rules. They termed this *simplification cycling*. By engaging in simplification cycling, people update their rules for changing conditions while maintaining their focus and flexibility by having only a few rules. An example comes from a Finnish team that sells point-of-sale products to retailers. Before internationalizing, the team created a how-to rule that specified using acquisitions to enter countries. The rationale was to jump-start entry with an existing business, run by locals. The team continued using acquisitions to enter several new countries, adding rules to make the acquisitions more effective. But the team ultimately realized that acquisitions did not make sense everywhere — either they were unavailable, as in the U.K., or too expensive, as in the U.S. The firm could have added more elaborate rules about when to do acquisitions and what to do if acquisitions were not appropriate. Instead, they just cut back their acquisition rules so that they could keep their focus on choosing which countries to enter and what products to sell. They didn't forget how to do acquisitions. Rather, their knowledge about acquisitions moved to the back burner so that they could focus their simple rules — and attention — where they mattered most. From then on, the firm kept a relatively small number of rules that they occasionally updated as they learned more or their focus of attention needed to shift.

This pattern of improving rules in organizations is also akin to how individuals improve their personal rules and become experts in domains ranging from bridge and physics to firefighting. Novices use simple rules that are superficial and easy to learn, whereas experts graduate to strategic and abstract ones. Experts in bridge count the number of cards played in each suit, a tactic that is strategically relevant to winning. In contrast, novices tend to count aces, which has a more distant relationship to success. Chess experts track the king, which is very germane to winning, while novices rarely use this rule. Experts also use abstract simple rules that reflect their deeper understanding of the domain than that of novices. Expert physicists diagnose problems using the abstract rules of physics, like the conservation of momentum, that apply across many situations. In contrast, novices use rules that relate to surface features like whether the problem is about a spring or an inclined plane, and are easily flummoxed if the superficial aspects of the situation change. Fire experts use intuitive simple rules for firefighting that focus their attention on the fire's trajectory — where it has been and is likely to go — which requires an abstract temporal understanding of fires. In contrast, novice firefighters look to concrete details like the fire's current color and intensity, which are less relevant to successful firefighting.

Experts are also more likely than novices to have rules that are difficult to learn. These rules — prioritizing, timing, and coordination — all involve tying together multiple experiences. People developing them must deal with several sets of inputs and simultaneously keep in mind information about them while making cognitive linkages among them. So these rules require more experience and cognitive sophistication to learn. Timing rules are especially likely to be learned later, because knowledge about time requires experiencing enough events over a sufficiently long period to recognize sequences of action or particular rhythms that make sense to use. A hallmark of experts is their efficient cognitive organization of relevant information into larger patterns or chunks than novices perceive. Organization of information into patterns enables experts to handle more information at once and link different pieces of information together faster than novices can. This means that experts can have greater temporal awareness and more implicit timing rules than novices. Expert fire commanders, for example, are better able to anticipate future events and formulate related timing rules than are new recruits.

Expert soccer players can anticipate how play will unfold, and use timing rules to get into the best positions on the pitch.

Like organizations, experts also keep their number of simple rules small, in a process similar to simplification cycling. Keeping the number of rules small is important because it simplifies the cognitive organization of the brain. When this organization is streamlined into a few patterns, it is easier for people to learn new information and locate existing knowledge. This is one reason why experts learn domain-specific information more quickly than novices. Experts keep their number of rules to a handful and information streamlined by frequently (and often automatically) reorganizing their information and chunking that information into large and more abstract patterns, in a process of progressive adaptation similar to simplification cycling.

TIME FOR REFLECTION

When Chris and Kathy (with Professor Nathan Furr of Brigham Young University) took the next step of looking at the performance numbers of their internationalizing entrepreneurs, they found that the teams with simple rules, especially the hard-to-master rules, had significantly more financial success in each of their countries than those with very few rules. In other words, success came to the teams with rules, especially rules like timing, prioritizing, and stopping. Simply gaining international experience was not enough for a strong performance, and instead the entrepreneurs had to translate that experience into simple rules. This finding further increased the credibility of simple rules, but did not explain exactly how the rules were improved.

Intriguingly, Chris and Kathy saw that some teams improved their rules while others made almost no progress. The secret for improvement was actually blindingly clear. Teams that consistently met with their key managers in each country on a regular basis, usually weekly, to update their progress improved their rules. Since the meetings combined in-country executives with deep knowledge of their specific countries, and corporate executives with a broad-brush understanding of multiple countries, the groups could have a rich discussion from multiple vantage points. They talked through successes and failures, leading to a common understanding of causality — of what worked and what didn't — and then to rules. In contrast, the teams that rarely improved didn't engage in consistent group meetings. To be sure, there were one-on-ones, and some in-country managers created their own rules, but for the most part, these teams rarely met as a group with their in-country managers.

The internationalizing teams reveal the importance of systematically reflecting on experience to improve rules. Just like Shannon Turley, who regularly added to his journal of ideas, the internationalizing teams that improved their rules did so by consciously reflecting on their experiences routinely within groups from multiple levels of their companies. Reflection on experience is, however, only one of several important learning processes. We now turn to probe more deeply a second key learning process — learning by doing something else.

LEARNING FASTER BY DOING SOMETHING ELSE

Victoria Coren Mitchell made history on Easter Sunday in 2014 when she became the first two-time winner of the European Poker Championship. The British journalist and BBC broadcaster first made history in 2006, when she became the first woman to win the event. This time, she came from eighth place to beat over 550 competitors to win a cash prize of close to 500,000 euros. Mitchell began playing as a teenager with her older brother and his friends in the family kitchen, with the aim of meeting boys. As she recalls, "I thought that if I learned how to play this game, I'd get to spend time with boys and figure out what they're like . . . Then I found that I was absolutely gripped by the game." Although she is now a U.K. television personality and claims that poker playing is not grown-up enough to be a real job, she admits, "I never really got up from the [poker] table."

Poker is a game of skill and luck, of mathematics and psychology, of reason and intuition. The trick is to combine all of these elements while operating in high uncertainty. In the long run the best players win, but in the short run the luckiest players can. The results of any particular hand are often driven by chance, but the results over many hands are mostly determined by skill. The best players learn the best simple rules, like Mitchell's number one rule for beginners: never play for an amount of money that you can't comfortably afford. Players like Mitchell live in the poker stratosphere, but at every level of the game, simple rules are being learned and improved. We were particularly interested in the remarkable story of one of Kathy's graduate students at Stanford, Raghu Shukla, who went from diligent scholar to professional-level poker player in the space of two years.

Raghu grew up in Chennai, and attended the University of Delhi before finishing his degree in math at the University of Southern California. He followed several cousins, and became a computer science graduate student at Stanford. After finishing an especially rough web-application assignment, he played his first poker game with other students one Saturday night. Yet unlike many of his equally smart friends, Raghu dramatically improved his poker-playing rules over time.

The poker-playing grad students favored Texas Hold'em. In this version of the game, each player gets two face-down cards at the start of the hand (the hole). Next, the table is dealt five cards in groups of three (the flop), one (the turn), and one more (the river). Of these seven cards — five that everyone shares and two that are unique — each player has to make a five-card hand. There is a hierarchy of hands, and the best hand wins. So a flush beats a straight, four aces beat four kings, and so on. There are four rounds of betting — after the hole, at the flop, at the turn, and at the river — and sometimes a showdown at the end. At each round, a player can fold, raise, or call. Texas Hold'em is a game that is easy to learn, but hard to master.

At first, Raghu found playing poker to be humbling. It wasn't that his grad student friends were such fabulous players, but rather that he was so new to the game. Determined to start winning, he began reading books like *Doyle Brunson's Super System: A Course in Power Poker,* and Action Dan Harrington's *Harrington on Hold'em.* Among other things, books like these teach players how to use the underlying probabilities of the game to gain an advantage. As a mathematics whiz, Raghu quickly learned the theory of how to play the odds. He picked up more knowledge by taking an online course on poker playing and competing in Internet poker, which let him (sometimes too conveniently) play a lot of hands at any conceivable time of day. Raghu took his game to the local casino, where he cleaned up in low-stakes games. Having learned some simple rules around card counting and probabilities, he became the king of the $1 and $2 tables.

Raghu moved up to the $5 and $10 tables, where richer and better players play, because, as he told us, "I don't like beating people who can't afford to lose." Unfortunately, though, Raghu had no clear advantage at these higher-stakes tables, because everyone else knew the same odds strategies. Also, the bigger financial stakes were a stretch for his graduate-student budget, creating pressure to win or at least not lose. In fact, without knowing it, Raghu was learning Victoria Mitchell's most important rule for beginners: never play for an amount of money you can't comfortably afford. The reason for Mitchell's rule is strategic, not just moral. The stress of too much money on the table makes for poor play. A big shock came when Raghu was too emotional after he lost to a player who played poorly but was lucky. Aggravated, Raghu played recklessly, and blew through his hard-earned graduate assistant's salary. Raghu remembered, "Eating cereal for two weeks until my next paycheck was a huge motivator to reexamine what I was doing." He realized that emotions — his and his opponents' — mattered. If he wagered too much money or had a run of too much bad luck, then he started playing emotionally. In poker terms, he played the tilt instead of the odds. When he played the tilt, he lost, and he realized a key to success was to avoid emotion.

Avoiding the tilt led Raghu to a couple of how-to rules. One was "Never use a credit card for gambling," and another was to bring to the casino only the cash that he could afford to lose. Raghu kept this money in his pocket, and when he lost that money, he was done. He also started focusing on the process — playing each hand well with regard to the odds — rather than worrying about the results of whether he won or not. To stay focused on the process, he made it a rule to write an analysis of his play (regardless of the outcome) in a journal after every casino trip — a lot like what Shannon Turley and the successful internationalizing entrepreneurs did. He had a related rule he described as "I could buy myself an Oreo shake at Jack-in-the-Box if I played well even if I didn't win. But if I played my hands poorly (even if I won), I could have no fast-food treats for two weeks." While we don't recommend fast food as a reward, Raghu's rules worked. He kept control of his own emotions and took advantage of others' when they tilted. Raghu was now playing better and winning more.

Raghu's next stop was to try his poker-playing skills at the gambling capital of the United States, Las Vegas. Las Vegas poker was a big step up from playing at his local casino. To be sure, there are a lot of unskilled players in Las Vegas, but there are also a lot of very good ones. To win, Raghu decided that it was essential to figure out how to play mostly against the poor players, and avoid the very good ones. As Raghu put it, "Las Vegas poker is a game of sharks and fish. If you're the shark, you win. But if you look around the table and see only sharks, then you're probably the fish and it's time to leave." So Raghu adjusted his rules so they focused on being at the right tables with the right players. One of his new timing rules was to play conservatively at a table for about an hour, and then decide whether there were enough "fish" to warrant staying. A new prioritizing rule was to prefer seats that let him play just after a fish — in other words, "Keep fish to the right and sharks to the left." He also learned some how-to rules for when to play unpredictably — mixing carefully playing the odds and taking unexpected risks — to confuse other players. As he described it, "I play conservatively with sharks because I don't want to make a mistake, but I mix up my strategies to confuse the fish."

Raghu is now back in India. While he has not yet reached the poker-playing heights of a Victoria Mitchell, he is now a professional-caliber player who sprinted ahead of his equally smart poker-playing friends. Raghu's improvements replicate the pattern of improving rules that we saw with the internationalizing entrepreneurs: his initial rules came from convenient and obvious sources, like reading famous books on poker, and improved — becoming more strategic and successful — as he reflected on his experience. He learned timing and stopping rules later than boundary and how-to rules, and cycled his emphasis from his initial probability-oriented rules to ones about emotion, and then later to rules about playing sharks and fish. Yet he always kept his rules to a handful.

More significantly though, Raghu's story highlights his use of lots of varied but related experiences, an important learning approach. He played with friends, in an online course, at a local casino, and in Las Vegas. His friends who only played with one another did not improve like Raghu. In fact, his experiences are a lot like Shannon Turley's journey through varied but related experiences in football, baseball, wrestling, volleyball, and back to football. They both improved their rules by doing something else.

Professor Melissa Schilling of New York University and her colleagues at Boston University conducted a clever study to explore how learning can be enhanced by doing something else. Their study compared three strategies for improving. The first, *specialized practice,* mirrors the old saying "Practice makes perfect," and repeats the same activity. The second, unrelated experience exploits what is known as *massed practice,* in which individuals take periodic breaks to do something completely different from what they are trying to learn. This strategy provides time to consolidate knowledge before moving on. The third strategy is *related experience,* which is what Shannon did by coaching different sports and Raghu did by practicing different kinds of poker playing.

Schilling and her colleagues pitted these three strategies for improving play against each other using the ancient Chinese game go. Go is a spatial game in which players place stones on a board and do not move them. The goal is to control territory. Like Texas Hold'em, go is easy to learn, but hard to master. The results intrigued and even surprised us. As expected, people improved by engaging in specialized practice — that is, playing only go. But unexpectedly, people who interspersed their playing of go with cribbage improved just as quickly, even though cribbage (a card game requiring math skills, played over rounds) is completely unrelated to go (a board game requiring spatial skills, played once). Finally, people improved most quickly when they played both go and reversi, a board game similar to go but not the same. In other words, the best strategy for improving was doing something else when that something else was related experience. So while very specialized practice might seem better for improving because it focuses time and energy on one task, it lacks the informative contrasts that enrich understanding. While unrelated activities may offer a helpful break, they are not germane to what is being learned. Instead, people improve most rapidly with varied but related experiences.

Learning from related experiences and learning by reflecting on past experience worked well for Shannon, Raghu, and the internationalizing teams, and these learning processes were essential for improving their simple rules. In the next section, we describe a further step. When they combine these and other learning processes like experiments and trial and error, people and organizations gain a particularly potent way to improve their rules.

MULTITASKING WAYS TO LEARN

You've probably heard of Airbnb. You may have used the site to rent a vacation house or an apartment in another city. Maybe you even know that its founders are the first billionaires of the so-called shared economy. You may not, however, have given much thought to the learning processes that helped propel Airbnb's founders to fortune and fame. Joe Gebbia and Brian Chesky met while they were industrial-design students at Rhode Island School of Design. Although they talked about starting a company together, they went their separate ways after graduation. Brian moved to Los Angeles, where he worked as a product designer (toilets were one of his products) with Simon Cowell's reality television show *American Inventor*, and Joe landed in San Francisco. Joe kept nagging Brian to move north, which Brian eventually did. When the two friends were short on cash, and a major design conference was coming to pricey San Francisco, they decided to place an ad offering affordable lodging in their apartment — breakfast plus an air mattress. They figured they might attract some young guys who were looking for cheap accommodations. Instead, they ended up hosting a forty-five-year-old father from Utah, a thirty-five-year-old woman from Boston, and a thirty-year-old Indian man. Brian and Joe realized this market might be bigger than they first thought. They soon launched Air Mattress Bed & Breakfast, later Airbnb.

Airbnb is among the most successful of the shared-economy companies. Unlike many traditional businesses, shared-economy companies have no single base of customers. Rather, these companies provide two-sided markets that connect sellers (or people with something to share) with buyers (who are willing to pay for the product or service) — like the transportation-network company Lyft, which connects passengers who need a ride to drivers who have a car, and TaskRabbit, an errand-outsourcing company that connects people who need something done with "taskers" who will do the job. For Airbnb, it's connecting local residents with room to spare and travelers who need a place to stay. To grow, shared-economy companies have to keep both sides of the market — sellers and buyers — happy. And growing matters, because these companies face what are known as *network effects* — in other words, the positively reinforcing cycle in which more buyers attract more sellers and vice versa. Network effects can create exploding growth for the first company or two in a market sector, but they can also make success impossible for later and slower ones. For Airbnb to succeed, the company needed lots of good hosts to attract guests, and lots of good guests to attract hosts. The challenge was to get this chicken-and-egg cycle of network effects going.

Joe and Brian brought in Nate Blecharczyk (Joe's former roommate) as the company's technical founder. Because of the success they'd had renting out their apartment space during the San Francisco design conference, they made it a rule to focus their young business on cities hosting conferences and festivals, with the rationale that these events attract lots of attendees on tight budgets. They also decided to use onsite credit card payments. They targeted Austin's huge South by Southwest (SXSW) media conference, and signed up hosts in the area with rooms to let. Unfortunately, only two guests booked rooms, one of whom was Brian. They had more success at the Democratic and Republican national political conventions later in the summer. Sales spiked, but that was the problem — it was only a spike. Joe and Brian kept Airbnb afloat by selling gimmicky breakfast cereal, and surprisingly sold several hundred boxes of "Obama O's" and "Cap'n McCain" on eBay. The big picture was, however, that Airbnb was floundering, with a few initial rules that cried out for improvement.

A much-needed turning point came when Airbnb joined Y Combinator. Y Combinator is a "seed accelerator" providing financing, advice, and connections to cohorts of early-stage ventures, but its headliner mission is helping entrepreneurs improve very fast. At this point, Airbnb's entrepreneurs began multitasking different ways to learn. One way was from weekly Tuesday-night dinners at Y Combinator. Each week, a famous founder or other luminary delivered an off-the-record speech full of stories and advise about building companies. It was an opportunity to learn vicariously from role models from the real world. During the mingling time at the dinner, entrepreneurs from various companies talked with each other to learn what their peers were doing across lots of markets, and to give and get advice. This was another opportunity to learn — this time through presenting Airbnb's story and getting feedback and insights from peers. These dinners created a relentless weekly rhythm of stepping back to reflect, getting feedback and ideas, and heading back to work.

Another way of learning was through tailored expert advice. The Airbnb founders gained two pivotal insights from Y Combinator cofounder Paul Graham that critically reframed their conception of what to do. One piece of advice was counterintuitive — forget about growing Airbnb, and instead focus on creating the perfect Airbnb experience. Graham's argument was, "It's better to have a hundred people love you than to have a million people like you." The second piece of advice was to stop organizing their business around conferences and get out into cities. As Brian recalled, "Go to New York. That was the best advice we ever got." Whether you call these tipping points, aha moments, or something else, these pieces of advice changed the course of Airbnb. Together, they crystallized the start of an action plan. Step one was creating a stellar host experience in destination cities.

A third way of learning was on the ground, through face-to-face experiences with potential hosts and guests. Like clockwork, the founders started flying to New York every Thursday or Friday for the weekend. Once there, they learned experientially by doing all sorts of activities — conducting interviews, going door-to-door, staying in living rooms, and passing out fliers in coffee shops and train stations. The founders coupled these activities with disciplined experiments to learn about specific practices, like testing whether professional photographs of lodging options were effective in luring guests. They were, and the founders let hosts know. The founders also had preconceived assumptions about what would work for Airbnb. For instance, they initially thought professional property managers would make good Airbnb hosts. They learned, however, that property managers were not the right fit for the company, whose quirky, personal vibe favored ordinary people who had never hosted before but were inspired to share their space and local knowledge.

Airbnb ended up with better simple rules: (1) enter international destination cities, (2) focus first on recruiting hosts, and (3) share with hosts Airbnb's hospitality principles, like providing professional-quality photos of their properties and having fresh soap on hand for guests. Airbnb's initial rule of targeting the host cities of major conferences was a reasonable place to start, but like most people and organizations, Joe and Brian needed time and real-world experience to craft better simple rules.

It is doubtful that the Airbnb founders had any idea what their company would become when they first opened up their apartment to paying guests. While they thought that the attraction of Airbnb would be low prices, travelers were instead lured by the quirky individuality and local flavor of the available properties, which now include castles, igloos, and treehouses as well as traditional houses and apartments. The founders initially conceived their target customer as young, male, and poor. In fact, Airbnb has more guests over fifty-five years old than between eighteen and twenty-five, and accommodations, including Italian villas and beachfront bungalows, are not always cheap.

Pursuing many ways of learning increases the likelihood of creative insights. The founders of Airbnb could not have predicted, for example, that Paul Graham's advice would be so essential to reimagining their simple rules. Yet by pursuing many avenues of learning, the founders improved their odds of experiencing the aha moments. Multitasking in learning also works because when people learn the same lesson in different ways, the learning is reinforced and better learned. This is reflected in teaching — our students learn best when they learn in multiple ways like reading articles, watching videos, having an in-class discussion, and hearing a lecture. It is also reflected on how Airbnb's founders improved when they went to New York City and participated in the Y Combinator dinners. By pursuing various ways to learn, the Airbnb founders accelerated the improvement of their initial simple rules. Airbnb has become one of the leading shared-economy companies in the world, operating in almost two hundred countries and about thirty-four thousand cities, and is used by an estimated fifty to sixty thousand people per night.

People improve their simple rules in a predictable pattern, and learning processes and combinations of processes can accelerate improvement. But occasionally a situation is so novel or demanding that just improving the current rules is not enough. Instead, it requires people to create a whole new understanding of their actions, and to revolutionize their simple rules. We turn to breaking the rules and remaking them in the next chapter.

8

Breaking the Rules

WHEN SPRING ARRIVED ON March 21, 2014, it marked the end of the third-driest winter in California history. San Francisco received only 8.6 inches of rain, well below its normal rainfall of 20.3 inches and its record-setting deluge of over 47 inches in 1997–98. After three years of below-normal rainfall, California braced for its worst drought in decades. Governor Jerry Brown asked for a voluntary, 20 percent water use reduction across California to avoid a summer shutoff of the spigot to the state's businesses, homes, and farms. Dry hillsides, emptying aquifers, the danger of explosive wildfires, and the prospect of soaring food prices in the nation's leading agricultural state had become impossible to ignore. In the face of the state's growing population, water restriction could become the new normal.

Much of California enjoys a Mediterranean climate of stunning blue skies, mild winters, and long periods of sunshine. It shares this moderate climate of few insects and rarely rained-out picnics with southern and southwestern Australia, central Chile, the Western Cape of South Africa, and of course the Mediterranean Sea region. The seasons of the Mediterranean zone differ dramatically from the temperate climate to the north and south. While the temperate climate has four seasons, the Mediterranean climate has only two. One is a rainy and cool winter with frost but little or no snow, while the other is a long, hot summer with little or no rain. Rainfall can vary significantly from year to year, with stretches of drought or deluge, plus occasional monsoons in Chile and Australia. But for the most part the Mediterranean climate consists of short, cool and wet winters coupled with long, hot and dry summers.

Although most Californians know they live in a Mediterranean zone, they don't always know what that entails, and they certainly don't always garden like they do. Kathy's friend Emily is typical. For years, Californians like Emily gardened as if they lived in a temperate climate of four seasons and year-round rain. Their vision of a perfect backyard was an English garden with rich soil and lush flowering plants surrounding a deliciously green lawn, or maybe a Japanese tea garden with winding paths through camellias, azaleas, and maples. Especially for Californians of northern European or North Asian heritage, these archetypes of ideal gardening were widely held. So it was common to see beautiful, well-fertilized, lush lawns surrounded by hydrangeas, dahlias, and other flowering plants that need a lot of watering. Since California had plenty of water, temperate-climate gardening was both beautiful and viable, and Emily's yard was spectacular.

Like millions of gardeners, Emily has, however, decided to change her ways in response to California's water shortage. The obvious moves were less lawn, more paving, and drought-tolerant plants. This response reflected a superficial understanding of the new situation, almost a gut reaction. Is a drab display of rocks and cactus the only answer? *Au contraire,* insisted Emily.

Rather, as Chris Woods, the internationally known horticulturalist, argued, "People have been cautious about gardening in drought. In my mind, drought presents an opportunity to rethink the garden." While some California gardeners took to paving and replaced their water-loving plants with cactus, others like Emily were more thoughtful. They took Woods's advice to heart and made an effort to deeply engage with their new situation, understanding it beyond a superficial level. They then renewed their passion, aligning it with a new vision of an ideal Mediterranean garden and new gardening rules to match.

Emily made a point of throwing out her dream of an ideal temperate-climate garden, and instead started actively learning about the Mediterranean climate and what it meant for gardening. Like the Airbnb founders profiled in the previous chapter, Emily combined learning approaches. She read Mediterranean gardening books, joined the Going Native Garden Tour, and experimented with new plants. She found out that the Mediterranean ecosystem supports a bewildering array of drought-tolerant plants from different parts of the world. She stumbled on insights that were counterintuitive to her, like the fact that many Mediterranean-zone plants can do well in poor soil, contravening Emily's rule that adding rich loam was always the way to go.

Emily's most critical insight revolved around the growing season. In temperate climates like northern Europe and Japan, the growing season begins in the spring, when warm rains awaken plants after a dormant winter. In contrast, in the Mediterranean zone the growing season begins in the fall. A wet fall gets plants going after a dormant summer as rain transforms hills from dingy brown to vibrant green. During the mild winter, stretches of rainy days alternate with sunny ones and there is an occasional nighttime frost. By late January, trees and flowers are beginning to bloom. The fall and winter rains bring a spectacular spring display of flowers, which is then followed by a long, hot summer in which many plants go dormant. The cycle then repeats.

With a deeper understanding of the Mediterranean climate, Emily began to reimagine her gardening possibilities beyond old directives like "use drip irrigation" and "more mulch," and to craft new rules in line with her new vision. Take, for example, Emily's old boundary rules for what to plant. When water was plentiful, it was fine to choose plants that collectively bloom for months — some in spring, others in summer, still others in fall — and Emily did just that. This stretched-out pattern of blooming yielded spectacular results, but required lots of watering, especially in summer. Instead, Emily's new rules recognize that plants from the Mediterranean climate bloom mostly in the spring. Since people spend time outdoors year-round in the Mediterranean zone, her plant-picking rules emphasize visual interest throughout the year and often favor choosing plants with intriguing leaf shapes, colors, and textures. One of Emily's new rules, for example, is to combine native grasses (which billow in the wind) with succulents (which have unusual leaves and plant shapes) and drought-tolerant flowering plants like lavenders and kangaroo paws. Another stipulates having five colorful pots filled with succulents on the deck year-round, to provide color bursts without much water.

The old timing rules were especially tough for Emily to abandon because they had become so ingrained over the years. Yet her old rules marched to the rhythm of spring planting and summer flowers, so they had to go. Her new timing rules exploit fall rains and dictate: "Plant bulbs in October and shrubs in November." The rhythm of the Mediterranean climate also called for new timing rules for watering. For example, April, not summer, becomes the critical time for watering, because April watering bolsters root systems just before the long, hot, dry summer. So Emily replaced the old adage of "April showers bring May flowers" with "April showers get plants through July and August," and added a timing rule: "Always deep water at least once in April." Another surprising insight with respect to the Mediterranean zone: many plants do poorly when watered during the dry summer season. Since they are dormant at this time, the combination of water and high heat can asphyxiate them. This insight led Emily, who thought that watering was always a positive, to a no-summer-watering rule for her native plants.

By taking the time to understand the Mediterranean climate and create a fresh vision of the ideal garden with new simple rules for key activities like watering and planting, Emily moved her gardening needles — ending up with a great-looking landscape and a much lower water bill. While the tendency is to pursue obvious alternatives in reaction to disruptive change, like building a garden around pavement and cactus in response to drought, this reflects only a superficial understanding of the new situation and leads to mediocre outcomes like a drab and boring landscape. To respond effectively to major change, it is essential to investigate the new situation actively, and create a reimagined vision that utilizes radically different rules.

The example of Emily's garden offers another lesson. Once she had decided to discard her old image of the ideal garden and replace it with a Mediterranean one, she had a choice of two paths toward change. She could, on the one hand, implement change slowly, gradually blending in drought-tolerant plants while keeping some temperate favorites like cherry trees and azaleas and maintaining a small lawn. On the other hand, she could implement change quickly, ripping out her old landscaping all at once and replacing it. The right choice is often to move to the new rules as quickly as possible. Performance will typically decline in the short run, but the transition to the new reality will be faster and more complete in the long run. In contrast, changing slowly often results in an awkward combination of the past and the future with neither fitting the other or working well. Emily took the fast path. She moved quickly, endured a dreary and bare yard as she made the switch, and ended up with an envy-producing new garden. By contrast, her slow-to-adapt neighbors tend gardens that are governed by two visions and thus have competing needs, making them more complicated to care for and less pleasing visually. The lesson is that major disruptions drive fundamental changes to rules, and that the best thing to do is to change quickly, all at once.

In the last chapter, we focused on how simple rules gradually improve with thoughtful experience and slowly adjust to incrementally shifting conditions. We described how people like Shannon Turley and Raghu Shukla and organizations like Airbnb and the internationalizing ventures used a variety of learning approaches to improve their initial simple rules. But occasionally the world changes in dramatic fashion and renders your understanding of what to do and your simple rules obsolete. Sometimes a health change like a pre-diabetes diagnosis forces you to rethink completely your exercise and diet. Sometimes a major life event like having kids suddenly shifts your main priorities to getting enough sleep and finding good childcare. Or, as California gardeners like Emily illustrate, sometimes big changes in your surroundings force you to reimagine your situation and drastically change your rules. Major disruptions are rare, but they require fundamental changes when they happen. This chapter is about figuring out the new game and reinventing your simple rules when a tsunami of change rolls in.

CHANGING THE VISION, CHANGING THE RULES

In many professional sports leagues, there are haves and have-nots. From European football clubs to Formula One racing, only the rich teams can afford the best players, and the rich teams disproportionately win. Poor teams rarely have a chance, especially if they simply copy the free-spending teams. To win, the poor teams need a novel vision and distinctly different rules. So it was a huge surprise in 2002 when the impoverished Oakland Athletics won both their division and an American League–record twenty games in a row.

The story begins with Sandy Alderson. Alderson, a former Marine with no baseball background, became the A's general manager in 1983. Unlike baseball traditionalists, Alderson saw scoring runs as a process, not an outcome, and imagined baseball as a factory with a flow of players moving along the bases. This view led Alderson and later his protégé and replacement, Billy Beane, to the insight that most teams overvalue batting average (hits only) and miss the relevance of on-base percentage (walks plus hits) to keeping the runners moving. Like many insightful rules, this boundary rule of picking players with a high on-base percentage has subtle second- and third-order effects. Hitters with a high on-base percentage are highly disciplined (i.e., patient, with a good eye for strikes). This means they get more walks, and their reputation for discipline encourages pitchers to throw strikes, which are easier to hit. They tire out pitchers by making them throw more pitches overall, and disciplined hitting does not erode much with age. These and other insights are at the heart of what author Michael Lewis famously described as *moneyball.*

Moneyball, the book and movie, is the ultimate sports fairy tale, with the A's playing the role of Cinderella. But unlike Cinderella, the A's did not live happily ever after. Moneyball's simple rules were just too easy to copy. By 2004, a free-spending team, the Boston Red Sox, co-opted the A's principles and won the World Series for the first time since 1918. In contrast, the A's went into decline, and by 2007 they were losing more games than they were winning. Moneyball had struck out.

Enter Farhan Zaidi, the A's director of baseball operations since 2009, who was named assistant general manager in 2014. Zaidi's background is rare by the standards of professional baseball. He is one of the few Muslims in the sport, grew up in the Philippines, and is Canadian. He also has a PhD in behavioral economics. But make no mistake, Zaidi is not just another quant jock. As his boss, Billy Beane, acknowledged, "Farhan could do whatever he wants to do, not just in this game, but in any sport or business. I'm more worried about losing him to Apple or Google than I am to another team." Zaidi's quantitative skills would prove essential as the A's tried to reverse their decline.

After the collapse of moneyball, Beane, Zaidi, and the rest of the A's brass needed to reimagine baseball and fundamentally change the team. They traded veterans for a boatload of inexperienced minor leaguers and fired the team's manager. At Zaidi's urging, they revamped their amateur draft rules to pay more attention to the five tools (i.e., specific physical skills like speed and throwing) that were discounted in moneyball, and broke another moneyball rule to avoid drafting high-school players. Meanwhile, on-field performance and fan attendance kept sinking. As with Emily's garden, the implementation of overall change brought about decline in the short term. As the 2012 season started, few predicted that the A's would win the division against the star-studded and free-spending Texas Rangers and Angels of Anaheim. Yet despite having no star players, the A's finished first.

Reflecting their formidable analytic skills, the A's brass had a new mindset that portrayed baseball as a financial market rife with arbitrage possibilities and simple rules to match. One was a how-to rule that dictated exploiting players with splits. Simply put, players with splits have substantially different performances in two seemingly similar situations. A common split is when a player hits very well against right-handed pitchers and poorly against left-handed pitchers, or vice versa. Players with splits are mediocre when they play every game, and are low paid. In contrast, most superstars play well regardless of the situation, and are paid handsomely for their versatility. The A's insight was that when a team has a player who can perform one side of the split well and a different player who excels at the opposite split, the two positives can create a cheap composite player. So the A's started using a boundary rule to pick players with splits and a how-to rule to exploit those splits with *platooning* — putting different players at the same position to take advantage of their splits against right- or left-handed pitching. Consider the A's first basemen in 2012. Nate Freiman hit .306 against lefties, while Brandon Moss hit .270 against righties. The two of them together formed an all-star player and came at a bargain price.

Exploiting splits was not a completely unknown rule, but no team used it as much or as successfully as the A's. Again, like most insightful simple rules, the splits rule for handedness has nuanced strategic effects. For example, exploiting these splits keeps players healthier during the long 162-game season because they don't play every day. The rule keeps everyone motivated because everyone has a role and plays often. It provides versatility when players are injured since players can fill in for each other. Finally, exploiting handedness splits works. Despite no all-star position players and a low payroll, the A's scored the most runs in the American League in 2012.

With their success in 2012, the A's might have rested on their laurels, but they didn't. Given the rivalry of professional baseball and easy imitation of successful simple rules, the A's had to keep changing their rules if they wanted to remain on top. In 2013 they added a new boundary rule to the player-selection activity: pick fly-ball hitters, meaning hitters who tend to hit the ball in the air and out of the infield (in contrast with ground-ball hitters). Sixty percent of the A's at-bats were by fly-ball hitters in 2013, the highest percentage in major-league baseball in almost a decade, and the A's had the highest ratio of fly balls to ground balls, by far. Why fly-ball hitters? Since one of ten fly balls is a home run, fly-ball hitters hit more home runs: an important factor in winning games. Fly-ball hitters also avoid ground-ball double plays, a rally killer if ever there was one. They are particularly effective against ground-ball pitchers because they tend to swing underneath the ball, taking away the advantage of these pitchers. In fact, the A's fly-ball hitters batted an all-star caliber .302 against ground-ball pitchers in 2013 on their way to their second consecutive division title despite having the fourth-lowest payroll in major-league baseball.

Since the A's have a low payroll, the team needs to have a mindset that is different from other teams if they want to win ball games. Moneyball was that vision until it was copied. Now the A's brass have the new mindset of financial arbitrage, and recognize that continually adjusting the rules is a necessity when rivals can easily imitate them. They keep shifting their simple rules to stay away from disruptions and a step ahead of their copycat rivals. As journalist Tim Kawakami writes, the A's "won't sit still because they can't sit still and that makes them experts at not sitting still."

Major disruptions call for understanding the new situation beyond a superficial level and creating a reimagined vision with brand-new simple rules, just like the California gardeners did when they embraced Mediterranean landscaping and as the Oakland A's did after the collapse of moneyball. Yet not everyone makes these fundamental adjustments, even when the need to change is stunningly obvious. Sometimes people become stuck, and as our next example demonstrates, the consequences of inertia can be substantial.

GETTING STUCK IN OLD RULES

At the turn of the twentieth century, Antarctica was the last great frontier of terrestrial exploration. The coast was barely charted, and it was just becoming clear that Antarctica was a continent, not a group of islands. Explorers were beginning to explore its impressive natural phenomena like its enormous ice shelf, lava lakes, and volcanoes. No one had yet penetrated very far into its interior, making the South Pole the ultimate prize for land explorers. In the Antarctic summer of 1911–12, Robert Scott led England's Terra Nova expedition in a legendary race against Roald Amundsen's Norwegian team to be the first to the South Pole.

To be first, Scott and Amundsen would have to travel over fifteen hundred miles across snow and ice in unforgiving weather. A betting person might have liked Scott's odds going into the race. He had more money than Amundsen and equipped his expedition with dogs, ponies, skis, and even cutting-edge motorized sleds. What's more, he had already traveled part of the route in an earlier expedition. Yet Scott lost both the race and his life. He and his men reached the pole, but several weeks after Amundsen's team got there, and then perished on their return journey. What accounted for this unexpected discrepancy between Amundsen, who made history, and Scott, who died tragically? On paper, both men looked like they had a good chance to win the race and would certainly survive it.

Perhaps Amundsen's biggest advantage was his willingness to shift his mindset from his prior sea experiences to the land, learn about land travel at the poles, and craft new simple rules. Amundsen began his South Pole preparations by attempting to understand the simple rules that Fridtjof Nansen had used in his landmark crossing of Greenland: use skiis, a small team, and sleds pulled by dogs. From his observation of Native arctic people, Amundsen continued to learn about polar land travel in depth, and gained the knowledge that he would later turn into how-to rules about nutrition, like "Eat fresh meat to avoid scurvy," and dog handling, such as "Have a lead skier whom the dogs can follow." As the trek to the South Pole unfolded, he added timing rules, including a consistent daily mileage that balanced progress with rest, and hourly stops to keep the dogs fresh.

In contrast, Scott failed to create a relevant vision with new simple rules. Instead, he remained stuck in the wrong mindset, with rules that didn't work and for reasons that are surprisingly universal. First, Scott could not escape the mindset of the Royal Navy. Scott was a career naval torpedo officer, trying to distinguish himself as a polar explorer at a time when there were few wars to fight. The Royal Navy operated with rules specifying top-down command, blind obedience to superiors, and strict separation of officers and men. So Scott was comfortable in the familiar hierarchy that supported literal obedience to orders and unquestioning respect based on rank. While these rules might have made sense on a ship, they were not helpful in Antarctic travel, where closely working together on small teams and sharing information in novel situations were vital. Scott was also trapped by the Royal Navy's ethos that there is nothing that English sailors cannot do. Consistent with this bravado, Scott tended to neglect careful preparation and preferred to wing it. Although Scott had an entire winter season to experiment with snow travel, he and his men were often busy with football games, scientific lectures, and work on their South Pole newspaper.

Consistent with the Royal Navy and English society at large, Scott saw heroism as intimately tied with adversity and self-sacrifice. This view unfortunately led Scott to glorify man-hauling, whereby people, not animals like dogs, do the arduous work of pulling heavy sleds packed with food and gear over the snow. In a telling quote, Scott observed, "In my mind no journey ever made with dogs can approach the height of that fine conception which is realized when a party of men go forth to face the hardships, dangers, and difficulties with their own unaided efforts, and by days and weeks of hard physical labor succeed in solving some of the problems of the great unknown." Although man-hauling was too slow, physically debilitating, and ultimately self-defeating, Scott, consistent with his time and place, perceived the extreme physical hardship of man-hauling as more valiant than relying on sled dogs as Amundsen and other successful polar explorers had done.

Second of all, Scott failed to make accurate attributions about the causes of his outcomes. Most of us tend to overattribute our successes to ourselves rather than to the circumstances, and conversely underattribute our failures to ourselves. A key to getting unstuck from old rules is, however, to avoid this tendency to never take the blame. In the case of Scott, he had ample opportunity to use the outcomes of his earlier Antarctic expedition to adjust his simple rules for polar land travel. That expedition had produced scientific successes, like finding the Cape Crozier emperor penguin colony, but also plenty of failures, including equipment breakdowns, scurvy, and sled-dog deaths, from which he could have learned.

Yet after returning to England, Scott wrote a triumphant book in which he often attributed the expedition's successes to his own skilled leadership and the heroism of courageous Englishmen, and blamed failures on unfortunate fate and the perils of Antarctica. He treated malnutrition, for example, as an inevitable challenge of polar travel that he and his men overcame. He failed to mention the bungled food rationing that brought on the calamity, as described in the men's private diaries. Scott blamed the failure to progress farther south on an ill team member, one Ernest Shackleton, without examining his own lack of planning that contributed to Shackleton's contracting scurvy. He attributed the poor performance of the dogs to their unsuitability to polar travel while leaving out his failure to understand how to handle sled-dogs. Research indicates that people learn best from their experience when they make accurate attributions, especially from failures. In Scott's case, it was difficult for him to learn new rules when he transformed failures into successes and misattributed the causes of relevant failures.

Third, Scott isolated himself from information. Consistent with command in the Royal Navy, Scott was aloof. He took few people into his confidence, and kept officers and men separated. People are more likely to develop correct attributions when they routinely discuss their experiences, and yet Scott's isolation impaired his ability to do this. He isolated himself in other ways too. There is no report that he engaged in brainstorming activities or personal reflection. As one account notes, "His [Scott's] naval training taught him form, routine, discipline, obedience, but stifled independent thought. He lacked the capacity to learn from experience." While Amundsen was interested in learning how Native people lived in the Arctic, Scott dismissed them as uncivilized and not a source of useful information. Even if he had been motivated to add to or change his rules, his lack of insight would have limited their effectiveness.

A pioneering journey to the South Pole demanded a new understanding with relevant simple rules. Amundsen studied up, shifted his mindset from sea to land travel, identified critical bottlenecks like dog handling and food provisioning, and filled in the rules. Scott, instead, stayed locked in the mindset of the British Navy, which was, at best, irrelevant to the expedition. Scott was undone by incorrect attributions that sapped his motivation to change, and spotty information about where to change. These are universal reasons for why some people cannot rethink their situations and simple rules even when the need to do so is blindingly obvious.

Scott got it wrong. When people face a major disruption, such as a water shortage that might be permanent or new terrain to traverse, the key is to recognize that the change is happening and to study its implications well beyond a surface understanding, then break the old rules and move on to the new ones quickly. There are situations, however, when it is unwise to wait passively for the next big change. In these situations, it makes sense to *be* the disruption, proactively shifting the bottlenecks to success and breaking the rules for everyone else.

CHANGING THE BOTTLENECKS, REWRITING THE RULES

Once upon a time, an amiable show called *Cheers* ruled television. When *Cheers,* set in a Boston bar "where everybody knows your name," debuted in September 1982, the critics loved it, but ordinary viewers were not so enamored. The show sank to the bottom of TV ratings. An undeterred NBC stuck with it, and the network's faith paid dividends. *Cheers* became a mainstay of NBC's blockbuster Thursday-night programming, along with *The Cosby Show* and *Family Ties. Cheers* stayed on prime-time television for eleven seasons, and forty million viewers watched its final episode.

Writing is a crucial bottleneck to quality television and was essential for *Cheers*'s success. Witty repartee among the show's memorable characters kept viewers tuning in. Bar owner Sam Malone was an unapologetic Lothario who constantly was wooing not-so-bright women. Sam's foil was a waitress named Diane Chambers, an intellectual snob stranded at the bar by a flyaway fiancé. Sam and Diane's unlikely chemistry provided one of the comedy's prime romantic tensions and left the audience wondering week after week: will they or won't they become a couple? The colorful ensemble cast members, including Carla, the sharp-tongued waitress, Norm, the stout everyman, and Cliff, the garrulous postal worker, changed remarkably little over the show's lengthy run.

Cheers writers used several simple how-to rules for writing. One was to develop characters with very distinct personality traits. The idea was to give the audience a sense of predictability and familiarity with each character. The writers often created particular situations, and then explored how each character would respond. In later seasons the writers purposefully surprised the audience by occasionally having the characters behave in the opposite way to what was expected. This rule let the writers develop characters' richness without diminishing their distinctiveness. A more challenging rule further distinguished each character. Each character had a unique way of speaking, and this rule was termed "write for radio" — meaning that the audience could know who was talking just by hearing the dialogue. Another rule was that every episode had to stand alone such that viewers could watch any episode at any time in any sequence and its story line would stand alone. This meant that writers had to create a complete story with a beginning, middle, and end for each episode.

When *Cheers* writers converged in the writers' room to share their own experiences, they wanted episode themes that aroused universal emotions like being embarrassed, amused, or scared. The rule was that anything with friction that resonates for lots of people was fair game for an episode. The writers were pragmatic and fast, and they often zoomed through creating rough drafts so they could take time detailing polished drafts. Within the rules, however, *Cheers* writers had extensive flexibility to explore all sorts of issues, including controversial ones. Despite being a light comedy, *Cheers* was among the first TV shows to address feminism, homosexuality, and addiction.

When the bar closed in May 1993, *Cheers* was one of the longest-running network series ever. The simple rules helped the writers to create the vivid characters, smart dialogue, and creative storylines that made the show such a hit. During its long run, *Cheers* was nominated for 117 Emmys, winning 26. In 2013 *TV Guide* named *Cheers* the eleventh-greatest show of all time, beating competition like *Star Trek*, *Saturday Night Live*, and *Mad Men*.

Cheers is a remarkably successful example of a show where viewers could tune in at almost any time and feel at home, even if they had missed a few episodes. Its simple rules for writing were geared around this promise: the stable cast of sympathetic (and predictable) characters did not change from episode to episode, each episode had a self-contained story, and shows were written with a brisk rhythm because episodes did not need to fit into a complex storyline. This instant familiarity was critical in a time before DVR, when viewers could not catch up on episodes they missed. Episodic simple rules are not limited to sitcoms like *Cheers* (or the vast number of comedies it has influenced, like *Friends* and *How I Met Your Mother*). They span television genres, notably procedural dramas in which familiar characters do the same thing in every episode, like solving a case in *CSI* or diagnosing an illness in *House*.

In March 2011 Netflix executives were surveying the new television landscape they had helped create. TV in the 2010s looked radically different from the heyday of *Cheers,* and Netflix was at the forefront of redefining television. With the sizable capital it had accumulated after destroying Blockbuster, Netflix was about to dive into original programming, offering television without a channel. It was a historic step, and a big risk. Netflix needed a hit to stand out from the crowd. The question was: How to create one?

Writing was an obvious place to start. After the advent of DVR and non-network channels like HBO, television entered what TV critic Brett Martin calls its "Third Golden Age." *The Sopranos* ushered in this era with serialized, not episodic, shows. While viewers could watch any episode of *Cheers* and know roughly what was going on, if they walked into a midseason episode of *The Sopranos* they would be constantly asking, "What's happening? Who is that guy?" Shows like *The Sopranos* darkened the tone with edgy storylines and took more risks than network shows, with their mass-market audiences. After *The Sopranos, The Wire, Breaking Bad, Mad Men,* and similar hits, audiences were primed for serialized shows that explored serious themes. Like *Cheers,* these shows relied on excellent writing, but to be successful, they had to redefine the rules.

Netflix, of course, could have followed the *Cheers*-style simple rules that were still driving some of the most popular entertainment on television. Procedural dramas like *NCIS* and sitcoms

like *Two and a Half Men* and *The Big Bang Theory*, which follow the simple rules of episodic writing so faithfully that critics
accuse them of being formulaic, dominated television. But Netflix executives realized that employing the same old rules would
not be enough to break out of the pack. Revolutionary times call
for revolutionary measures. In order to change how television
worked and skyrocket a non-channel show to stardom, Netflix
would have to change the game. It would have to join the revolution of the Third Golden Age of television, and then push that
revolution one step further.

In February 2013, Netflix's longshot debuted. *House of Cards*
stars two-time Oscar winner Kevin Spacey as Francis "Frank"
Underwood, a conniving politician from rural South Carolina.
In the series premiere, Frank is passed over for secretary of state
and embarks on a path of power and revenge. To tell Frank's
story, *House of Cards*'s writers embraced the serialized format.
They used event foreshadowing and wove characters in and out
of the story. A character could appear in episode two and then
disappear until episode eight (something that Sam's character
in *Cheers* would never do). Instead of stable character development, as expressed through the characters' predictable reactions
to common situations, *House of Cards*'s characters develop in
lengthy side-segments, like when a vice-prone congressman is
portrayed hanging out with his kids.

While excellent writing is part of the *House of Cards* story, the
bigger story is Netflix and its re-envisioning of television. In earlier chapters, we defined bottlenecks as decisions or activities that
hinder value creation. In essence, Netflix attacked critical bottlenecks that others had accepted as the status quo. For example,
rather than focusing primarily on writing as the key bottleneck,
Netflix and its partner, Media Rights Capital, made the strategic
bet that world-class directing could help *House of Cards* stand

out among the vast array of choices available to viewers. To stand out, *House of Cards* did something very rare in television: the show recruited an A-list Hollywood director. That director was David Fincher, a two-time Oscar nominee who had directed top films like *The Social Network, The Curious Life of Benjamin Button,* and *The Girl with the Dragon Tattoo.* As the story goes, Fincher was on the prowl for new projects when a remake of the British political thriller *House of Cards* crossed his path. Media Rights Capital owned the rights to the show and wanted Fincher at the helm of a U.S. remake. Fincher loved the BBC version, stating, "The way it was structured was so smart. Meeting him [the lead character, played by Ian Richardson] at his lowest point and watching him gain traction as he begins to move all the pieces on the chess board."

Netflix and its partners gave Fincher the directorial control that is common in moviemaking. With a twenty-six-episode commitment from Netflix, Fincher had the freedom to establish a creative process that was freeing for directors. He signed up five leading directors, including Charles McDougall (*Desperate Housewives, The Office*) and Allen Coulter (*The Sopranos*), to direct their own episodes. Fincher directed the first two episodes to set the tone, and then left the director's chair. The rules called for each director to be responsible for two sequential episodes and a twenty-day shoot. The directors were also required to watch Fincher's first two episodes to get a feel for the show, and read the scripts leading up to their own episodes. Fincher strongly suggested that the directors use the more cinematic stationary camera, a classic moviemaking technique that emphasizes framing shots with intriguing angles, lighting, and actor movement. After that, Fincher left the directors alone. They could take their episodes wherever they liked within the story arc, had the flexibility to cast their own day players for characters introduced in their episodes, and could do their final cuts. The result is the signature and Emmy-winning cinematic quality of *House of Cards*.

Beyond directing, Netflix tackled another novel and neglected bottleneck: programming. Picking winning TV shows is a major bottleneck to the success of media companies because viewers will simply avoid shows that don't interest them. Yet since the dawn of television, picking winners has been more art than science, and has rested on guesswork and luck. That is why media companies rely on well-worn rules for programming that commit them to shows in stages — first a pilot, then a few shows, and then a single season. Netflix broke those rules and did so with technology that didn't exist in the days of *Cheers*. It committed to two full seasons in advance — no pilot, no stages. Why? As one pundit claims, "Netflix knew you would like *House of Cards* before you did." While this downplays the very real risk Netflix was taking in launching a major new show, there is more than a sliver of truth in it. With about thirty million subscribers, Netflix understood what its members were watching, and with a granularity that executives in other media companies could only envy. Its analytics, for instance, picked up on the success of the British version of *House of Cards*, and the popularity of David Fincher and Kevin Spacey movies on Netflix. The new programming rule to buy shows sight unseen was innovative and let Netflix obtain *House of Cards* before other buyers were ready to commit. It's an intriguing rule as well because it exploits Netflix's unique "big data" capabilities, making it a less risky rule than it would be for a conventional television network. By exploiting its unique capabilities, Netflix proactively redefined the boundary rules for choosing television programming.

Netflix broke the rules of programming again by releasing the entire season at once, an innovative rule that the company used again with shows like *Orange Is the New Black*. The rule seemed risky at the time. After all, viewers traditionally watched new shows with breaks in between episodes, which built anticipation and excitement into the viewing experience. Releasing an entire series all at once might temper the romance. But again, this practice exploited the unique expertise of Netflix. The company had data on millions of searches, pauses, rewinds, and fast-forwards, and knew how frequently people already streamed multiple shows in one sitting. In other words, Netflix knew from its vast data that many viewers were already "binge watching" shows. As important, the all-at-once rule made *House of Cards* stand out in the media and break away from the pack, just as Netflix wanted.

As if breaking the rules of two bottlenecks were not enough disruption of the industry, Netflix tackled a third novel bottleneck: hiring. The creators of successful shows like *Cheers,* of course, pay attention to talent, and hiring appropriate people is critical to success. Yet Netflix changed the rules of talent acquisition, signing Fincher, one of the only A-list directors to ever take on a television show, and Spacey, one of the biggest A-list actors to ever star in a television show. Even the relatively novice creator, Beau Willimon, had an Oscar nomination for screenwriting a George Clooney movie, *The Ides of March.* The rule of hiring such high-quality talent seemed risky from the outside. Netflix has, however, long focused on the hiring bottleneck in its existing businesses and was simply exploiting familiar boundary and how-to rules: hire the very best, pay them top dollar, and leave them alone. Netflix applied those rules to *House of Cards,* and its star talent generated extensive media attention, just as Netflix executives had hoped.

Individually, many of the *House of Cards* rules had some precedence. The serialization writing rules were similar to those of other shows with intricate and edgy plots. Although star directors are rare, *House of Cards* followed ABC's *Twin Peaks,* directed by David Lynch in the early 1990s. Yet taken collectively, the *House of Cards* rules, including its unique programming and talent rules, produced something unusual in television history. *House of Cards* was a stunning success that became the first Emmy-winning show never seen on traditional "television," getting twelve nods and winning three. It also picked up four Golden Globe nominations, including a win for Robin Wright. The show moved the needles that Netflix wanted to shift: achieving a leading position on the map for top-notch creative content and a heftier subscriber base.

Sometimes it is enough to adapt to a dramatic change, like re-envisioning a garden in the face of a water shortage. Other situations demand proactive change. Just as the Oakland A's initially changed their vision of baseball with the moneyball rules and then changed their vision and rules again when moneyball faltered, *House of Cards* proactively tried to alter the landscape of television. *Cheers* perfected the simple rules for episodic television writing that are still in use today. In contrast, Netflix broke away from the industry with a disruptive focus on neglected bottlenecks: directing, programming, and talent acquisition. The company's adaptiveness and willingness to change the bottlenecks gave it the freedom to rewrite its rules.

Conclusion

WHEN JANET YELLEN WAS sworn in as the fifteenth chair of the Board of Governors of the Federal Reserve System in February 2014, she took on one of the toughest jobs in the world. The Federal Reserve Board is charged with keeping the U.S. economy on track. This is a demanding job in the best of conditions, but Yellen took charge as the economy was clawing its way out of the deepest downturn since the Great Depression. The board's decisions on whether to raise or cut interest rates may seem far removed from the day-to-day lives of most Americans, but they have profound consequences. In addition to keeping inflation under control, the Federal Reserve Board is charged with maximizing employment, a critical issue when more than ten million Americans were out of work. As chair, Yellen understood the human costs of joblessness. "Long-term unemployment is devastating to workers and their families," she noted in a 2013 speech. "The toll is simply terrible on the mental and physical health of workers, on their marriages, and on their children."

If ever there was a system too complex for simple rules, it

would be the U.S. economy, which consists of hundreds of government agencies, thousands of banks, tens of millions of companies, and over a hundred million households interacting with one another every day. And yet, within three months of taking office, Yellen outlined a framework for making decisions on interest rates, which Bloomberg.com dubbed her "mind the gap" rule. This timing rule, in essence, states that the Federal Reserve Board will not increase interest rates until the economy achieves target levels of employment and inflation. Yellen's mind-the-gap rule is a variant of an earlier guideline, developed in 1992 by Stanford economist John Taylor as a practical tool to guide monetary policy. Within a few years, Taylor's rule was being used, along with other rules of thumb, as a benchmark to guide and evaluate policy decisions not only by the Federal Reserve, but also by central bankers around the world.

Simple rules to manage economic complexity are far from new. In fifteenth-century Europe, there were over five hundred mints supplying nearly one hundred currencies. Medieval princes routinely reduced the silver or gold content of their coins, and passed the diluted currency on to their subjects, thereby fueling price inflation. Under pressure from merchants who refused to accept debased currency, some princes transferred their right of coinage to autonomous city councils, a forerunner of the modern central bank, some of which relied on simple rules to regulate currency. The rules used to manage monetary policy grew more sophisticated over time. As England's master of the mint in 1717, Sir Isaac Newton decreed the "golden rule" that paper currency must be convertible to an equivalent amount of gold. Eight decades later, England abandoned Newton's golden rule and proceeded to print pounds to fund the Napoleonic wars. The financial chaos that followed inspired English bankers to develop new rules to stabilize England's economy: (1) limit the amount of paper money,

(2) never reduce circulating cash but "vibrate within limits," (3) expand cash as trade expands, and (4) allow temporary increases in emergencies.

OVERCOMING THE BARRIERS TO SIMPLICITY

The simple rules used by central bankers bring us full circle to where we began this book. Like battlefield medics, central bankers use simple rules to make critical decisions in the face of daunting complexity. The use of simple rules when the stakes are so high — millions of jobs, for example, or the difference between life and death — illustrates their power in even the most complex situations. These rules also raise an important question: if simple rules are so effective in so many situations, why do complex solutions remain so prevalent? Regulators churn out ever more detailed rules, personnel departments promulgate thick policy manuals, and self-styled experts promote ever more arcane diet and exercise regimes. People crave simplicity and, as we've argued throughout this book, simple rules often outperform more complicated approaches. Why aren't simple rules even more common? What are the obstacles to simplifying our lives, corporations, and societies? And, most important, how can we overcome these obstacles to achieve simplicity?

The first obstacle is the effort required to develop simple rules. Like most worthwhile endeavors, it takes time and energy to get them right. The process of developing simple rules requires ruthless prioritization — honing in on the essential and decluttering the peripheral. You must identify which of many objectives will move the needles, identify the specific activity or decision that represents a critical bottleneck, and prune dozens of potential rules down to a handful. Each step requires you to make difficult tradeoffs and ask hard questions. But when you consider the costs of developing simple rules, don't ignore the costs of *not* using them — the enervation of complicated solutions, for example, or the frustration of failing to achieve your objectives year after year. When explaining how he led Apple's resurgence from near-bankruptcy, Steve Jobs emphasized the power of simplicity. "You have to work hard to get your thinking clear to make it simple," Jobs said. "But it is worth it in the end because once you get there you can move mountains." The payoffs of simplification often dwarf the costs of getting there.

The people who benefit from complexity pose a second obstacle to simplicity. The costs of complex solutions are distributed across many people while the benefits of complexity tend to be concentrated in the hands of a few. These beneficiaries have, as a consequence, strong incentives to resist simplification. Much of the complexity of the U.S. tax code, for example, exists because special-interest groups secure tax breaks, including write-offs for owning a racehorse or building a race track, that benefit a small number of individuals. These special-interest groups obviously benefit from complexity, but so do the lobbyists who make their case to legislators, as well as the lawmakers themselves. After creating a labyrinth of rules, regulators and politicians often walk through the revolving door to join the companies they formerly supervised. In the private sector they can guide their new employers through the maze of regulations they themselves helped build. And the revolving door between government and business is likely to spin faster as regulatory complexity increases. A recent study found that the number of former regulators hired by financial service firms increased by 55 percent between 2001 and 2013.

The third obstacle to simplicity is what we call the "myth of requisite complexity," the mistaken belief that complex problems demand complicated solutions. There are, naturally, situations when complicated solutions are appropriate — recall the detailed checklists used by pilots and surgeons. But detailed rules and regulations aren't the only possible way to deal with complexity. The U.S. Congress responded to the 2008 financial crisis by drafting tens of thousands of pages of detailed regulations covering financial service organizations. That may be the best approach to avert future crises, but it is certainly not the only option. Andy Haldane is the chief economist at the Bank of England and was named one of the world's most influential people by *Time* magazine. At a recent conference of central bankers from around the world, Haldane argued that simple rules could prevent future banking crises more effectively than voluminous regulation. Haldane may be right and he may be wrong, but surely this is a debate worth having. Complicated solutions should be a considered choice, not the result of regulatory autopilot.

Whether simple rules or detailed regulations are more effective is ultimately an empirical question that should be resolved by testing them to see which works better in the real world. Such studies are rare, and the few done to date underscore the danger of assuming that more rules are always better. Consider the results of a recent study that analyzed legal systems around the world. The authors compared how well the judicial systems in 109 countries resolved two of the most common legal disputes — evicting a tenant who stops paying rent and chasing down payment on a bounced check. Their study revealed enormous variation across countries in terms of the number of rules limiting a judge's discretion, with more rule-laden systems taking an order of magnitude longer to mete out justice. In the United States, a landlord could evict a delinquent tenant in under two months, a process that took eighteen months in Austria. The authors measured justice along several dimensions, including whether citizens considered their legal systems impartial, free from corruption, affordable, and consistent. The number of rules was negatively correlated with all measures of justice. Any way the authors cut the data, the result was the same — more rules, less justice.

Often, complex rules and regulations arise out of a distrust of human nature. If people cannot be trusted to do the right thing, detailed regulations are necessary to prevent malfeasance. Many corporations, for example, rely on thick policy manuals to control people who might abuse their discretion. But these bad apples represent a tiny fraction of all employees. After studying their human resources policies, executives at Netflix determined that 97 percent of their employees were trustworthy. Nearly all of the company's time writing, monitoring, and enforcing detailed personnel policies was directed at the remaining 3 percent. Rather than continue to produce binders of detailed regulations, Netflix executives concentrated on not hiring people who would cause problems, and removing them quickly when hiring mistakes were made. This change allowed the company to replace thick manuals with simple rules. The company's policy for expenses, travel, gifts, and conducting personal business at work, for example, was reduced to four rules: (1) expense what you would not otherwise spend, (2) travel as if it were your own money, (3) disclose nontrivial gifts from vendors, and (4) do personal stuff at work when it is inefficient not to.

RULES TO LIBERATE

We typically equate rules with restrictions that limit our options and keep us from doing what we want to do. But rules enable as well as constrain. By following simple rules, parents and investors can resist short-term temptations and achieve their long-term objectives. Using simple rules, entrepreneurs and managers can seize opportunities to grow their business without losing sight of their overall strategy. Rules can help us make better decisions, on the fly, when information is limited. Artists like Elmore Leonard and Claude Monet unleashed their creativity by following a handful of rules. As members of organizations, communities, and societies, we can coordinate our activities even as we pursue our personal objectives. Following the rule to drive on the right-hand side of the road, everyone can arrive at their destination while minimizing the odds of an accident.

As we have seen throughout this book, simple rules work because they provide a threshold level of structure while leaving ample scope to exercise discretion. Complex rules, in contrast, attempt to anticipate every contingency and dictate what to do in each scenario, thereby reducing people to automatons who do what they are told. But human discretion is not a defect to be eliminated, it is our greatest hope in the battle against complexity. Close to the facts on the ground, individuals can draw on their judgment and creativity to manage risks and seize unexpected opportunities. The latitude to exercise discretion not only makes simple rules effective, it makes them attractive. People thrive when given the opportunity to apply their judgment and creativity to the situations they face from day to day. And if they benefit from simple rules, they are more likely to use them and use them well.

In many areas of our lives — both professional and personal — we face an apparently unpalatable choice between the simplicity we crave and complicated solutions that seem necessary. This tradeoff is often false. For many of our most important activities and decisions, simple rules are both more desirable and more effective than complicated solutions. We wrote this book to open readers' eyes to the myriad possibilities they have to tackle complexity with simplicity, and to provide concrete guidance on how to seize these opportunities. For those who wield the power of simple rules, complexity is not destiny.

Acknowledgments

One of the great pleasures of researching and writing a book is that it provides an opportunity to work with, and learn from, so many people. We are deeply indebted to the many colleagues, students, entrepreneurs, executives, and friends with whom we collaborated in writing this book.

First we would like to thank our outstanding agent Larry Weissman, who helped translate an interesting idea into a fully fledged proposal that served as a roadmap for writing the book. Courtney Young commissioned *Simple Rules* as an editor at Houghton Mifflin Harcourt and then provided two rounds of detailed feedback that led to quantum-change improvements in the quality of the book. Rick Wolff took the reins from Courtney, and leveraged his deep experience and enthusiasm to shepherd the book through production and marketing. We appreciate Courtney's and Rick's invaluable help. We also thank the publicity and marketing team at Houghton Mifflin Harcourt, led by Taryn Roeder, Katrina Kruse, and Lori Glazer, for helping to ensure that the book reaches a wide audience. We appreciate Melissa Dobson's expert efforts in thorough copyediting and diligent fact checking of the final manuscript. Sarah Cliffe, our editor at the *Harvard Business Review* for two articles on simple rules, supported the initial concept and provided much helpful and needed feedback.

In addition to our joint thanks, each of us owes collaborators and colleagues a special debt of gratitude. Don would like to begin by thanking his son Charlie, who leveraged his experience as the former president of the *Harvard Lampoon* and coauthor of a *New York Times* best-selling parody to help research and write this book. Parental pride aside, Charlie provided some of the most vivid examples and memorable prose in the book. If a particular phrase caught your attention or an example stayed with you, the odds are very high that Charlie wrote it.

The action research project described in chapter 5 began in 2010, when Ran Sharon knocked on Don's office door at the London Business School and threatened not to leave until he agreed to help develop a program that would disrupt traditional executive education. The simple rules program (officially called the Active Learning Program) was a first for the Young Presidents' Organization, and like all innovations, experienced its share of setbacks and surprises. The initiative would never have gotten off the ground or stayed aloft without the commitment of time and energy provided by Ran, as well as the other program champions, Alessandro Di Fiore, Joerg von Weiler, and Paolo Kalaw. All of them took time from their day jobs of running a company to recruit fellow YPOers, manage the process, reflect on what was working and what wasn't, and continuously improve the simple rules program. Stefano Turconi, a former student and later colleague, worked on the simple rules program from its inception, and along the way became an extremely skilled facilitator of simple rules interventions.

The YPO members who participated in the simple rules program committed their time and considerable energy to making it work. Our thanks to Padraig O Ceidigh, Jeremy Coller, Kobi Tadmor, Martin Ott, Itamar Levy, Gilbert Frizberg, Przemek Gacek, Stefan von Weiler, Martin Friz, Anar Aligulov, Gummi Palmason, Vincent Lo Cicero, Alexander Tremmel, Franz-Joseph Miller, Eduardo Aziz Nader, Ludger Kleyboldt, Jochen Werz, Janis Oslejs, Yoni Assia, Federico Bausone, George Konstantinidis, Gaggai Barel, Francois Moreau de Saint Martin, Richard Torriani, Sanjiv Suri, Sunil Lalvani, David Beck, Karen Flavelle, Jeff Fuller, David Heffernan, Randy Pratt, Nilesh Ved, Tushar Ved, and Vivian Zalkow.

One of the distinctive aspects of the simple rules program was that the YPO members brought members of their management team to ensure the changes took root in their organizations. Don would like to thank the executives who brought so much insight and enthusiasm to the simple rules program, including Ralf Wenzel, Paul Shutz, Charles Hippsley, Gracjan Fiedorowicz, Andreas Mac, Jabir Jumshudov, Andreas Toerschen, Christoph Tremmel, Arne Schulke, Nei Tremarin, Jan Obenbrink, Jens-André Warnecke, Marite Seite, Guy Ben Yossef, Jacqueline Powell, Ivan Gonzalez, Saul Guzman, Michael Melachrinidis, Emmanouil Margaritis, Nikos Lambrou, Rony Gihan, David Leporini, Dris Warreyn, Idoia Rodes Torrontegui, Oscar Cerezales, Petra Kandertova, Renata Lukasova, Libor Pavlicek, Kathleen Chan, John McGrath, Robert Watkins, Steve Pavelich, Grant Bettesworth, Duncan Johnston, Peter Higgins, Kriston Dean, Tyson Rideout, Layne Krienke, Al Jessa, Britt Innes, Glenn Green, Geoff Boyd, Katherine Angus, Marcello Lo Cicero, Bill Downing, Neeraj Teckchandani, Manoj Nakra, Azim Mohammed, Kamal Kotak, Siddharth Dixit, Jitendra Bulani, Sachin Banodkar, Arun Pagarani, Santosh Bhatia, Ross Moncur, Ravi Rao, Ghosa Biswajeet, Pat Wilkinson, Lauren Walker, Peter Thomson, Nelson Nogales, and Doug McLean.

A great thing about being a teacher is the opportunity to work with, and learn from, a steady stream of talented and enthusiastic students. Don would like to acknowledge the following London Business School students who participated on the YPO study or other simple rules projects: Daniel Sacerdoti, Simon Wintels, Ido Hochman, Assaf Shlush, Avinash Samtani, Kathryn Farmer, Mamello Selamolela, Aline Hochman, Mohsin Drabu, Uri Zahavi, Torsten Wolter, Kunal Shah, Daniela Scur, Shivani Parmar, Payal Patel, Uri Meirovich, Yonatan Puterman, Felipe Koechlin, and James Samworth. At MIT Sloan, it was a great pleasure to work with Leila Zreik, David Hoyme, Esteban Lubensky, and Jenny Larios Berlin. Don would also like to thank his students at London Business School and MIT Sloan School of Management, who posed great questions, offered surprising insights, and provided unexpected examples of simple rules in action.

Don completed much of the research on this book while a professor at the London Business School, and the ideas in this book were sharpened considerably through many discussions with his colleagues. He would particularly like to thank current and former London Business School colleagues Julian Birkinshaw, Kevin Boudreau, Donal Crilly, Dan Goldstein, Ben Hallen, Dominic Houlder, Ioannis Ioannou, Michael Jacobides, Costas Markides, Yiorgos Mylonaids, and Freek Vermeulen. Don's London Business School colleague Rebecca Homkes contributed her great energy to leading simple rules interventions in a few of the YPO companies. The leadership team of London Business School Executive Education, especially Sabine Vinck and Samantha Bown, demonstrated great enthusiasm for simple rules and used them to help run that business. Don would also like to thank the hundreds of executives who participated in the Achieving Strategic Agility and Executing Strategy for Results courses. Although they are too numerous to mention by name, these leaders road-tested simple rules in their own companies and provided many practical tips on what works in the real world.

Several current and former students, friends, and family members carved time out of their busy schedules to read early drafts of the manuscript, and Don would like to thank in particular his mother, Kathleen Sull, brother, Mark Sull, and wife, Theresa Sull, for providing invaluable feedback long after they were sick of discussing "the book." Grateful thanks also to other readers, including Alejandro Ruelas Gossi, Bill Borgia, Tommy Nebl, Kelly Basner, Mark McDonald, and Temple Fennell, as well as many of the YPO members and students mentioned above, who took the time to read early drafts and provide extremely helpful insights.

Kathy would like to thank her friends, family members, students, and colleagues who helped to create this book. Several of her former PhD students stand out as essential contributors to the simple rules ideas. Kathy's simple rules journey began when she and Shona Brown began studying the strategies of technology-based companies as Shona worked on her dissertation. They were searching for fresh ideas that would break away from the stale paradigms of traditional strategy and organization theory. They found those ideas at the "edge of chaos" in complexity theory, and penned *Competing on the Edge: Strategy as Structured Chaos*. This project became a precursor to the simple rules research. Kathy is also indebted to another former PhD student, Professor Chris Bingham of the University of North Carolina. Chris was the perfect research partner, and together they pushed forward insights into how simple rules are learned and why they work so well. Nathan Furr, now a professor at Brigham Young University, pitched in with a thoughtful analysis showing the power of learning simple rules over simply accumulating experience. Another former PhD student, Professor Jason Davis of INSEAD, helped lift the conceptual foundation of simple rules to a higher intellectual plane when he coded a simple rules simulation over one Thanksgiving break. The richness of the results was stunning. Although the simulation itself is on the geeky side for the aims of this book, it's a central piece of the simple rules' conceptual base. Professor Gerardo Okhuysen's dissertation research proved unexpectedly useful for clarifying why better rules matter. Now a professor at the University of California at Irvine, Gerardo's laboratory study provided an ideal setting to explore the quality of rules. Kathy will never forget that the results were so powerful, they could be seen visually on graphs without any statistical analysis. Current PhD student Mike Leatherbee is exploring simple rules in Start-Up Chile, the hugely successful national experiment to ignite entrepreneurship in that country. Kathy appreciates Mike's help, especially in clarifying how simple rules work and evolve within a government policy.

Kathy is also grateful for the help of several individuals who generously gave their time and personal stories. Lynne Barre of NOAA shared the agency's careful process to develop simple rules to protect killer whales, the threatened cultural icons of the Pacific Northwest. Shannon Turley of Stanford lent his journey along a path of improving simple rules from undergraduate volunteer to the height of his profession as a football strength coach. Former Stanford student Raghu Shukla graciously described (through his avatar) how he became a top-notch poker player by learning better simple rules. Cheri Steinkellner colorfully recounted her simple rules as a writer for *Cheers*, while the anonymous Emily told the story of remaking her garden during the California drought. Several others contributed rich background to simple rules examples, but prefer to stay out of the spotlight. To all of these generous people, Kathy gives her deep thanks.

Kathy is also indebted to terrific undergraduate and master's students from Stanford's School of Engineering. Andrew Stutz improved Kathy's football acumen, and would not rest until she heard Shannon Turley's story. Nick Manousos gave Kathy a quick education in screenwriting for movies and television, and connected her with Cheri Steinkellner. Annie Case diligently researched simple rules for crowdfunding at Indiegogo and Kickstarter, while Lauryn Isford and Florence Koskas clarified how simple rules work in shared-economy companies. Luke Pappas provided revealing baseball insights. Although their material did not make the final version of the book, Kathy appreciates the terrific efforts of Andrea Sy on Wikipedia and Michael Heinrich on the Lean Startup. Their work will shine somewhere — soon. Finally, successive cohorts of master's students in Kathy's course, Strategy in Technology-based Companies (MS&E 270), challenged and immeasurably sharpened the conceptual foundation of simple rules.

For Kathy, the book could not have happened without the help of family members, friends, and colleagues. She appreciates the insights of Jim Colton (golf), Bob Eberhart (poker), Ruth Satterthwaite and Lois Lin (music), Athene Eisenhardt (gardening and firefighting), and Eric Eisenhardt (fish and killer whales). Kathy's dedicated and savvy book group of longtime friends (Sheryl Cassella, Mary Jo Colton, Lois Lin, Nancy Madsen, Ruth Satterthwaite, and Margaret Zuanich) gave an unvarnished critique of the working manuscript. When everyone had diligently read the almost-finished draft and not an assigned book, a discussion of simple rules completely took over one August meeting. The book is much better for it. More of "the Neighborhood" (Dick Carlson, Pat Carlson, Helen Gracon, Steve Madsen, Shannon Madsen, Ed Satterthwaite, and Dick Zuanich), plus Margaret Ann and Don Fidler, weighed in with insightful ideas about what was working and what was not. Kathy's sister, Beth Fahey, chimed in with smart comments even though she barely had time. Her comments are very much appreciated. Kathy's executive colleagues in various corporations lent their insights and feedback over the years during consulting engagements, board meetings, and executive education. As Don mentions above, Charlie Sull was just an extraordinary help. Kathy deeply appreciates the insights of these people.

Books are often influenced by where they are written. Kathy found the Helen R. Whiteley Center at the University of Washington's Friday Harbor Laboratories to be the ideal venue for creativity as she began writing the book. She appreciates the hospitality of Kathy Cowell and others at FHL for making her stay so productive. Kathy also found inspiration in the Fontainebleau forest when she visited at INSEAD, and is grateful for being a member of the school's visiting faculty in France and Singapore. Ideas came as well in Lake Tahoe, Palo Alto, and on the Roswell porch of her brother and sister-in-law, Bill and Colette Kennedy. Kathy thanks Stanford's School of Engineering, where she is a faculty member. She is especially indebted to the Stanford Technology Ventures Program, where she serves as codirector, for its significant support of her research, teaching, and this book. Tina Seelig, Matt Harvey, and Josh Tennefoss, in particular, took time to provide superb comments on the manuscript. Mike Pena expertly provided help with communications, while Bob Sutton gave numerous tips on publishing excellent books, as he has himself done so often.

On the larger stage, Kathy is particularly grateful for the timeless inspiration of Liv and Given Eisenhardt, who shine as the bright promise of the future, and Athene and Eric, who are always there. Kathy is especially fortunate for having a lifetime of loving support from her parents, Bill and Marie Kennedy. They wrote their final chapters as Kathy worked on this book. Kathy is certain that her dad would love the book, and that her mom would love that she wrote it.

Endnotes

INTRODUCTION

1 *The Sixty-Seventh Combat Support Hospital:* Christine Hauser, "At U.S.
Hospital, Reflections on 11 Hours and 91 Casualties," *New York Times,*
December 29, 2004; Dave Hnida, *Paradise General: Riding the Surge at a
Combat Hospital in Iraq* (New York: Simon & Schuster, 2010); Roosevelt
J. Mitchell, "The Deployment of Bravo Company 21st Combat Support
Hospital," U.S. Army Sergeant Majors Academy Digital Library, Personal
Experience Papers, October 5, 2006, http://cgsc.contentdm.oclc.org/cdm/
singleitem/collection/p15040coll2/id/635/rec/14.

2 *At noon on December:* Blog of Sgt. Edward Montoya Jr., a U.S. Army
medic who was in the mess hall when the explosion took place. http://
gene-afterthemilitary.blogspot.com/2011/12/day-of-hell-on-fob-marez-
by-sgt-edward.html.

3 *In 2004 the Army:* Atul Gawande, "Casualties of War — Military Care
for the Wounded from Iraq and Afghanistan," *New England Journal of
Medicine* 351 (2004): 2471–75.
Only one out of every ten: Ibid.

4 *After the first:* M. M. Manring et al., "Treatment of War Wounds: A
Historic Review," *Clinical Orthopaedics and Related Research* 467, no. 8
(2004): 2168–91.
Simple guidelines: There are no universally accepted standards for use in
emergency triage, but common criteria include systolic blood pressure,

pulse rate, respiration, ability to respond to commands, and the motor
component of the Glasgow Coma Scale. See Brian J. Eastridge et al.,
"Field Triage Score (FTS) in Battlefield Casualties: Validation of a Novel
Triage Technique in a Combat Environment," *American Journal of Surgery* 200, no. 6 (2010): 724–27.

5   *After the Boston:* Deborah Kotz, "Injury Toll from Marathon Bombings
Rises," *Boston Globe,* April 23, 2013.

8   *Complexity arises:* The term *complexity* has been defined in many different ways across multiple disciplines, ranging from the amount of
computation required to describe an object (Kolmogorov complexity in
computer science) to the energy flow per second per gram of material
(energy-rate density in physics). We define complexity as an attribute of a
system composed of multiple parts that interact with one another in unpredictable ways. See Jan W. Rivkin, "Imitation of Complex Strategies,"
Management Science 46, no. 6 (2000), for a fuller discussion of system
complexity.

Integrating more parts: Average number of remotes per household from
William Grimes, "Pushing All Our Buttons," *New York Times,* May 30,
2012.

A search for the word: Google Books Ngram viewer, accessed October 12,
2012, http://books.google.com/ngrams.

The upsurge in interest: Warren Weaver, "Science and Complexity,"
American Scientist 36, no. 4 (1948): 536–44.

Warren Weaver is not: Information on Warren Weaver's life and career
from Warren Weaver, *Scene of Change: A Lifetime in American Science*
(New York: Charles Scribner's Sons, 1970); Lily E. Kay, *The Molecular Vision of Life: Caltech, the Rockefeller Foundation, and the Rise of the New
Biology* (New York: Oxford University Press, 1996); Raymond Fosdick,
The Story of the Rockefeller Foundation (New York: Harper & Brothers,
1952); Linus Pauling, "How My Interest in Proteins Developed," *Protein
Science* 2 (1993): 1060–63; and Barbara Marianacci, *Linus Pauling in His
Own Words* (New York: Simon & Schuster, 1995).

9   *Over his three:* Fosdick, *The Story of the Rockefeller Foundation,* 159.

Eighteen scientists: Weaver, *Scene of Change,* 73.

He wrote a seminal: Warren Weaver, "Translation" (unpublished memorandum, Rockefeller Foundation, July 15, 1949), available at Machine
Translation Archive, http://www.mt-archive.info/Weaver-1949.pdf; and
Matt Novak, "The Cold War Origins of Google Translate," *BBC Online,*
May 30, 2012, http://www.bbc.com/future/story/20120529-a-cold-war-

google-translate. Weaver also coauthored, with Claude E. Shannon, *The Mathematical Theory of Communication* (Champaign: University of Illinois Press, 1949), which laid out the principles required to build modern telecommunications networks, including the Internet.

When India and: Justin Gillis, "Norman Borlaug, Plant Scientist Who Fought Famine, Dies at 95," *New York Times,* September 13, 2009.

In his 1948 article: Weaver, "Science and Complexity," 536–44. Weaver used the term *disorganized complexity* to describe problems we call "uncertain," and *organized complexity* to denote those we refer to as "complex." While Weaver's classification is brilliant, his terminology is a bit confusing. For clarity, we use more intuitive terms — such as *simple, uncertain,* and *complex* — to describe Weaver's three categories.

10 *But what about the messy:* The distinction between uncertain and complex problems does not hinge per se on the number of components in the system, but rather on the number of interdependencies among these components. Uncertain problems, in Weaver's words, exist when "the number of variables is very large, and . . . each of the many variables has a behavior which is individually erratic, or perhaps totally unknown . . . in spite of this helter-skelter, or unknown, behavior of all the individual variables, the system as a whole possesses certain orderly and analyzable average properties." Ibid., 538. Complex problems, in contrast, consist of components that do not behave in a random fashion, but rather their behavior is influenced by other parts of the system.

Since the fall: Number of international trade agreements from Karen J. Alter and Sophie Meunier, "The Politics of International Regime Complexity," *Perspectives on Politics* 7, no. 1 (2009): 13–24; and World Trade Organization, "Regional Trade Agreements," June 15, 2014, http://www.wto.org/english/tratop_e/region_e/region_e.htm.

Over the same time: World Bank, "Data: Air Transport, Passengers Carried," accessed January 5, 2013, http://data.worldbank.org/indicator/IS.AIR.PSGR/countries/1W?page=4&display=default.

Capital has followed trade: Correlations on equity returns across forty-eight markets and exposure to foreign debt from Kristin J. Forbes, "The 'Big C': Identifying and Mitigating Contagion" (MIT Sloan Research Paper no. 4970-12, 2012), http://papers.ssrn.com/sol3/papers.cfm?abstract_id=2149908.

11 *And of course the Internet:* World Bank, "Data: Internet Users (Per 100 People)," accessed January 5, 2012, http://data.worldbank.org/indicator/IT.NET.USER.P2.

High default rates: Barry Eichengreen et al., "How the Subprime Crisis Went Global: Evidence from Bank Credit Default Swaps," *Journal of International Money and Finance* 31 (2012): 1299–1318.

12 *In 1988 bankers:* Andrew G. Haldane and Vasileios Madouros, "The Dog and the Frisbee" (speech given at the Federal Reserve Bank of Kansas City's annual economic policy symposium, Jackson Hole, Wyoming, August 31, 2012), www.kansascityfed.org/publicat/sympos/2012/ah.pdf.
Its successor: Ibid., 8.
The policies governing: Arthur B. Laffer, Wayne H. Weingarden, and John Childs, *The Economic Burden Caused by Tax Code Complexity* (Austin, TX: Laffer Center, 2011), 8. Number of books calculated assuming 250 words per page and 250 pages per volume.
And yet, when forty-five: Teresa Tritch, "Why Your Tax Return Could Cost You a Bundle: We Asked 45 Tax Preparers to Fill Out One Hypothetical Family's Tax Return — And We Got 45 Different Answers," *Money,* March 1, 1997, available at *Interesting Texts Preserved for Prosperity,* http://textosdeinteresse.blogspot.com/2008/05/45-tax-preparers-filled-out-for.html.

13 *The tax code is so:* Gordon C. Milbourn, "Customer Service at the Taxpayer Assistance Centers Is Improving but Is Still Not Meeting Expectations" (Memorandum for Commissioner, Wage and Investment Division, U.S. Department of the Treasury, December 28, 2004), http://www.treasury.gov/tigta/auditreports/2005reports/200540021fr.pdf.
To navigate this labyrinth: "Complex U.S. Tax Code Spawns an Industry: More Than a Million Tax Preparers Now Make Their Living Navigating a Complex U.S. Tax Code," Face the Facts USA, George Washington University, March 22, 2013, http://www.facethefactsusa.org/facts/when-tax-complexity-puts-dinner-on-the-table/.
To illustrate how: A standard Lego block is two prongs wide by four prongs long and of a single color. See Bergfinnur Durhuus and Soren Eilers, "On the Entropy of LEGO," *Journal of Applied Mathematics and Computing* 45 (2014): 1–16.
A study of personal: Grant Richardson, "Determinants of Tax Evasion: A Cross-Country Investigation," *Journal of International Accounting, Auditing, and Taxation* 15, no. 2 (2006): 150–69.

14 *According to the:* "Retirement Savings Assessment 2013," Fidelity, accessed January 23, 2014, http://www.fidelity.com/inside-fidelity/individual-investing/fidelity-unveils-new-retirement-preparedness-measure.

When employers offered: Sheena S. Iyengar and Emir Kamenica, "Choice Proliferation, Simplicity Seeking, and Asset Allocation," *Journal of Public Economics* 94, no. 7–8 (2010): 530–39. For a broader review of the related literature, see Roy Yong-Joo Chua and Sheena S. Iyengar, "Empowerment Through Choice? A Critical Analysis of the Effects of Choice in Organizations," *Research in Organizational Behavior* 27 (2006): 41–79.

Overwhelmed by complexity: The perceived complexity of a choice is influenced not only by the number of options, but also by other factors including how the options are categorized, the number of attributes per option, and ease of comparison across options. See Benjamin Scheibehenne, Rainer Greifeneder, and Peter M. Todd, "Can There Ever Be Too Many Options?: A Meta-Analytic Review of Choice Overload," *Journal of Consumer Research* 37 (2010): 409–25.

At present there are: A partial list of journals focused on complex systems include *Complexity, Journal of Complexity, Journal of Systems Science and Complexity, International Journal of Complexity in Applied Science and Engineering, Complex Systems, International Journal of Computational Complexity and Intelligent Algorithms, Emergence: Complexity & Organization, Chaos and Complexity Letters, International Journal of Complexity in Leadership and Management, Journal of Complex Networks, Computational Complexity,* and *Journal on Policy and Complex Systems.* For a partial list of research centers on complex systems see Wikipedia entry on complex systems, at http://en.wikipedia.org/wiki/Complex_systems, accessed June 30, 2014.

15 *Kathy had just:* Shona L. Brown and Kathleen M. Eisenhardt, *Competing on the Edge: Strategy as Structured Chaos* (Boston: Harvard Business Review Press, 1998).

16 *We wrote up:* Kathleen M. Eisenhardt and Donald Sull, "Strategy as Simple Rules," *Harvard Business Review,* January 2001, 107–16.

Simple rules allow: A 2005 study in *Nature* found that Wikipedia articles on scientific topics were nearly as accurate as those found in the *Encyclopaedia Britannica.* See Jim Giles, "Internet Encyclopedias Go Head to Head," *Nature* 438 (2005): 900–901. For a review of studies comparing Wikipedia with encyclopedias across topics and languages, see Imogen Casebourne et al., *Assessing the Accuracy and Quality of Wikipedia Entries Compared to Popular Online Encyclopaedias* (Brighton, UK: EPIC/University of Oxford, 2012), https://commons.wikimedia.org/wiki/File:EPIC_Oxford_report.pdf.

1. WHY SIMPLE RULES WORK

21 *After publishing a string:* Pollan first introduced his simple rules for eating well in Michael Pollan, *In Defense of Food: An Eater's Manifesto* (New York: Penguin Press, 2008).
    Pollan's rules: In a follow-on book, *Food Rules,* Pollan introduced sixty-four variations on his three simple rules. See *Food Rules: An Eater's Manual* (New York: Penguin, 2009).

22 *A comprehensive review:* David L. Katz and Stephanie Meller, "Can We Say What Diet Is Best for Health?" *Annual Review of Public Health* 35 (2014): 83–103.
    To be used: Nelson Cowan, "The Magical Number 4 in Short-Term Memory: A Reconsideration of Mental Storage Capacity," *Behavioral and Brain Sciences* 24, no. 1 (2001): 87–119.
    The National Academy: Committee on Quality of Health Care in America, *Crossing the Quality Chasm: A New Healthcare System for the 21st Century* (Washington, DC: National Academy Press, 2001). The rules for redesigning health-care processes are listed on pages 8–9.
    The panel developed: To be reimbursed for their services, doctors treating Medicare and Medicaid patients must assign a code to every diagnosis and procedure they provide, ranging from administering a flu vaccine to open-heart surgery. The current version of the International Classification of Diseases lists approximately sixty-eight thousand distinct codes, and even that large number does not include outpatient treatment or administrative processes necessary for delivery. "ICD-10 Changes from ICD-9," Medicaid.gov, accessed January 23, 2014, http://www.medicaid.gov/Medicaid-CHIP-Program-Information/By-Topics/Data-and-Systems/ICD-Coding/ICD-10-Changes-from-ICD-9.html.

24 *One of the longest wars in modern history:* Peter Hamish Wilson, *The Thirty Years' War: Europe's Tragedy* (London: Penguin, 2009), 4.

25 *Over 217 million:* Eltjo Buringh and Jan Luiten van Zanden, "Charting the 'Rise of the West': Manuscripts and Printed Books in Europe, a Long-Term Perspective from the Sixth Through Eighteenth Centuries," *Journal of Economic History* 69, no. 2 (2009): 409–45.
    The Catholic Church: John W. O'Malley, *The First Jesuits* (Cambridge, MA: Harvard University Press, 1993), 35.
    Within two decades: John W. Padberg, "Development of the Ratio Studiorum," in *The Jesuit Ratio Studiorum of 1599: 400th Anniversary Perspec-*

tives, edited by Vincent J. Duminunco (New York: Fordham University
Press, 1990), 80.

The Jesuits run: Society of Jesus, *Summary of Statistics 2012* (Rome: Sec-
retariat for Secondary and Pre-Secondary Education, 2012).

26 *The Jesuits' founder:* James van Dyke, *Ignatius Loyola: The Founder of
the Jesuits* (New York: Charles Scribner's Sons, 1927); James Brodrick, *The
Origin of the Jesuits* (1940; repr., Chicago: Loyola University Press, 1997);
Michael Foss, *The Founding of the Jesuits* (New York: Weybright and Tal-
ley, 1969); John Olin, ed., *The Autobiography of St. Ignatius Loyola* (New
York: Fordham University Press, 1992); John W. O'Malley, *The First Jesu-
its* (Cambridge, MA: Harvard University Press, 1993); Victor Hoagland,
The Book of Saints (New York: Regina Press, 1986).

27 *Rules prescribed:* Order of Saint Benedict, "The Rule of Benedict," accessed April 11, 2014, http://www.osb.org/rb/text/toc.html#toc.

The Benedictine's rules: Order of Preachers, "The Primitive Constitutions of the Order of Friars Preachers," accessed February 1, 2014,
http://www.op.org/sites/www.op.org/files/public/documents/fichier/
primitive_consti_en.pdf.

The Jesuits' foundational: Antonio M. de Aldama, *The Formula of the
Institute: Notes for a Commentary,* translated by Ignacio Echaniz (Rome:
Centrum Ignatianum Spiritualitatis, 1990).

The most important rule: Ibid., 8.

28 *The first generation:* John Patrick Donnelly, trans., *Year by Year with
the Early Jesuits (1537–1556): Selections from the "Chronicon" of Juan de
Polanco, S.J.* (St. Louis: Institute of Jesuit Studies, 2004).

Even sympathetic commentators: O'Malley, *The First Jesuits,* 81, 85.

29 *A decade after the order's:* Ibid., 82.

30 *Both flexibility and consistency:* Jason P. Davis, Kathleen M. Eisenhardt,
and Christopher B. Bingham, "Optimal Structure, Market Dynamism,
and the Strategy of Simple Rules," *Administrative Science Quarterly* 54,
no. 3 (2009): 413–52.

Although these errors: Atul Gawande, *The Checklist Manifesto: How to
Get Things Right* (New York: Metropolitan, 2009).

31 *The chain's selling point:* McDonald's has ranked last for seventeen of
the last eighteen years in the American Customer Satisfaction Index. American Customer Satisfaction Index, "Benchmarks by Industry: Limited-Service Restaurants," http://www.theacsi.org/index.
php?option=com_content&view=article&id=147&catid=&Itemid=212&i
=Limited-Service+Restaurants. A 2013 survey of two thousand consum-

ers by Goldman Sachs found McDonald's ranked dead last among twenty-three fast-food chains in food quality, healthfulness, and customers' willingness to pay more for the food. Julie Jargon, "Losing the Taste for McDonald's," *Corporate Intelligence* blog, *Wall Street Journal,* October 15, 2013, http://blogs.wsj.com/corporate-intelligence/2013/10/15/losing-the-taste-for-mcdonalds/. In a separate online survey of twenty-eight hundred consumers, McDonald's burgers ranked last among eighteen fast-food restaurants. "Our Readers Reveal: Best Burgers," *Consumer Reports,* October 2010.

Rather, McDonald's offers: Mona Chalabi and John Burn-Murdoch, "McDonalds 34,492 Restaurants: Where Are They," *Guardian Datablog,* July 17, 2013, http://www.theguardian.com/news/datablog/2013/jul/17/mcdonalds-restaurants-where-are-they.

Nine out of ten McDonald's: Josh Sanborn, "Fast Food Strikes: Unable to Unionize, Workers Borrow Tactics from 'Occupy,'" *Time,* July 30, 2013, http://business.time.com/2013/07/30/fast-food-strikes-unable-to-unionize-workers-borrow-tactics-from-occupy/.

33 *A simple rule:* Brent Snook, Paul J. Taylor, and Craig Bennell, "Geographic Profiling: The Fast, Frugal, and Accurate Way," *Applied Cognitive Psychology* 18, no. 1 (2004): 105–21.

Another study compared: Markus Wuebben and Florian von Wangenheim, "Instant Customer Base Analysis: Managerial Heuristics Often Get It Right," *Journal of Marketing* 72, no. 3 (2008): 82–93.

Other research finds: L. Green and D. R. Mehr, "What Alters Physicians' Decisions to Admit to the Coronary Care Unit?" *Journal of Family Practice* 45, no. 3 (1997): 219–26; Rocio Garcia-Retamero and Mandeep K. Dhami, "Take-the-Best in Expert-Novice Decision Strategies for Residential Burglary," *Psychonomic Bulletin & Review* 16, no. 1 (2009): 163–69.

34 *Fitting a model too:* "Overfitting the data" is shorthand for a model that has high variance, when random noise is mistaken for signal. High variance is a risk when generalizing predictions outside a small sample of a larger population, such as polling a subset of voters, when the cause-and-effect relationships among variables are poorly understood, or when causal relationships shift in unexpected ways over time. Poorly understood causal relationships that shift over time are common among complex social systems. See Stuart Geman, Elie Bienenstock, and René Doursat, "Neural Networks and the Bias/Variance Dilemma," *Neural Computation* 4, no. 1 (1992): 1–58.

IBM recently released: IBM, "IBM Social Media Analysis Points to Lower

Heels, Bucking Economic Trend," press release, November 17, 2011, http://www-03.ibm.com/press/us/en/pressrelease/35985.wss.

Despite their simplicity: Brian J. Eastridge et al., "Field Triage Scores (FTS) in Battlefield Casualties: Validation of a Novel Triage Technique in a Combat Environment," *American Journal of Surgery* 200, no. 6 (2010): 724–27. Emergency room triage practices have also proven robust in civilian settings; see Jolande Elshove-Bolk et al., "Validation of the Emergency Severity Index (ESI) in Self-Referred Patients in a European Emergency Department," *Emergency Medicine Journal* 24, no. 3 (2007): 170–74.

Statisticians have found: Professor Scott Armstrong of the Wharton School reviewed thirty-three studies comparing simple and complex statistical models used to forecast business and economic outcomes. He found no difference in forecasting accuracy in twenty-one of the studies. Sophisticated models did better in five studies, while simple models outperformed complex ones in seven cases. See J. Scott Armstrong, "Forecasting by Extrapolation: Conclusions from 25 Years of Research," *Interfaces* 14 (1984): 52–66. Spyros Makridakis has hosted a series of competitions for statistical models over two decades, and consistently found that complex models fail to outperform simpler approaches. The history of the competitions is summarized in Spyros Makridakis and Michèle Hibon, "The M3-Competition: Results, Conclusions, and Implications," *International Journal of Forecasting* 16, no. 4 (2000): 451–76.

35 *When it comes to modeling*: In statistical terms, a model that closely approximates the underlying function that generates observed data is said to have low bias. Complex models are better able to minimize bias than simple ones. But complex models are also more likely to have high variance because they treat noise as signal. When modeling complex systems where the underlying causality is not understood, every model faces a tradeoff between bias and variance. See Geman et al., "Neural Networks and the Bias/Variance Dilemma."

For example, Kathy: Christopher B. Bingham and Kathleen M. Eisenhardt, "Rational Heuristics: The 'Simple Rules' That Strategists Learn from Process Experience," *Strategic Management Journal* 32, no. 13 (2011): 1437–64.

One study, for example: Timothy D. Wilson and Jonathan W. Schooler, "Thinking Too Much: Introspection Can Reduce the Quality of Preferences and Decisions," *Journal of Personality and Social Psychology* 60, no. 2 (1991): 181–92.

36 *Each entrepreneur:* Alejandro Drexler, Greg Fischer, and Antoinette Schoar, "Keeping It Simple: Financial Literacy and Rules of Thumb," *American Economic Journal: Applied Economics* 6, no. 2 (2014): 1–31.
One study of dieting: Jutta Mata, Peter M. Todd, and Sonia Lippke, "When Weight Management Lasts: Lower Perceived Rule Complexity Increases Adherence," *Appetite* 54, no. 1 (2010): 37–43.

37 *If we deploy:* Roy F. Baumeister and John Tierney, *Willpower: Rediscovering the Greatest Human Strength* (New York: Penguin, 2012).
But research finds: Stefanie J. Salmon et al., "Health on Impulse: When Low Self-Control Promotes Healthy Food Choices," *Health Psychology* 33, no. 2 (2013): 103–9, http://www.medscape.com/medline/abstract/2347758.
In contrast, people: Brian Wansink, David R. Rust, and Collin R. Payne, "Mindless Eating and Healthy Heuristics for the Irrational," *American Economic Review: Papers and Proceedings* 99, no. 2 (2009): 165–69.

38 *Meteorologists make:* Nate Silver, *The Signal and the Noise* (New York: Penguin, 2012), 126–27.

39 *Japanese honeybees:* Atsushi Ugajin et al., "Detection of Neural Activity in the Brains of Japanese Honeybee Workers During the Formation of a 'Hot Defensive Bee Ball,'" *PLoS One* 7, no. 3 (2012), available at the website of the National Center for Biotechnology Information, http://www.ncbi.nlm.nih.gov/pmc/articles/PMC3303784/.
As an example of: Our account of the bees' choice of new nest is based on the research of Thomas Seeley, especially Thomas D. Seeley, *Honeybee Democracy* (Princeton, NJ: Princeton University Press, 2010), and Seeley et al., "Stop Signals Provide Cross Inhibition in Collective Decision-Making by Honeybee Swarms," *Science* 6 (January 2012), 108–11.

42 *Instead, for its first:* Since its acquisition by Avis Budget, Zipcar's six simple rules have been incorporated into fifty-one frequently asked questions, which were themselves organized into ten categories, including "driving rates, billing and fees," "insurance and vehicle damage," and "manual driving record checks." The rules are no longer simple. "No smoking" was stretched out to 26 words (plus an appendix), "pets in carriers" to 73 words, and "return on time" to a 142-word statement of policy. Accessed January 28, 2014, http://www.zipcar.com/how#faqs.
Students might use them: Examples of how people use Zipcars from company website, http://www.zipcar.com/?redirect_p=0, accessed August 4, 2014.
A study of dozens: Emmanuelle Fauchart and Eric von Hippel, "Norms-

Based Intellectual Property Systems: The Case of French Chefs," *Organization Science* 19, no. 2 (2008): 187–201.

43 *One chef explained:* Ibid., 193.
The offending chef: Ibid., 198.

44 *PayPal's terms and conditions:* Rich Parris, "Online T&Cs Longer Than Shakespeare Plays — Who Reads Them?" *Which?* March 23, 2012, http:// conversation.which.co.uk/technology/length-of-website-terms-and-conditions/. With amendments, the U.S. Constitution has about 7,600 words.
Property rights are: This rule is known as the *ad coelum* rule of property.
Simple and clear property: Thomas W. Merrill and Henry E. Smith, "What Happened to Property in Law and Economics," *Yale Law Journal* 111 (2001): 357–98.

2. MAKING BETTER DECISIONS

47 *In most countries:* David Berry, *The Socioeconomic Impact of Pretrial Detention* (New York: Open Society Foundation, 2011).

48 *A study in England:* HM Chief Inspector of Prisons, *Unjust Deserts: A Thematic Review by HM Chief Inspector of Prisons of the Treatment and Conditions for Unsentenced Prisoners in England and Wales* (London: HM Inspectorate of Prisons for England and Wales, 2000).
Prison is often: Barry Holman and Jason Ziedenberg, *The Dangers of Detention: The Impact of Incarcerating Youth in Detention and Other Secure Facilities* (Washington, DC: Justice Policy Institute, 2006).
They also served sentences: Laura and John Arnold Foundation, *Pretrial Criminal Justice Research* (Houston, TX: Laura and John Arnold Foundation, November 2013), http://www.arnoldfoundation.org/sites/default/ files/pdf/LJAF-Pretrial-CJ-Research-brief_FNL.pdf; C. Davies, "Pre-Trial Imprisonment: A Liverpool Study," *British Journal of Criminology* 11, no. 1 (1971): 32–48.
To assess the risks: Marie Van Nostrand and Christopher T. Lowenkamp, *Assessing Pretrial Risk Without a Defendant Interview* (Houston, TX: Laura and John Arnold Foundation, November 2013), http://www. arnoldfoundation.org/sites/default/files/pdf/LJAF_Report_no-interview_FNL.pdf.
Did a previous: Mandeep K. Dhami, "Psychological Models of Profes-

sional Decision Making," *Psychological Science in the Public Interest* 14, no. 2 (2003): 175–80.

50 *Even female hyenas:* Thorsten Pachur and Gianmarco Marinello, "Expert Intuitions: How to Model the Decision Strategies of Airport Customs Officers," *Acta Psychologica* 144, no. 1 (2013): 97–103; Brent Snook and Jamison C. Mercer, "Modeling Police Officers' Judgements of the Veracity of Suicide Notes," *Canadian Journal of Criminology and Criminal Justice* 52, no. 1 (2010): 79–95.

In one study, Texas: Paul Cromwell and James N. Olson, "The Reasoning Burglar: Motives and Decision-Making Strategies," in *In Their Own Words: Criminals on Crime,* edited by Paul Cromwell (New York: Oxford University Press, 2009), http://cooley.libarts.wsu.edu/soc3611/Documents/The_Reasoning_Burglar.pdf.

In a recent study, researchers: Brent Snook, Mandeep K. Dhami, and Jennifer M. Kavanagh, "Simply Criminal: Predicting Burglars' Occupancy Decisions with a Simple Heuristic," *Law and Human Behavior* 35, no. 4 (2011): 316–26.

52 *The agency's ongoing projects:* One Shot XG: DARPA, Adaptive Execution Office, "One Shot XG," accessed July 2014, http://www.darpa.mil/Our_Work/AEO/Programs/One_Shot_XG.aspx; Guinness World Records, "Longest Confirmed Sniper Kill," accessed March 12, 2014, http://www.guinnessworldrecords.com/world-records/12000/longest-confirmed-sniper-kill. Z-Man: DARPA, Defense Sciences Office, "Z-Man," accessed July 2014, http://www.darpa.mil/Our_Work/DSO/Programs/Z_Man.aspx. Brain-controlled prosthetics: DARPA, Biological Technologies Office, "Revolutionizing Prosthetics," http://www.darpa.mil/Our_Work/BTO/Programs/Revolutionizing_Prosthetics.aspx. Robotic horse: DARPA, Tactical Technology Office, "Legged Squad Support System (LS3)," http://www.darpa.mil/Our_Work/TTO/Programs/Legged_Squad_Support_System_(LS3).aspx. Plan X: DARPA, Information Innovation Office, "Plan X," accessed July 2014, http://www.darpa.mil/Our_Work/I2O/Programs/Plan_X.aspx.

They are all the: Sharon Weinberger, "Ten Extraordinary Pentagon Mind Experiments," BBC, March 12, 2013, http://www.bbc.com/future/story/20130311-ten-military-mind-experiments; DARPA, "DARPA's Cheetah Robot Bolts Past the Competition," press release, September 5, 2012, http://www.darpa.mil/NewsEvents/Releases/2012/09/05.aspx.

Its permanent personnel: Regina E. Dugan and Kaigham J. Gabriel, "'Special Forces' Innovation: How DARPA Attacks Problems," *Harvard Business Review* (October 2013), 2–11; U.S. Department of Defense, "Pentagon Tours," accessed January 27, 2014, https://pentagontours.osd.mil/facts.jsp.

Its annual budget: Adam L Penenberg, "Siri-ously DARPA," *Fast-Company,* October 5, 2011, http://www.fastcompany.com/1785221/siri-ously-darpa.

Considering the jaw-gaping: Dugan and Gabriel, "'Special Forces' Innovation."

53 *The model for DARPA's:* Ibid.

Boundary rules are also used: Gerd Gigerenzer, *Calculated Risks: How to Know When Numbers Deceive You* (New York: Simon & Schuster, 2002).

There are, for example: Jorge C. Kattah et al., "HINTS to Diagnose Stroke in the Acute Vestibular Syndrome: Three-Step Bedside Oculomotor Examination More Sensitive Than Early MRI Diffusion-Weighted Imaging," *Stroke* 40, no. 11 (2009): 3504–10.

Consider the case: World Health Organization, "Media Center: Fact Sheets: Depression," October 2012, http://www.who.int/mediacentre/factsheets/fs369/en/.

Symptoms can be as subtle: WebMD, "Symptoms of Depression," accessed March 12, 2014, http://www.webmd.com/depression/guide/detecting-depression.

54 *Patients who answer:* Mirjam A. Jenny et al., "Simple Rules for Detecting Depression," *Journal of Applied Research in Memory and Cognition* 2 (2013): 149–57.

As a physician: G. Gigerenzer et al., "Helping Doctors and Patients Make Sense of Health Statistics," *Psychological Science in the Public Interest* 8 (2007): 53–96.

55 *And the correct answer:* To see why this is true, imagine that 1,000 patients were being screened. One percent of them, or 10, actually have breast cancer. The test picks up on 90 percent of those, meaning 9 have been correctly identified. Of the 990 women who do not have breast cancer, the test falsely says that 9 percent of them do. So 89 women test false positive for breast cancer. In total, 98 women test positive for breast cancer, but only 9 women actually have breast cancer. So only about 9 percent (9 out of 98) of women who test positive for breast cancer actually have it . . . a huge relief for those who test positive.

In a 2013 speech: "Out of the Shadows," *Economist,* June 1, 2013, http://

www.economist.com/news/united-states/21578689-barack-obamas-rules-drones-could-shape-new-global-laws-war-out-shadows?frsc=dg|c.

56 *In 2013, the year Obama:* "Report: Sharp Decline in Confirmed Civilian Casualties by Drone Strikes," Voice of America, January 21, 2014, http://www.voanews.com/content/report-sharp-decline-in-confirmed-civilian-casualties-by-drone-strikes/1834807.html.

The United States has enjoyed: Sarah Kreps and Micah Zenko, "The Next Drone Wars: Preparing for Proliferation," *Foreign Affairs* 93 (2014).

57 *In the late 1990s:* Donald Sull, Fernando Martins, and Andre Delben Silva, "América Latina Logística" (Harvard Business School Case, Cambridge, MA, 2003); Sergio de Azevedo Marques, *Privatização do Sistema Ferroviário Brasileiro* (Sao Paulo: IPEA, 1996).

60 *In the ensuing centuries:* John F. Matthews, *Laying Down the Law: A Study of the Theodosian Code* (New Haven: Yale University Press, 2000): 10–30; James A. Brundage, *The Medieval Origins of the Legal Profession: Canonists, Civilians, and Court* (Chicago: University of Chicago Press, 2010).

The Law of Citations: Alan Watson, *Roman Law & Comparative Law* (Athens: University of Georgia Press, 1991), 82–83.

(1) when the jurists: Papinian was a legendary jurist who, according to the historian Edward Gibbon, possessed "intrepid virtue, which had escaped pure and unsullied from the intrigues of courts, the habits of business, and the arts of his profession." Despite his virtue, Papinian was beheaded and his body was dragged through the streets of Rome. Edward Gibbon, *The History of the Decline and Fall of the Roman Empire* (London: John Murray, 1862).

The Law of Citations: Alan Watson, *Law out of Context* (Athens: University of Georgia Press, 2000), 14. While the "fall" of the western Roman Empire is typically dated at 476 AD, many of the Roman institutions, including its legal system, continued on and the Law of Citations was still in force at least through the time of the Byzantine emperor Justinian, who reigned from 527 to 565 AD.

61 *A typical sentence reads:* Harry Markowitz, "Portfolio Selection," *Journal of Finance* 7, no. 1 (1952): 77–91, http://www.math.ust.hk/~maykwok/courses/ma362/07F/markowitz_JF.pdf.

Markowitz went on: "This Year's Laureates Are Pioneers in the Theory of Financial Economics and Corporate Finance," NobelPrize.org, press release, October 16, 1990, http://www.nobelprize.org/nobel_prizes/economic-sciences/laureates/1990/press.html.

According to this rule: Ran Duchin and Haim Levy, "Markowitz Versus the Talmudic Portfolio Diversification Strategies," *Journal of Portfolio Management* 35, no. 2 (2009): 71–74.

This research ran: Jun Tu and Guofu Zhou, "Markowitz Meets Talmud: A Combination of Sophisticated and Naive Diversification Strategies," *Journal of Financial Economics* 99, no. 1 (2011): 204–15. See table 6 for summary of tests of rules against real data sets.

The 1/N rule earned: Ibid. When provided with twenty years of data, the financial models did a bit better, beating the 1/N rule just over one-third of the time.

62 *Other studies have run:* Victor DeMiguel, Lorenzo Garlappi, and Raman Uppal, "Optimal Versus Naïve Diversification: How Inefficient Is the 1/N Portfolio Strategy," *Review of Financial Studies* 22, no. 5 (2007): 1915–53; Victor DeMiguel et al., "A Generalized Approach to Portfolio Optimization: Improving Performance by Constraining Portfolio Norms," *Management Science* 55, no. 5 (2009): 798–812; Michael Gallmeyer and Marcel Marekwica, "Heuristic Portfolio Trading Rules with Capital Gains Tax," Social Science Research Network, May 18, 2013, http://ssrn.com/abstract=2172396.

Instead, as he later confessed: Jason Zweig, "Investing Experts Urge 'Do as I Say, Not as I Do,'" *Wall Street Journal,* January 3, 2009.

When choosing a mate: Oliver M. Beckers and William E. Wagner Jr., "Mate Sampling Strategy in a Field Cricket: Evidence for a Fixed Threshold Strategy with Last Chance Option," *Animal Behavior* 81, no. 3 (2011): 519–27.

63 *Females directly benefit:* William E. Wagner Jr. and Christopher J. Harper, "Female Life Span and Fertility are Increased by the Ejaculates of Preferred Males," *Evolution* 57, no. 9 (2009): 2054–66.

64 *Studies of cockroaches:* Patricia J. Moore and Allen J. Moore, "Reproductive Aging and Mating: The Ticking of the Biological Clock in Female Cockroaches," *Proceedings of the Natural Academy of Sciences* 98 (2001): 9171–76. For decline in choosiness in other species, see references 15–17 in this article.

65 *Instead, like crickets:* Herbert A. Simon, *Administrative Behavior: A Study of Decision-Making Processes in Administrative Organizations* (New York: Macmillan, 1947).

A well-documented tendency: William Samuelson and Richard Zeckhauser, "Status Quo Bias in Decision Making," *Journal of Risk and Uncertainty* 1, no. 1 (1988): 7–59.

These stay-versus-go: Brigitte C. Madrian and Dennis F. Shea, "The Power of Suggestion: Inertia in 401(k) Participation and Savings Behavior," *Quarterly Journal of Economics* 116, no. 4 (2001): 1149–87; Alexander Kempf and Stefan Ruenzi, "Status Quo Bias and the Number of Alternatives: An Empirical Illustration from the Mutual Fund Industry," *Journal of Behavioral Finance* 7, no. 4 (2006): 204–13.

While images of financiers: Nina Rastogi, "Wall Street Suicides," *Slate,* September 22, 2008, http://www.slate.com/articles/news_and_politics/ explainer/2008/09/wall_street_suicides.html.

The first edition of Loeb's: Peter Krass, ed. *The Book of Investing Wisdom: Classic Writings by Great Stock-Pickers and Legends of Wall Street* (New York: John Wiley & Sons, 1999), http://books.google.com/ books?id=b5GhHdVEoosC&q=Loeb.

66 *"The most important single":* Ibid.

"If you make": Gerald M. Loeb, *The Battle for Investment Survival* (Burlington, VT: Fraser, 1995), 91–92.

When Chicago's civic leaders: Caroline Nye Stevens, "Plan of Chicago: Paris on the Prairie," Blueprint Chicago, December 22, 2009, http://www. blueprintchicago.org/2009/12/22/plan-of-chicago-paris-on-the-prairie/.

But walking through: World Health Organization, "Global Database on Body Mass Index," accessed February 18, 2014, http://apps.who.int/bmi/ index.jsp.

67 *One study suggests:* Brian Wansink, Collin R. Payne, and Pierre Chandon, "Internal and External Cues of Meal Cessation: The French Paradox Redux," *Obesity* 15, no. 12 (2006): 2920–24.

Escalating commitment: For a recent review of the literature on the escalating-commitment error, see Dustin J. Sleesman et al., "Cleaning Up the Big Muddy: A Meta-Analytic Review of the Determinants of Escalation of Commitment," *Academy of Management Journal* 55, no. 3 (2012): 541–62. As applied to NBA players see Barry M. Staw and Ha Hoang, "Sunk Costs in the NBA: Why Draft Order Affects Playing Time and Survival in Professional Basketball," *Administrative Science Quarterly* 40, no. 3 (1995): 474–94.

68 *The founder of one tour:* Michael A. Roberto and Gina M. Carioggia, "Mount Everest—1996" (Harvard Business School Case, Cambridge, MA, 2002), 4.

Against this apparently benign: Jon Krakauer, *Into Thin Air* (New York: Anchor Books, 1998); Broughton Coburn, *Everest: Mountain Without Mercy* (Des Moines, IA: National Geographic, 1997); Anatoli Boukreev and G. Weston DeWalt, *The Climb: Tragic Ambitions on Everest* (New York: St. Martin's Griffin, 1997); Harsimran Julka, "Everyone Has His Own Everest to Climb: Jamling Norway," *Economic Times,* April 10, 2012, http://articles.economictimes.indiatimes.com/2012-04-10/news/31318771_1_jamling-tenzing-norgay-climber-beck-weathers.

3. DOING THINGS BETTER

74 *ESPN, whose flagship:* Kurt Badenhausen, "Why ESPN Is Worth $40 Billion as the World's Most Valuable Media Property," *Forbes,* November 9, 2012, http://www.forbes.com/sites/kurtbadenhausen/2012/11/09/why-espn-is-the-worlds-most-valuable-media-property-and-worth-40-billion/. Value of world's top sport franchises from Kurt Badenhausen, "Real Madrid Tops the World's Most Valuable Sports Teams," *Forbes,* July 15, 2013, http://www.forbes.com/sites/kurtbadenhausen/2013/07/15/real-madrid-tops-the-worlds-most-valuable-sports-teams.
In the early days: Richard Haynes, "'Lobby' and the Formative Years of Radio Sports Commentary, 1935–52," *Sport in History* 29, no. 1 (2009): 25–48. Background on history of sports commentating on BBC from "History of the BBC," accessed February 25, 2014, http://www.bbc.co.uk/historyofthebbc/resources/index.shtml.

76 *How-to rules are:* Norman Maclean, *Young Men and Fire* (Chicago: University of Chicago, 1992).
At the time of the Mann Gulch: Karl E. Weick, "The Collapse of Sensemaking in Organizations: The Mann Gulch Disaster," *Administrative Science Quarterly* 38, no. 4 (1993): 629–52.

77 *A recent study experimented:* Weihua Niu and Dan Liu, "Enhancing Creativity: A Comparison Between Effects of an Indicative Instruction 'To Be Creative' and a More Elaborate Heuristic Instruction on Chinese Student Creativity," *Psychology of Aesthetics, Creativity, and the Arts* 3, no. 2 (2009): 93–98.

78 *Patricia Stokes, a painter:* Patricia D. Stokes, *Creativity from Constraints: The Psychology of Breakthrough* (New York: Springer, 2006).
In the span of two years: Andrew Perry, "What's Eating Jack?," *Guardian,* November 13, 2004, http://www.theguardian.com/music/2004/nov/14/popandrock.thewhitestripes. *Rolling Stone* ranked *White Blood Cells* no. 19 and *Elephant* no. 5 in its "100 Best Albums of the 2000s," http://www.rollingstone.com/music/lists/100-best-albums-of-the-2000s-20110718/

the-white-stripes-elephant-20110707). A *Pitchfork* poll of nearly 28,000 voters ranked *White Blood Cells* no. 22 and *Elephant* no. 21 in its "People's List: Top Albums 1996–2011," http://pitchfork.com/peopleslist/.

"The whole point": David Fricke, "The Mysterious Case of the White Stripes: Jack White Comes Clean," *Rolling Stone,* September 8, 2005, http://www.rollingstone.com/music/news/white-on-white-20050908.

Their breakout album: Jennifer Maerz, "Sister Lover? An Interview with the White Stripes," *Spin,* June 5, 2001, accessed February 26, 2014. http://www.whitestripes.net/articles-show.php?id=04.

79 *"I'm disgusted"*: Josh Eells, "Jack Outside the Box," *New York Times,* April 5, 2012, http://www.nytimes.com/2012/04/08/magazine/jack-white-is-the-savviest-rock-star-of-our-time.html?pagewanted=all&_r=0.

Elmore Leonard was working: Marilyn Stasio, "A Novelist Who Made Crime an Art, and His Bad Guys 'Fun,'" *New York Times,* August 20, 2013, http://www.nytimes.com/2013/08/21/books/elmore-leonard-master-of-crime-fiction-dies-at-87.html?pagewanted=all. Also available at http://www.elmoreleonard.com.

At the prodding: Elmore Leonard, "Easy on the Adverbs, Exclamation Points, and Especially Hooptedoodle," *New York Times,* July 16, 2001, http://www.nytimes.com/2001/07/16/arts/writers-writing-easy-adverbs-exclamation-points-especially-hooptedoodle.html.

80 *Based on their global:* Brown and Eisenhardt, *Competing on the Edge.*

The environment of: Jason P. Davis, Kathleen M. Eisenhardt, and Christopher B. Bingham, "Optimal Structure, Market Dynamism, and the Strategy of Simple Rules," *Administrative Science Quarterly* 54, no. 3 (2009): 413–52.

The more successful firms: Eisenhardt and Sull, "Strategy as Simple Rules."

81 *One journalist commented:* Adam Lashinsky, "Chaos by Design: The Inside Story of Disorder, Disarray and Uncertainty at Google. And Why It's All Part of the Plan. (They Hope)," *Fortune,* October 2, 2006.

Early on, Google formulated: Shona L. Brown, senior vice president of business operations at Google for ten years, interviewed June 5, 2014.

82 *Starlings in flight:* Andrew J. King and David J. T. Sumpter, "Murmurations," *Current Biology* 22, no. 4 (2012): 112–14.

Starlings in vast flights: Richard Holmes, *Coleridge: Early Visions, 1772–1804* (New York: Pantheon Books, 1989), 253.

Edmund Selous, an English naturalist: K. E. L. Simmons, "Edmund Selous (1857–1934): Fragments for a Biography," *IBIS* 126 (1984): 595–96;

and David Lack, "Some British Pioneers in Ornithological Research, 1859–1939," *IBIS* 101 (1959): 71–81.

83 *After three decades:* Edmund Selous, *Thought-transference (or What?) in Birds* (London: Constable & Co, 1931).
Reynolds created avian: Craig Reynolds, "Flocks, Herds, and Schools: A Distributed Behavioral Model," *Computer Graphics* 21 (1987): 25–34.

84 *Behavioral biologists:* Ballerini et al. review the models of collective animal behavior and summarize that all agree on three behavioral rules: "move in the same direction as your neighbors, remain close to them, avoid collisions." Michele Ballerini et al., "Interaction Ruling Animal Collective Behaviour Depends on Topological Rather than Metric Distance: Evidence From a Field Study," *Proceedings of the National Academy of Science USA* 105 (2008): 1232–37.
In flocks, however: C. C. Ioannou, V. Guttal, and I. D. Couzin, "Predatory Fish Select for Coordinated Collective Motion in Virtual Prey," *Science* 337 (2012): 1212–15.
Even today, locusts: Vishwesha Guttal et al., "Cannibalism Can Drive the Evolution of Behavioral Phase Polyphenism in Locusts," *Ecology Letters* 15 (2012): 1158–66.

85 *In 1955 a group:* Janet Coleman, *The Compass: The Improvisational Theatre That Revolutionized American Comedy* (Chicago: University of Chicago Press, 1991). See also "History of the Second City," accessed March 2, 2014, http://www.secondcity.com/history/overview/.

86 *While comedians:* A brief survey of some of the more prominent "rules of improv" reveals a large area of common ground. While most lists contain the odd esoteric rule like "Never underestimate or condescend to your audience," they converge on a handful of rules. See Charna Halpern, Del Close, and Kim Johnson, *Truth in Comedy: The Manual of Improvisation* (Colorado Springs, CO: Meriwether, 1994), and Tina Fey, *Bossypants* (New York: Little, Brown, 2011).

88 *The Exxon Valdez:* Australasian Broadcasting Corporation, "40 Facts About Sleep You Probably Didn't Know," accessed February 6, 2014, http://www.abc.net.au/science/facts/htm.
Thankfully, recent research: Daniel J. Buysse et al., "The Efficacy of Brief Behavioral Treatment for Chronic Insomnia in Older Adults," *Archives of Internal Medicine* 171, no. 10 (2011): 887–95.

89 *Timing rules sometimes:* Kathleen M. Eisenhardt and Shona Brown, "Time Pacing: Competing in Markets That Won't Stand Still," *Harvard Business Review,* March 1998; Connie J. G. Gersick, "Pacing Strategic

Change: The Case of a New Venture," *Academy of Management Journal*
37, no. 1 (1994): 9–45; and M. Anjali Sastry, "Problems and Paradoxes in
a Model of Punctuated Organizational Change," *Administrative Science
Quarterly* 42, no. 2 (1997): 237–75.

Approximately fifty of them: Martin Wikelski et al., "Simple Rules Guide
Dragonfly Migration," *Biology Letters* 2, no. 3 (2006): 325–29.

91 *Take Pixar:* Ed Catmull and Amy Wallace, *Creativity Inc: Overcoming
the Unseen Forces That Stand in the Way of True Inspiration* (New York:
Random House, 2014); Karen Paik, *To Infinity and Beyond: The Story of
Pixar Animation Studios* (London: Virgin Books, 2007); Linda Hill et al.,
Collective Genius: The Art and Practice of Leading Innovation (Boston:
Harvard Business Review Press, 2014).

By getting the right people: Chris Bell, "Pixar's Ed Catmull: Interview,"
Telegraph, April 5, 2014, http://www.telegraph.co.uk/culture/pixar/
10719241. Pixar continues to adjust its timing rules, such as synchroniz-
ing its releases with the summer peak of movie going and occasionally
pausing its rhythm to prioritize movie quality.

92 *Stanford engineering professor:* Riitta Katila and Eric L. Chen, "The Effects of Search Timing on Innovation: The Value of Not Being in Sync
with Rivals," *Administrative Science Quarterly* 53, no. 4 (2008): 593–625.

93 *Nathan Rothschild was very rich:* Niall Ferguson, *The Ascent of Money: A
Financial History of the World* (New York: Penguin Books, 2008); World
Bank, "Data: GDP (current US$)," last modified 2014, http://data.
worldbank.org/indicator/NY.GDP.MKTP.CD.

Initially, SUP's idea: "The Lure of Chilecon Valley," *Economist,* October
13, 2012, http://www.economist.com/node/21564589; Ricardo Geromel,
"Start-Up Chile: Importing Entrepreneurs to Become the Silicon Valley
of Latin America," *Forbes,* October 5, 2012, http://www.forbes.com/sites/
ricardogeromel/2012/10/05; Lynda Applegate et al., "Start-Up Chile: April
2012" (Harvard Business School Case, Cambridge, MA, 2012).

The dream was: Michael Leatherbee and Charles E. Eesley, "Boulevard of
Broken Behaviors: Socio-psychological Mechanisms of Entrepreneurial
Policies" (working paper, Stanford Technology Ventures Program, Stan-
ford University, Stanford, CA, 2014).

The fear was that: Vivek Wadhwa, "Want More Startups? Learn
from Chile," *Bloomberg Businessweek,* April 11, 2012, http://www.
businessweek.com/printer/articles/72608.

94 *The six types of rules:* Interviews and emails during summer 2014 with
Michael Leatherbee, secretary general of Start-Up Chile's advisory board

and assistant professor of entrepreneurship and innovation at Pontificia Universidad Católica de Chile.

95 *In 2010 the first cohort:* Start-Up Chile, CORFO, Government of Chile, accessed September 22, 2014, http://www.startupchile.org.
The SUP startups: Leatherbee and Eesley, "Boulevard of Broken Behaviors."

4. WHERE SIMPLE RULES COME FROM

98 *These are complex:* Average size of a cabbage white butterfly brain is 0.44 mm³. See Emilie C. Snell-Rood, Daniel R. Papaj, and Wulfila Gronenberg, "Brain Size: A Global or Induced Cost of Learning," *Brain, Behavior and Evolution* 73, no. 2 (2009): 111–28, appendix 1.
To see whether butterflies: Guy Pe'er et al., "Response to Topography in a Hilltopping Butterfly and Implications for Modeling Nonrandom Dispersal," *Animal Behavior* 68, no. 4 (October 2004): 825–39.

99 *The Nobel prize–winning:* Friedrich Hayek, "Notes on the Evolution of Systems and Rules of Conduct," in his *Studies in Philosophy, Politics, and Economics* (Chicago: University of Chicago Press, 1967), 66–81.

100 *In one 2005:* Dotan Oliar and Christopher Sprigman, "There's No Free Laugh (Anymore): The Emergence of Intellectual Property Norms and the Transformation of Stand-Up Comedy," *Virginia Law Review* 94, no. 8 (2008): 1797.
Hope was widely accused: Ibid., 1849–50.

101 *In the case of:* Ibid., 1825.

103 *In an insightful article:* Tina Fey, "Lessons from Late Night," *New Yorker,* March 7, 2011.
Indiegogo's rules reflect: Kathy is grateful for the superb research help of Annie Case in comparing Indiegogo and Kickstarter. Christina Farr, "Indiegogo Founder Danae Ringelmann: 'We Will Never Lose Sight of Our Vision to Democratize Finance,'" *Venture Beat,* February 21, 2014, http://venturebeat.com/2014/02/21/; Dan Schawbel, "Slava Rubin on How Indiegogo Has Created Jobs," *Forbes,* October 4, 2012, http://www.forbes.com/sites/danschawbel/2012/10/04/; Jessica Hullinger, "Crowdfunding Clash: How Indiegogo Wants to Kick Kickstarter's @$$," *Fiscal Times,* May 30, 2014, http://thefiscaltimes.com/Articles/2014/05/30.
Parenting is another domain: Diane Sonntag, "10 Golden Rules of Positive Parenting," accessed July 31, 2014, http://www.babyzone.com/kids/

positive-parenting_222185; Alyssa S. Fu and Hazel Rose Markus, "My Mother and Me: Why Tiger Mothers Motivate Asian Americans but Not European Americans," *Personality and Social Psychology Bulletin* 40 (2014): 739–49.

104 *In a study she conducted:* Leslie A. Perlow, "The Time Famine: Toward a Sociology of Work Time," *Administrative Science Quarterly* 44, no. 1 (1999): 57–81.

106 *When people face an unfamiliar situation:* Giovanni Gavetti, Daniel A. Levinthal, and Jan W. Rivkin, "Strategy Making in Novel and Complex Worlds: The Power of Analogy," *Strategic Management Journal* 26, no. 8 (2005): 691–712; Giovanni Gavetti and Jan W. Rivkin, "How Strategists Really Think: Tapping the Power of Analogy," *Harvard Business Review,* April 2005; Michael Shayne Gary, Robert E. Wood, and Tracey Pillinger, "Enhancing Mental Models, Analogical Transfer, and Performance in Strategic Decision Making," *Strategic Management Journal* 33, no. 11 (2012): 1229–46.

In 1997 Reed Hastings was annoyed: Willy Shih, Stephen Kaufman, and David Spinola, "Netflix" (Harvard Business School Case, Cambridge, MA, 2007).

107 *A cross-disciplinary team:* Atsushi Tero et al., "Rules for Biologically Inspired Adaptive Network Design," *Science* 327, no. 5964 (2010), 439–42.

108 *Yet occasionally the slime:* Toshiyuki Nakagak, Hiroyasu Yamada, and Agota Toth, "Intelligence: Maze-Solving by an Amoeboid Organism," *Nature* 47 (2000); Tetsu Saigusa et al., "Amoebae Anticipate Periodic Events," *Physical Review Letters* 100 (2008); John Tyler Bonner, "Brainless Behavior: A Myxomycete Chooses a Balanced Diet," *Proceedings of the National Academy of Science* 107 (2010): 5267–68.

109 *They have enough collective intelligence:* Termites are another example of social insects as a source of simple rules. Jonathan Amos, "Termites Inspire Robot Builders," *BBC News,* February 13, 2014, http://www.bbc.com/news/science-environment-26025566.

Roomba, a vacuum cleaner: Alan S. Brown, "From Simple Rules, Complex Behavior," *Mechanical Engineering* 131 (2009): 22–27.

In one study: Thomas Gilovich, "Seeing the Past in the Present: The Effect of Associations to Familiar Events on Judgments and Decisions," *Journal of Personality and Social Psychology* 40, no. 5 (1981): 797–808.

111 *Well under 1 percent:* Ann Van den Bruel et al., "Diagnostic Value of Clinical Features at Presentation to Identify Serious Infection in Developed Countries: A Systematic Review," *Lancet* 375 (2010): 834–45.

112 *California passed a law:* California Department of Fish and Wildlife, "Introduction to the Marine Life Protection Act," accessed December 6, 2012, http://www.dfg.ca.gov/mlpa/intro.asp#q1; Christopher M. Weible, Paul A. Sabatier, and Mark N. Lubell, "A Comparison of a Collaborative and Top-Down Approach to the Use of Science in Policy: Establishing Marine Protected Areas in California," *Policy Studies Journal* 32, no. 2 (2004): 187–207; Christopher M. Weible and Paul A. Sabatier, "Comparing Policy Networks: Marine Protected Areas in California," *Policy Studies Journal* 33, no. 2 (2005): 181–202.

One study, for example: Eric Eisenhardt, "Effect of the San Juan Islands Marine Preserves on Demographic Patterns of Nearshore Rocky Reef Fish" (master's thesis, University of Washington, 2001).

115 *James Buchanan:* For a concise summary of Buchanan's argument, see Geoffrey Brennan and James M. Buchanan, *The Reason of Rules: Constitutional Political Economy* (New York: Cambridge University Press, 1985).

The southern resident killer whales: Deborah A. Giles and Kari L. Koski, "Managing Vessel-Based Killer Whale Watching: A Critical Assessment of the Evolution from Voluntary Guidelines to Regulations in the Salish Sea," *Journal of International Wildlife Law & Policy* 15 (2012): 125–51.

116 *The southern residents' favorite meal:* An interview with Lynne Barre of National Marine Fisheries Service on July 31, 2014, as well as follow-up emails, clarified this example. We thank Lynne for her gracious help. See also the *Final Environmental Assessment: New Regulations to Protect Killer Whales from Vessel Effects in the Inland Waters of Washington* (National Marine Fisheries Service, Northwest Region, November 2010).

After determining the need: To evaluate the need for regulation, NOAA started with a notice of proposed rule-making to gather initial information from the public on whether regulations were needed and what type of rules would be appropriate. This was helpful in gathering information, gauging acceptance, and being transparent.

117 *NOAA settled on:* Ibid. NOAA used a very effective "stop sign" analogy to communicate its rationale for the rules; in other words, the regulations apply to all watercraft, just as stop signs apply to all modes of transport—bikes, cars, buses, and trucks—on roads. In the final regulations, exemptions were, however, made for cargo ships in shipping lanes, commercial and tribal fishermen actively fishing, and certain government and scientific vessels with permits. Otherwise, the rules are the same for all watercraft.

5. STRATEGY AS SIMPLE RULES

119 *Yoni Assia was only:* Donald Sull and Yonatan Puterman, "eToro: Simple Rules (A)," London Business School case study and author's interview with eToro executives, 2012.

121 *In 2014 the YPO:* Young Presidents' Organization, http://www.ypo. org/, accessed August 2, 2014. The median YPO member has $41 million in revenues and 250 employees. The YPO, however, also includes large enterprises with billions in revenues and thousands of employees, which explains why the combined employees and revenue exceed the median numbers multiplied by the number of members.

The simple rules program: For a good overview of action research, see David Bargal, "Personal and Intellectual Influences Leading to Lewin's Paradigm of Action Research," *Action Research* 4, no. 4 (2009): 367–88.

122 *In a recent survey of over four hundred:* Linda Barrington, *CEO Challenge 2010: Top Ten Challenges,* report no. R-1461-10-RR (New York: Conference Board, February 2010). The CEO challenge consists of eighty-four challenges that CEOs rate on a six-point scale ranging from 0 (not applicable) to 5 (my greatest concern). The sample consisted of 444 CEOs.

A separate survey of one thousand: Gary L. Neilson, Karla L. Martin, and Elizabeth Powers, "The Secrets to Successful Strategy Execution," *Harvard Business Review,* June 2008, 61–70.

Our 2001 Harvard Business Review *article:* Eisenhardt and Sull, "Strategy as Simple Rules," and Donald Sull and Kathleen M. Eisenhardt, "Simple Rules for a Complex World," *Harvard Business Review,* September 2012.

125 *When asked to list:* Unpublished results of survey conducted by Donald Sull and Rebecca Homkes. As of June 2014, 7,577 managers responsible for executing strategy across 249 companies were asked to list their company's top three to five objectives over the following few years. On average only 52 percent of these managers listed the same top priority for the company. Donald Sull, Rebecca Homkes, and Charles Sull, "Why Strategy Execution Unravels — And What to Do About It," *Harvard Business Review,* March 2015.

Economic value is: Adam M. Brandenburger and Harborne W. Stuart, "Value-Based Business Strategy," *Journal of Economics & Management Strategy* 5, no. 1 (1996): 5–24. Strategy is about both how a firm creates economic value and how it captures that value in the face of competition. Much of the research in the strategy field focuses on how to capture value through barriers to entry, bargaining power, or resources and capabilities. In practice, however, we found that managers struggled to articulate how they could create economic value in the first place, which renders capturing and sustaining it a moot point. Thus our analysis centered on value creation, with value capture introduced later in the discussions.

126 *For another example of:* Donald Sull and Uri Meirovich, "Primekss: Simple Rules for Selecting Partners," London Business School case study and author's interview with Primekss executives, 2012.

127 *When Janis looked for:* Facts on concrete from James Mitchell Crow, "The Concrete Conundrum," *Chemistry World,* March 2008, 62–66; and Nobuo Tanaka and Bjorn Stigson, *Cement Technology Roadmap 2009* (Paris: International Energy Agency, 2009).

128 *How will we provide:* These three questions (or close variants) have been used to articulate a company's strategy for decades. See Constantinos Markides, *All the Right Moves: A Guide to Crafting Breakthrough Strategy* (Boston: Harvard Business School Press, 2000).

129 *Consider, for example, the case:* Author's interviews with Zatisi executives.
Sanjiv went on: The Zatisi Group's restaurants were ranked first (Bellevue Restaurant), sixth (Mlynec Restaurant), and seventh (V Zatisi Wine Restaurant) on the "Best Restaurants in Prague" list on http://www.pragueexperience.com/restaurants/highlights/restaurants_best.asp, accessed April 29, 2014.

132 *By focusing on:* In January 2012 eToro's leading trader (user name NMarijus, from Lithuania) had 2,868 followers. The leading trader in July 2014 (Malsolo, from Spain) was followed by 140,000 traders. Data from https://openbook.etoro.com, accessed July 31, 2014.

133 *This was the approach:* Author's interviews with Grupo Multimedia executives.

134 *Consider Weima:* Donald Sull and Mohsin Drabu, "Developing Simple Rules at Weima Maschinenbau," London Business School case study and author's interviews with Weima executives, 2012.

136 *Consider, as an example, the VLS-Group:* Donald Sull, Assaf Shlush, and Ido Hochman, "VLS: Prioritizing Projects in a Turnaround," London Business School case study and author's interviews with VLS executives, 2011.

138 *A close look at:* Herkimer Corporation is a fictitious name for a YPO company that requested anonymity, and Victor Belmondo is a pseudonym.

141 *Frontier Dental:* Author's interviews with Frontier executives.

6. GETTING PERSONAL

147 *Increasing these activities:* The upper needle, as we use the term, corresponds to activities that increase what psychologists call *positive affect,* or the extent to which a person feels happy, energized, and engaged versus lethargic or sad. The lower needle corresponds to *negative affect,* characterized by anxiety, stress, or fear versus a sense of calm or serenity. See David Watson, Lee Anna Clark, and Auke Tellegen, "Development and Validation of Brief Measures of Positive and Negative Affect: The PANAS Scales," *Journal of Personality and Social Psychology* 54, no. 6 (1988): 1063–70.

152 *In his book* Slim by Design: Brian Wansink, *Slim by Design: Mindless Eating Solutions for Everyday Life* (New York: William Morrow, 2014).

160 *He found an analysis:* Christian Rudder, "Exactly What To Say In A First Message," OkCupid, accessed July 9, 2014, http://blog.okcupid.com/ index.php/online-dating-advice-exactly-what-to-say-in-a-first-message.

162 *Extensive evidence has established:* For recent and comprehensive reviews that document the benefits of cognitive behavioral therapy, see Stefan G. Hofmann et al., "The Efficacy of Cognitive Behavioral Therapy: A Review of Meta-analyses," *Cognitive Therapy and Research* 36, no. 5 (2012): 427–40; and David F. Tolin, "Is Cognitive-Behavioral Therapy More Effective Than Other Therapies?: A Meta-Analytic Review," *Clinical Psychology Review* 30, no. 6 (2010): 710–20.

166 *Daniel searched Amazon:* Olivia Fox Cabane, *The Charisma Myth: How Anyone Can Master the Art and Science of Personal Magnetism* (New York: Portfolio Trade, 2013).

7. RULES FOR IMPROVEMENT

171 *To understand the importance:* Gerardo A. Okhuysen and Kathleen M. Eisenhardt, "Integrating Knowledge in Groups: How Formal Interventions Enable Flexibility," *Organization Science* 13, no. 4 (2002): 370–86.

173 *Shannon Turley was:* Much of the material on Shannon Turley is drawn from interviews on March 12, 2014, and July 1, 2014. Kathy appreciates the superb assistance of Andrew Stutz in understanding and writing about Stanford's training program. See also Greg Bishop, "Stanford's Distinct Training Regimen Redefines Strength," *New York Times,* December 31, 2013, http://www.nytimes.com/2013/12/31/sports/

ncaafootball; Max Rausch, "How to Build a Bully: Inside the Stanford Football Strength Program," BleacherReport.com, August 16, 2013, http://bleacherreport.com/articles/1739903; Joseph Beyda, "Turley Named NSCA Coach of the Year," *Stanford Daily*, November 20, 2013, http://www.stanforddaily.com/2013/11/20; and Tom FitzGerald, "Stanford Strength Coach Helps Players Avoid Injuries," *SFGate*, December 28, 2013, http://www.sfgate.com/collegesports/article/Stanford-strength-coach-helps-players-avoid-5098841.php. Winston Shi wrote a three-article series on Turley for the *Stanford Daily*: "Shannon Turley, Part I: Sometimes It Rains," *Stanford Daily*, April 22, 2013, http://www.stanforddaily.com/2013/04/22; "Shannon Turley, Part II: It Pays to Be Different," April 24, 2013, http://www.stanforddaily.com/2013/04/24; and "Shannon Turley, Part III: The Student Teaches the Master," April 26, 2013, http://www.stanforddaily.com/2013/04/26.

178 *The team had only won:* Beyda, "Turley Named NSCA Coach of the Year"; and Bishop, "Stanford's Distinct Training Regimen Redefines Strength."

180 *Chris Bingham, a professor:* Christopher B. Bingham and Kathleen M. Eisenhardt, "Rational Heuristics: The 'Simple Rules' that Strategists Learn from Process Experience," *Strategic Management Journal* 32, no. 13 (2011): 1437–64.

181 *They lack the information:* Daniel Kahneman, *Thinking Fast and Thinking Slow* (New York: Farrar, Straus and Giroux, 2011). See also Amos Tversky and Daniel Kahneman, "Judgment Under Uncertainty: Heuristics and Biases," *Science* 185, no. 4157 (1974): 1124–31.

184 *This pattern of improving:* Paul J. Feltovich, Michael J. Prietula, and K. Anders Ericsson, "Studies of Expertise from Psychological Perspectives," in *Cambridge Handbook of Expertise and Expert Performance,* edited by K. A. Ericsson et al. (New York: Cambridge University Press, 2006); K. Anders Ericsson and Neil Charness, "Expert Performance: Its Structure and Acquisition," *American Psychologist* 49, no. 8 (1994): 725–47; Chess: William G. Chase and Herbert A. Simon, "Perception in Chess," *Cognitive Psychology* 1 (1973): 33–81; Herbert A. Simon and William G. Chase, "Skill in Chess," *American Scientist* 61 (1973): 394–403; Neil Charness et al., "The Perceptual Aspect of Skilled Performance in Chess: Evidence from Eye Movements," *Memory and Cognition* 29 (2001): 1146–52. Bridge: Neil Charness, "Components of Skill in Bridge," *Canadian Journal of Psychology* 33 (1979): 1–50. Physics: Michelene T. H. Chi, Paul J. Feltovich, and Robert Glaser, "Categorization of Physics Problems by Experts and Novices," *Cognitive Science* 5 (1981): 121–52. Firefighters: Gary Klein,

Sources of Power: How People Make Decisions (Cambridge, MA: MIT Press, 1998). Entrepreneurship: Robert A. Baron and Michael D. Ensley, "Opportunity Recognition as the Detection of Meaningful Patterns: Evidence from Comparisons of Novice and Expert Entrepreneurs," *Management Science* 52 (2006): 1331–44. Time: Jamie S. North et al. "Perceiving Patterns in Dynamic Action Sequences: Investigating the Processes Underpinning Stimulus Recognition and Anticipation Skill," *Applied Cognitive Psychology* 23 (2009): 878–94. Chunking: Nelson Cowan, "The Magical Number 4 in Short-Term Memory: A Reconsideration of Mental Storage Capacity," *Behavioral and Brain Sciences* 24 (2001): 87–185; K. Anders Ericsson, Vimla L. Patel, and Walter Kintsch, "How Experts' Adaptation to Representative Task Demands Account for the Expertise Effect in Memory Recall: Comment on Vicente and Wang (1998)," *Psychological Review* 107 (2000): 578–92.

186 *When Chris and Kathy:* Professor Nathan Furr joined our team and helped immensely in understanding the financial performance implications of simple rules for internationalizing entrepreneurs. Christopher B. Bingham, Kathleen M. Eisenhardt, and Nathan R. Furr, "What Makes a Process a Capability? Heuristics, Strategy, and Effective Capture of Opportunities," *Strategic Entrepreneurship Journal* 1, no. 1–2 (2007): 27–47.

187 *Teams that consistently met:* Christopher B. Bingham and Jerayr (John) Haleblian, "How Firms Learn Heuristics: Uncovering Missing Components of Organizational Learning," *Strategic Entrepreneurship Journal* 6, no. 2 (2012): 152–77.

Victoria Coren Mitchell: Megan Gibson, "How Europe's First Female Poker Champ Made History and Learned How to Compete with the Guys," *Time*, April 23, 2014, http://time.com/tag/profiles/.

188 *As she recalls:* Ibid.

Although she is now: Ibid.

Poker is a game: Kyle Siler, "Social and Psychological Challenges of Poker," *Journal of Gambling Studies* 26, no. 3 (2010): 401–20.

The results of any: Steven D. Levitt and Thomas J. Miles, "The Role of Skill Versus Luck in Poker: Evidence from the World Series of Poker" (working paper, National Bureau of Economic Research, May 2011).

The best players: Gibson, "How Europe's First Female Poker Champ Made History."

Raghu grew up: Raghu's story is based on interviews with him on March 17, 2014, and June 6, 2014, emails, and other conversations. At his request, we have used a pseudonym for him, and changed some identifying details. Raghu would like readers to know that he spent his college summers working as an intern with a consulting firm in Dubai, at a tech startup, and with a winemaker in Clovis, California, and that the web-application assignment was for CS 142.

189 *The poker-playing grad students*: Kathy thanks Bob Eberhart for significantly improving her strategic knowledge of poker.

191 *He also learned*: Keeping opponents off-balance by switching these strategies is also recommended by poker coach Corwin Cole. Corwin Cole, "Unpredictability Keeps Opponents Off Balance," *San Jose Mercury News*, April 18, 2014.

192 *Professor Melissa Schilling*: Melissa A. Schilling et al., "Learning by Doing Something Else: Variation, Relatedness, and the Learning Curve," *Management Science* 49, no. 1 (2003): 139–56.

193 *Maybe you even know*: Alex Konrad and Ryan Mac, "Airbnb Cofounders to Become First Sharing Economy Billionaires as Company Nears $10 Billion Valuation," *Forbes*, March 20, 2014, http://www.forbes.com/sites/alexkonrad/2014/03/20/.

You may not, however: Kathy especially thanks Florence Koskas for sharing her thoughts and bibliography. Two revealing firsthand video accounts from the founders are "1000 Days of Airbnb, Airbnb Founder — Brian Chesky — Startup School 2010," 2010, www.youtube.com, accessed September 19, 2014; and "Joe Gebbia — The Airbnb Story," 2013, www.youtube.com, accessed September 19, 2014. See also Matt Vella and Ryan Bradley, "Airbnb CEO — 'Grow Fast but not Too Fast,'" *Fortune*, July 18, 2012, http://fortune.com/2012/07/18/.

194 *Joe Gebbia and Brian Chesky*: Jared Tame, "From Toilet Seats to $1 Billion: Lessons from Airbnb's Brian Chesky," in *Startups Open Sourced: Stories to Inspire & Educate*, May 30, 2011.

When the two friends: Jessica Salter, "Airbnb: The Story Behind the $1.3bn Room-Letting Website," *Telegraph*, September 7, 2012, http://www.telegraph.co.uk/technology/news/9525267/Airbnb-The-story-behind-the-1.3bn-room-letting-website.html.

195 *Because of the success*: Ibid.

Y Combinator is a "seed accelerator": Benjamin L. Hallen, Christopher B. Bingham, and Susan L. Cohen, "Do Accelerators Accelerate? A Study of Venture Accelerators as a Path to Success" (working paper, University of Washington, Seattle, 2013).

At this point: Paul Graham, October 2013, "What Happens at Y Combinator," http:// ycombinator.com/atyc.html, accessed April 28, 2014;

and Freedman, 2013, "YC Without Being in YC," http://blog.42floors.com, accessed April 28, 2014. Firsthand account of how former Y Combinator entrepreneurs mimicked the Y Combinator experience by pretending that they had just been accepted again.

196 *Another way of learning:* Derek Thompson, "Airbnb CEO Brian Chesky on Building a Company and Starting a Sharing Revolution," *Atlantic,* August 13, 2013, http://www.theatlantic.com/business/archive/2013/08/airbnb-ceo-brian-chesky-on-building-a-company-and-starting-a-sharing-revolution/278635/.
As Brian recalled: Ibid.
Like clockwork: Tame, "From Toilet Seats to $1 Billion."

197 *The founders coupled these:* Jessie Hempel, "More Than a Place to Crash," *Fortune,* May 3, 2012, http://fortune.com/2012/05/03/airbnb-more-than-a-place-to-crash/.
The founders also had: Vella and Bradley, "Airbnb CEO — 'Grow Fast but not Too Fast.'"
Airbnb ended up with: Tomio Geron, "Airbnb Hires Joie de Vivre's Chip Conley as Head of Hospitality," *Forbes,* September 17, 2013, http://www.Forbes.com/sites/tomiogeron/2013/09/17.
In fact, Airbnb: Salter, "Airbnb: The Story Behind the $1.3bn Room-Letting Website."

198 *Airbnb has become:* Thompson, "Airbnb CEO Brian Chesky on Building a Company and Starting a Sharing Revolution."

8. BREAKING THE RULES

199 *When spring arrived:* "Politics Drowns Water Bonds," *San Jose Mercury News,* March 23, 2014.
After three years: Josh Richman and Paul Rogers, "Brown Declares California Drought Emergency," *San Jose Mercury News,* January 17, 2014, http://www.mercurynews.com/science/ci_24933924/.
Much of California: Heidi Gildemeister, "What Is a Mediterranean Climate?," Mediterranean Garden Society, http://www.mediterranean gardensociety.org/climate.html; Olivier Filippi, "Drought: Introduction," Mediterranean Garden Society, http://www.mediterraneangardensociety.org/drought.html.

201 *Rather, as Chris Woods:* Debbie Arlington, "Garden Reimagined," *San Jose Mercury News,* March 22, 2014.

She read Mediterranean: Leslie Griffy, "Seeing Is Believing: Low-Water Natives Are Easy on the Eye," *San Jose Mercury News,* April 19, 2014.

She stumbled on insights: David Beauliu, "Drought-Tolerant Perennials," About.com Landscaping, accessed March 22, 2014, http://landscaping. about.com/cs/landscapeplans/a/drought_plan.html.

Emily's most critical insight: Gildemeister, "What Is a Mediterranean climate?"

202 *Another stipulated:* "The All-Container Garden," *Sunset Magazine,* April 2014, p. 42.

The rhythm of: Filippi, "Drought: Introduction."

203 *Since they are dormant:* Ibid.

204 *The right choice is often:* For a review of relevant research, see Nicolaj Siggelkow, "Change in the Presence of Fit: The Rise, the Fall and the Renaissance of Liz Claiborne," *Academy of Management Journal,* 44, no. 4 (2001): 838–57.

205 *Alderson, a former Marine:* Michael Lewis, *Moneyball: The Art of Winning an Unfair Game* (New York: W. W. Norton, 2004).

These and other insights: Ibid.

206 *Enter Farhan Zaidi:* Susan Slusser, "A Beautiful Mind," *San Jose Mercury News,* February 5, 2014. As this book went into production, the L.A. Dodgers hired away Zaidi to be their general manager, to the dismay of A's fans.

As his boss, Billy Beane: Ibid.

After the collapse: David Laurila, "Sloan Analytics: Farhan Zaidi on A's Analytics," accessed September 27, 2014, http://www.fangraphs.com/blogs/sloan-analytics-farhan-zaidi-on-as-analytics/print/.

At Zaidi's urging: Slusser, "A Beautiful Mind." The five tools are described more fully in Michael Lewis's book *Moneyball.*

207 *One was a how-to rule:* Alexander Smith, "Billy Beane's Finest Work Yet: How the Oakland A's Won the AL West," BleacherReport.com, October 19, 2012, http://bleacherreport.com/articles/1377486.

The two of them: Andrew Brown, "A's Platoon System New Moneyball," SwinginA's.com, September 20, 2013, http://swinginas.com/2013/09/23.

208 *In 2013, they added:* Rob Neyer, "Those A's Found Another Edge?", December 31, 2013, *Baseball Nation,* accessed March 22, 2014, http://www.sbnation.com/2013/12/31/5261940/oakland-athletics-moneyball-platoon-switch-hitters-flyball.

In fact, the A's: Andrew Koo, "A Decade after *Moneyball,* Have the A's Found a New Market Efficiency?," accessed July 23, 2014, http://

regressing.deadspin.com/a-decade-after-moneyball-have-the-as-found-a-new-mark-1489963694.

As journalist Tim: Tim Kawakami, "Beane, Staff Become Experts at Playing the Roster Game," May 23, 2014, *San Jose Mercury News.*

209 *At the turn of the twentieth:* David Roberts, "Into the Unknown," *National Geographic,* January 2013, pp. 120–34.

To be first: Roland Huntsford, *The Last Place on Earth* (New York: Modern Library, 1999).

210 *As the trek:* Ibid.

First, Scott could: Ibid.

211 *In a telling quote:* Ibid. p. 379.

A key to getting unstuck: Christopher B. Bingham and Jerayr (John) Haleblian, "How Firms Learn Heuristics: Uncovering Missing Components of Organizational Learning," *Strategic Entrepreneurship Journal* 6, no. 2 (2012): 152–77.

212 *Yet after returning:* Robert Falcon Scott, *Voyage of Discovery* (London: Chatham Publishing, 1905), as cited in Huntsford, *The Last Place on Earth.*

Research indicates that: See, for evidence and a research review, Bingham and Haleblian, "How Firms Learn Heuristics," and Amy C. Edmondson, Richard H. Bohmer, and Gary P. Pisano, "Disrupted Routines: Team Learning and New Technology Implementation in Hospitals," *Administrative Science Quarterly* 46, no. 4 (2001): 685–716.

People are more likely: Ibid.

As one account notes: Huntsford, *The Last Place on Earth,* 161.

213 *When* Cheers, *set:* Dave Nemetz, "'*Cheers*' 30th Anniversary: What You Never Knew About the Show," *Yahoo TV,* September 29, 2012, https://tv.yahoo.com/news-cheers'-30th-anniversary:what-you-never-knew-about-the-show.html; "The Best TV Show That's Ever Been," *Gentlemen's Quarterly,* October 2012, http://www.gq.com/entertainment/movies-and-tv/201210/cheers-oral-history-extended/.

214 Cheers *writers used:* Much of this material is drawn from interviews with Cheri Steinkellner (a former writer for *Cheers*), with Nick Manousos, and with Kathy on June 17, 2014. We appreciate Cheri's gracious and wise insights as well as Nick Manousos's superb help in improving Kathy's understanding of writing for television and movies. See also Angelique Dakkak, "'*Cheers*' Writer on Comedy" *Stanford Daily,* February 4, 2014.

215 *During its long run:* Bruce Fretts and Matt Roush, "TV Guide Magazine's 60 Best Series of All Time," *TV Guide,* December 23, 2013,

http://www.tvguide.com/news/tv-guide-magazine-60-best-series-1074962.aspx.

216 *In March 2011:* Kate Stanhope, "Netflix and Kevin Spacey on Deck with *House of Cards*," *TV Guide,* March 15, 2011, http://www.tvguide.com/News/Netflix-Kevin-Spacey-1030752.aspx?rss=breakingnews.

After the advent: Hope Reese, "Why Is the Golden Age of TV So Dark?," July 2013, *Atlantic,* http://www.theatlantic.com/entertainment/archive/2013/07/why-is-the-golden-age-of-tv-so-dark/277696/.

Procedural dramas like: Nellie Andreeva, "Full 2011–2012 TV Season Series Rankings," *Deadline.com,* http://www.deadline.com/2012/05/full-2011-2012-tv-season-series-rankings/.

217 *In the series premiere:* Adam Sternbergh, "The Post-Hope Politics of 'House of Cards.'" *New York Times,* February 2, 2014, http://www.nytimes.com/2014/02/02/magazine/.

218 *Fincher loved the BBC version:* Nev Pierce, "David Fincher Exclusive: The Making of *House of Cards*," *Empire Magazine,* March 2013, http://www.empireonline.com/interviews/interview.asp?IID=1636/.

Netflix and its partners: Robert Abele, "Playing with a New Deck," Director's Guild of America, http://www.dga.org/Craft/DGAQ/All-Articles/1301-Winter-2013/House-of-Cards.aspx.

219 *As one pundit claims:* David Carr, "Giving Viewers What They Want," *New York Times,* February 25, 2013, http://www.nytimes.com/2013/02/25/business/media/for-house-of-cards-using-big-data-to-guarantee-its-popularity.html.

Its analytics, for instance: Ibid.

220 *The company had data:* Ibid.

Netflix has, however: Robert I. Sutton and Hayagreeva Rao, *Scaling Up Excellence* (New York: Crown, 2014).

CONCLUSION

222 *In addition to keeping:* When Janet Yellen took office, unemployment stood at ten million. Federal Reserve Bank of St. Louis, Economic Database, "Graph: Unemployed," accessed July 17, 2014, http://research.stlouisfed.org/fred2/graph/?id=UNEMPLOY.

"Long-term unemployment": Janet L. Yellen, "A Painfully Slow Recovery for America's Workers: Causes, Implications, and the Federal Reserve's

Response" (transcript of speech delivered at Trans-Atlantic Agenda for Shared Prosperity conference, sponsored by AFL-CIO, Friedrich Ebert Stiftung, and the IMK Macroeconomic Policy Institute, Washington, DC, February 11, 2013), p. 10.

223 *And yet, within three months:* Janet L. Yellen, "Monetary Policy and Economic Recovery" (speech at the Economic Club of New York, New York, April 16, 2014); and Craig Torres, "Yellen's Mind-the-Gap Goals Rule Says Rates Stay Low," Bloomberg.com, April 16, 2014, http://www.bloomberg.com/news/2014-04-16/yellen-says-rates-to-stay-low-as-long-as-jobs-price-gaps-remain.html.

Within a few years: Pier Francesco Asso, George A. Kahn, and Robert Leeson, "The Taylor Rule and the Practice of Central Banking" (research working paper, RWP 10-05, Federal Reserve Bank of Kansas City, February 2010).

In fifteenth-century Europe: Oliver Volckart and David Chilosi, "Money, States and Empire: Financial Integration and Institutional Change in Central Europe, 1400–1520," *Journal of Economic History* 71, no. 3 (2011): 762–91.

Under pressure from merchants: Oliver Volckart, "Rules, Discretion, or Reputation? Monetary Policies and the Efficiency of Financial Markets in Germany, 14th to 16th Centuries" (SFB Discussion Paper 649, Sonderforschungsbereich, Humboldt University, Berlin, February 2007).

As England's master: Walter Eltis, "Lord Overstone and the Establishment of British Nineteenth-Century Monetary Orthodoxy" (working paper no. 2001-W42, Economics Group, Nuffield College, University of Oxford, December 2001).

The financial chaos: Robert L. Hetzel, "Henry Thornton: Seminal Monetary Theorist and Father of the Modern Central Bank," *FRB Richmond Economic Review* 73, no. 4 (1987): 3–16.

225 *"You have to work:* Andy Reinhardt, "Steve Jobs on Apple's Resurgence: 'Not a One-Man Show,'" *Business Week Online,* May 12, 1998, http://www.businessweek.com/bwdaily/dnflash/may1998/nf80512d.htm.

Much of the complexity: Scott A. Hodge, "Out with the Extenders, In with the New Obamacare Taxes," Tax Foundation, *Tax Policy Blog,* December 31, 2013, http://taxfoundation.org/blog/out-extenders-new-obamacare-taxes.

A recent study found: Sophie Shive and Margaret Forster, "The Revolving Door for Financial Regulators" (working paper, University of

Notre Dame, May 17, 2014), available at Social Science Research Network, http://ssrn.com/abstract=2348968 or http://dx.doi.org/10.2139/ssrn.2348968.

226 *Andy Haldane is:* John Cassidy, "The Hundred Most Influential People: Andy Haldane," *Time,* April 23, 2014, http://time.com/70833/andy-haldane-2014-time-100/.

At a recent conference: Andrew G. Haldane and Vasileios Madouros, "The Dog and the Frisbee" (speech at the Federal Reserve Bank of Kansas City's 366th Economic Policy Symposium, "The Changing Policy Landscape," Jackson Hole, Wyoming, August 31, 2012), available at website of the Bank for International Settlements, http://www.bis.org/review/r120905a.pdf.

Consider the results: Simeon Djankov et al., "Courts," *Quarterly Journal of Economics* 118, no. 2 (2003): 453–517.

227 *After studying:* Reed Hastings, the cofounder and CEO of Netflix, created (along with some colleagues) a PowerPoint presentation describing the company's approach to managing people, a document that had been viewed nearly nine million times online by September 2014. See Patty McCord, "How Netflix Reinvented HR," *Harvard Business Review,* January–February 2014. Original document available online at http://www.slideshare.net/reed2001/culture-1798664.

Index